"Spiritual formation has both a deeply personal and a profoundly collective dimension. If the personal has been at the forefront of many churches in the last generation, there is a surging, vital interest in church, or ecclesial, formation. This book moves a person and a church from personal formation into formation of community. In particular, Ruth Haley Barton has moved her well-known studies of the personal into the community. Genuine Christian community formation involves fellowship, generosity, forgiveness, and love. For leaders and churches willing to enter the process of formation as a group, this book is a wonderful catalyst. Those leaders and churches will never be the same. They will experience transformation, both slowly and at times suddenly."

**Scot McKnight,** visiting professor of New Testament at Houston Theological Seminary

"Ruth Haley Barton invites us to discover the miracles of God's transformation that unfold through practices pursued in community rhythms. Spiritual formation is the way we can experience Christ's abundant life in a fallen world, and I am grateful Ruth has distilled her considerable, hard-won wisdom into this guide. It will be a gift to so many communities that long for a path of lasting change, together."

**Gary A. Haugen,** founder and CEO of International Justice Mission

"Ruth Haley Barton offers a compelling vision for holistic, trinitarian spiritual transformation lived out in authentic community. She addresses challenges that hinder spiritual growth while providing both sound theology and guidance for genuine transformation. She invites us to examine the tensions within our ecclesial structures while holding hope for what is possible when communities yield to the Spirit. This is a resource for those who long to cultivate environments where spiritual disciplines are not performative but transformative. Barton desires redeemed people reflecting God's glory."

**Barbara L. Peacock,** author of *Soul Care in African American Practice* and founder of Peacock Soul Care Institute

"This is a manifesto, the crescendo of decades' worth of seed sown and wisdom won in the inner lives of leaders from every swath of the church. Ruth Haley Barton invites leaders to think deeply about their own formation, the traditions they've inherited, and the communities they lead. Most poignantly, she challenges the misappropriations of success and tragic status quos that serve as cheap substitutes for resilient discipleship in the modern, Western church. I received the invitations of this book first as a member of a transforming community, its yeast kneaded into the dough of my life and leadership years ago. I'm delighted that the gift I received has been crafted into written form, that it might be shared more broadly."

**Tyler Staton,** lead pastor of Bridgetown Church and author of *After Amen* and *The Familiar Stranger*

"Ruth Haley Barton's *Leading a Transforming Community* is a deeply engaging read that masterfully unpacks the integral connection between the inner work of spiritual formation with the outer work of mission. I would recommend it to anyone seeking to go deeper in their inward and outward journeys."

**Adam Russell Taylor,** president of Sojourners and author of *A More Perfect Union: A New Vision for Building the Beloved Community*

"*Leading a Transforming Community* is a work of breadth, depth, and clarity, all wrapped in stories that convey the reality of the longings and the griefs in the church as it is. With it, Ruth Haley Barton offers us yet another volume of wisdom acquired, not as a distant observer of what she writes but as one who continues to do the very hard work of formation while remaining faithful—as is Jesus—to the church that he began and she occupies. For those among us who long for durable transformation in our communities, what you hold in your hands is a gift to us that will long provide bread and water for our hungry and thirsty souls."

**Curt Thompson, MD,** psychiatrist and author of *The Soul of Desire* and *The Deepest Place*

# LEADING A TRANSFORMING COMMUNITY

Foundations, Practices, and Strategies for Opening to God Together

RUTH HALEY BARTON

*Foreword by Prince Rainey Rivers*

ivp

An imprint of InterVarsity Press
Downers Grove, Illinois

InterVarsity Press
P.O. Box 1400 | Downers Grove, IL 60515-1426
ivpress.com | email@ivpress.com



InterVarsity Press® is the publishing division of InterVarsity Christian Fellowship/USA®. For more information, visit intervarsity.org.



Cover design: Faceout Studio
Interior design: Jeanna Wiggins
Images: Moment via Getty Images: © oxygen, © Sapphire, © Katsumi Murouchi; © Billion Photos via Shutterstock

ISBN 978-0-8308-4601-6 (print) | ISBN 978-0-8308-9820-6 (digital)

Printed in the United States of America ♾

**Library of Congress Cataloging-in-Publication Data**
Names: Barton, R. Ruth, 1960- author
Title: Leading a transforming community : foundations, practices, and strategies for opening to God together / Ruth Haley Barton.
Description: Downers Grove, IL : IVP, [2026] | Includes bibliographical references.
Identifiers: LCCN 2026016470 (print) | LCCN 2026016471 (ebook) | ISBN 9780830846016 hardcover | ISBN 9780830898206 ebook
Subjects: LCSH: Christian leadership | Communities–Religious aspects–Christianity | Spiritual life–Christianity
Classification: LCC BV652.1 .B37 2026 (print) | LCC BV652.1 (ebook)
LC record available at https://lccn.loc.gov/2026016470
LC ebook record available at https://lccn.loc.gov/2026016471

33 32 31 30 29 28 27 26 | 11 10 9 8 7 6 5 4 3 2 1

TO M. ROBERT MULHOLLAND JR.
(1936–2022)

New Testament theologian, teacher,
ministry colleague, and friend,
with gratitude

*Every teacher needs a teacher,*
*and you have been mine.*

*Christianity needs to clarify and exemplify methods for human transformation. It must show how ordinary individuals who make up the human race today can become, through the grace of Christ, a love-filled, effective, powerful community.*

Dallas Willard

# CONTENTS

# CONTENTS

# FOREWORD

*Prince Raney Rivers*

Years ago, at the recommendation of my friend and fellow pastor David Hughes, I applied to join one of the Transforming Center's transforming community cohorts. I had no idea then how profoundly that decision would shape my life and leadership. It was there that I first met Ruth Haley Barton, and it was there that my understanding of Christian leadership began to shift in deep, transformative ways.

Over nine quarterly retreats, our cohort sustained rhythms of worship, silence, teaching, and community. Each retreat carried its own theme, but all of them invited us to pay attention to God's presence in places we often overlook. One retreat explored the ways we discern God through our bodies, an essential teaching we often overlook in the West because faith is sometimes practiced in disembodied ways. Using the incarnation as a point of departure, Ruth helped us reconnect that important theological truth with our lived experience.

During the retreat that focused on the body, Ruth candidly shared about her experience as a woman navigating ministry and leadership. As I listened and looked around our largely White cohort, I reflected on how my own story had been shaped more significantly by race than by gender, growing up as an African American man in the South. After the session, I shared this observation with Ruth, and she received my comments with genuine gratitude. Ultimately, her sensitivity to the Spirit transformed a passing conversation into the beginning of a meaningful friendship and a catalyst for transformation.

Later that day, Ruth invited me to share my reflections with the entire community. By then, our cohort had become a safe, prayerful space, and that conversation strengthened our collective understanding of what it means to attend to God in embodied, culturally diverse ways. Other participants shared what it was like to live in their bodies as Asian American men and African American women. Moments like this are characteristic of Ruth's leadership. She is discerning and willing to shift direction as the Holy Spirit leads.

Since that retreat, my involvement as a Transforming Center board member, Ruth's published works, and our occasional partnership in ministry have shaped the contours of my leadership in profound ways. I regularly use *Strengthening the Soul of Your Leadership* as a core text in courses I teach in the doctor of ministry program I direct at Duke Divinity School because Ruth brings together spiritual depth and practical wisdom in a way few leadership authors do.

*Leading a Transforming Community* places that hard-earned wisdom in your hands. At a time when organizational life can become preoccupied with metrics, outcomes, and performance, Ruth offers a model of leadership grounded in discernment, humility, and attentiveness to the Spirit. She reminds us that true transformation happens not through control or strategy alone but through communities committed to prayerful listening, silence, and corporate discernment.

Whether you are a new leader or a seasoned one, this book will challenge, guide, and encourage you. It's an ideal field guide for your leadership team. Ruth has faithfully followed God's call on her life, and through this work she offers trustworthy companionship for anyone seeking to lead others toward authentic transformation.

I am grateful for Ruth's faithfulness to God's call and the gift she offers in this work, and I trust you will be too.

# 1

# LONGING FOR MORE IN COMMUNITY

*For me, talking about church in front of a bunch of Christians means approaching the microphone and attempting to explain the most important, complicated, beautiful, and heart-wrenching relationship of my life in thirty minutes or less without yelling or crying or saying any cuss words. Sometimes I wish they would find someone with a bit more emotional distance to give these lectures, someone who doesn't have to break herself open and bleed all over the place every time someone asks, innocently enough, "So where have you been going to church these days?"*

Rachel Held Evans

---

**Recently, while signing books** at a conference on spiritual formation, a mature, sharply dressed woman approached the table with no apparent interest in purchasing a book. Instead, she blurted out, "I have given up on church. Completely. What do you have to say to someone like me?"

All I could think to say was, "I don't blame you. I get it." Because the truth is, I do.

Not long after that encounter, I was talking with a youngish former pastor about a ministry he had helped start. He described a house-sized group of couples and families who gathered regularly to be in community with one another, to learn and experience spiritual practices that would further their transformation, and to minister to the real needs of others in their neighborhood. Several times he mentioned "his elders" who seemed to provide leadership and accountability for the whole undertaking. Innocently enough I said, "That sounds a lot like a church! If someone were to ask, would you say that this is your church?" He said yes, he would identify this gathering as a church, *but* he said with emphasis, "We are not a church or anything like that. . . . We have no intention of ever owning a building or starting lots of programs."

While I was sobered by the fact that this young pastor seemed to have reduced the idea of church to buildings and programs, I could relate to his desire to distance himself from "church" to have any hope at all of experiencing the change and transformation for which his soul longed. I have done the same thing myself. I, too, got to the end of my hopes and expectations that church could be a place where change and transformation take place regularly. I, too, got so desperate for a community that would support and catalyze the transformational journey that I started something I still insist is not a church, and yet it has become my primary community for spiritual transformation over the last twenty-five years.

Even as I resonated deeply with this young man and his description of what he was trying to do, it disturbed me to acknowledge that transformation—the very thing that could (and *should)* be central to the church—is so missing in many people's experiences of church that they no longer expect to find it there. These days, when people are looking for real-life change, they routinely turn elsewhere—to a yoga class, a spirituality center, a runner's club, an informal gathering of like-minded friends who want to "go deeper," or even online communities! Today's spiritually savvy seeker seems to know intuitively that calling something a church or letting it become a church has the potential to doom the whole endeavor from the get-go. We can judge the "spiritual but not religious" folks all we want, but those who are in touch with their deepest spiritual longings have no problem voting with their feet. And this is not for lack of desire but because the desire is so deep.

Clarence Heller captures the poignancy of the situation in this poem that we can all, perhaps, relate to.

**So Far**

*I have drifted so far from church*
*that I have lost touch with the liturgical seasons*
*and the markers that distinguish ordinary time.*
*When was Pentecost this year?*
*I miss wearing red and dancing/singing*
*in the flow of the Holy Spirit.*
*I miss hearing the familiar readings and*
*perhaps receiving a fleeting invigoration,*
*a new or newly remembered insight.*
*I miss being with people, especially the ones*
*I know well, especially the ones who know*
*and still love me.*
*I miss the rhythm of the week,*
*a moment set aside to gather and reflect,*
*to stop, to connect, to belong.*
*Yet it is human nature to allow painful memories*
*to fade sooner, farther.*
*Yet there were times that hurt, when my church*
*rejected me, when the graced decision was to leave . . .*
*and so far, it is not yet time to return.*[1]

For those who have been raised in church or spent a good portion of their lives committed to church; struggling with church; weathering church splits, scandals, and disappointments; and trying to help; the choice to listen to a favorite preacher online or rely on the latest pick-your-own-practice app is understandable.

## TELLING THE TRUTH ABOUT CHURCH

To be fair, churches are good for a great many things. Some are good at discipleship, providing structure for the fledgling journeys of new Christians. Others do an amazing job of attracting unchurched seekers through high-tech worship services, quality programming for children and youth, and ministries to a wide variety of human needs. Some are havens of traditional worship for those who love liturgy and enjoy a well-rehearsed robed choir, a pipe organ, and a ten-minute homily. Still others have moved into specific neighborhoods for the express purpose of engaging with the needs of that community in Jesus' name. Most desire to be a community in which the ministry of Word and sacrament is offered to parishioners from birth to death and (if all goes well) at significant moments in between—although this kind of stability is becoming more and more rare in our consumeristic culture. But the church as a place where people are routinely experiencing spiritual transformation, where they are discovering a way of life that works and produces good fruit in them? Not so much.

All it takes is living through one church split or denominational meltdown to understand that even folks who have been in church all their lives are not functioning much beyond the capacity of their reptilian brain with its fight, flight, or freeze responses to old wounds and deeply ingrained false-self patterns. When push comes to shove, those who have been in church all their lives often don't behave much better than anyone else. The Covid-19 pandemic exposed this in a most striking way. A recent survey describes the stress endured by pastors and congregations during the pandemic as divisions over public health restrictions transformed (or should we say deformed?) many churches into culture war–battlefields. "Polarization decreased the middle ground, diminished trust in pastoral decision-making, and created a general culture of contempt in churches," the authors of the study write.

> The middle area in many church communities thinned to a fine line—devolving into "Our Side" or "Their Side." Applying

> pandemic requirements to their church required leaders to navigate a political, religious, and social minefield. . . . The reality is that many wounds have not been healed, many churches are still struggling to find a new normal, and presidential election cycles have reopened many of these wounds.[2]

One pastor observed, "I think COVID revealed that we have a lot more idols in our life than we realize. And so, where I was hoping to see the body of Christ come together and lead in the areas of loving people, having compassion and caring for those in need, I was disappointed to see fractions and division . . . right down party lines politically."[3] Turns out, what Covid exposed about deep divisions within the church and among Christians was only the tip of the iceberg. We currently find ourselves navigating issues that have to do with basic morality, the economy, health care, holding billionaires and high-level leaders accountable for sexual abuse and misconduct, immigration and how we treat "strangers" who are also our fellow human beings, government paralysis and shutdown, the global impact of tariffs, vaccines and the use of Tylenol, the limits of executive powers, human sexuality and abortion. The list of issues that expose divisions in the church and Christians' inability to have meaningful dialogue about these things goes on and on.

Observing this, one is tempted to ask: Does the church really make a difference when it comes to the transformation of human beings into the image of Christ? Does being part of a Christian community make us better or just busier? Does it affect who we fundamentally *are*? Do our well-crafted statements of faith really matter if nobody is actually changing? And that's not even to mention the layers of Christian busyness that seem to be part and parcel of anything having to do with church these days. Many are hesitant to cross the threshold of a church for fear of getting roped into a new set of demands that—when added to a pace of life that is already unmanageable—threaten to completely overwhelm them. What does one do when what you want *more than anything* is a way of life that *works,* and organized church seems to work against that? Are good Christians even allowed to ask such questions? I sure hope so because I just did!

It is not easy to talk about what's missing when everything is supposed to be going up and to the right. It's not easy to write about it either, given how long I have loved and served the church. I know that some who are reading these words may be uncomfortable, feeling like I've said too much about what's not working while others might feel I haven't been strong enough in my truth-telling about where the church is at right now. But I am encouraged by Brian McClaren's perspective that to be part of a life-giving tradition brings with it a moral responsibility to make it even better as we pass it on to future generations. He writes,

> How will we help our traditions to grow, mature, and expand its influence for good? How will we enrich and improve the tradition as it stands? How can we discern its present weakness, not in order to criticize and condemn the tradition, but in order to heal, strengthen, and energize it for greater fruitfulness in the future? What might the growing edges of our tradition be?[4]

I believe Christianity is a life-giving tradition and that the body of Christ is meant to be its ever-growing, ever-transforming life-giving expression. As someone who has been around for a while, I am trying to participate in the process McClaren describes—the process of responding to the questions about how the tradition I am a part of can grow, mature, and expand its influence for good. Let me hasten to add that I *have* experienced *some* transformation in church—in fact, it's hard to know who or what I would be without it! But it is also true that growing up in the church has contributed to the care and feeding of my false self almost as effectively as it has nurtured my true self. The tares have definitely grown up with the wheat.

But as I passed from the early stages of basic Christian discipleship into the more challenging stages of faith, there came a point when I had to admit that even though I had been in church all my life (both as a "lay person" and as a "professional") there was something seriously missing. Amid my most unsettling spiritual questions, greatest brokenness, and deepest spiritual longings, I had to look beyond current expressions of institutionalized church to the broader historic faith to discover next steps for my journey. I was longing for a particular kind of community—one whose very aim was to hold space and provide guidance in the spiritual practices that open us to God's transforming work. One that would foster *participation* in the divine nature, also known as *theosis* in the orthodox Christian tradition. *Sanctification* or *transformation* as the apostle Paul describes it. *Union* or *oneness* as the contemplative traditions articulate. Or as Jesus taught it, the kingdom of God *here now* if we can only find ways to open to it (Luke 17:21; John 17:11; Romans 12:2; 2 Peter 1:4, respectively).

Where does one go to find a community that orders its life around *that*?

## HOW BAD DO YOU WANT IT?

Those of us who founded the Transforming Center many years ago were leaders from a variety of church and ministry settings who sought each other out because we were holding similar questions and longings for levels of transformation we were not experiencing in the communities we were a part of. Just as Nicodemus came to Jesus under the cover of night to ask his dangerous questions, we found each other outside our professional religious contexts. In quiet conversations where we risked telling the truth about what was happening and not happening in our spiritual lives, we dared to express our longing for deeper levels of transformation through spiritual practices that were not being offered meaningfully in our settings. We were tired of being so driven and worn out in ministry and wanted desperately to experience discernment together as the heart of our spiritual leadership. We were spiritual seekers on a stealth mission to find the "treasure" of real spiritual transformation hidden in the field of our life together in Christ.

We also had a sense that if we *as leaders* could take some next steps spiritually—toward deeper intimacy with God, toward real change in our trust structures and core motivations, toward an increasing capacity to surrender to Love—it would be the best thing we could do, not only for ourselves but for the churches and communities we were a part of. So, we began meeting based on one desire and one desire alone: to experience deeper levels of transformation through spiritual practices that were not being offered meaningfully in the settings we were in. We said to each other, "Okay, we love the church, and we're still committed to giving our best there, but we're going to have to set up some sort of community outside our current contexts to create space for the deeper journey of spiritual transformation. Otherwise, we will never get to ask the questions we need to ask, we will never be able to be honest about what's really going on inside, and we will never find the safety to risk vulnerability."

In some ways this only highlighted the problem: that here we were as leaders in churches and Christian ministries admitting we needed to go outside the religious institutions we were a part of to pursue our longing for deeper transformation. We knew there had to be more to the spiritual life than what we were experiencing, and like Nicodemus, we were desperate enough to do something radical to find it.

The power of this kind of desire seems to be what Jesus was illustrating when he used the metaphor of a merchant who has been searching all his life for the pearl of great price or the treasure hidden in a field (Matthew 13:44-45). When he finds it, Jesus says, he sells everything he has in order to buy it—in other words, a radical reprioritization of his life. Several other biblical narratives (for example, Jesus' question to blind Bartimaeus in Mark 10:51, "What do you want me to do for you?") led us to realize that anything of real significance in the spiritual life begins with desire—our desire for God and God's desire for us. And like the paralytic at the pool of Bethsaida, sometimes Jesus walks right up to us and asks, "Do you really want to be made well?"

While it might *seem* like something as personal as desire originates with us, the truth is that the very presence of spiritual desire and our awareness of it is a great grace. It is a manifestation of God's presence already at work within us. We love God because he first loved us. We long for God because he first longed for us. We reach for God because he first reached for us. Even though unmet desire and longing can be uncomfortable to acknowledge and live with, their very presence indicates that God is already at work, drawing us to himself. Saint Augustine writes, "The entire life of a good Christian is never less than holy desire"—God's and ours. The psalmist assures us in Psalm 37:4 that there are desires God has placed within us that God longs to meet. This is true for individuals, and it is true for whole communities.

## IT'S COMPLICATED

One of things that complicated matters for me early on is that even as I was acknowledging the limits of church relative to my own and others' spiritual transformation, I was also trying to make church work as a vocation. I discovered the hard way that "the powers that be" didn't really want to hear me (or anyone else) say that, for all our religious activity, people were not really changing. It was like trying to talk about the fact that the emperor wasn't wearing any clothes. The idea that some of us who had been Christians for a long time were quite stuck and that some of our beliefs and practices were, in fact, deforming was a truly inconvenient truth.

Add to that the performance orientation attached to the "job" of vocational Christian ministry; it was simply not wise to talk about longing for more, the emptiness and stuckness we were experiencing, and what was or was not happening in our own spiritual lives. After all, a leader's spirituality was part of how success was measured. If you were a leader in the church, there was simply no safe place for naming and attending to the deeper desires we were now in touch with. And that's exactly what caused the intrepid little group of leaders that eventually founded the Transforming Center to start meeting "off the grid" to create safe space for attending to our deepest spiritual questions and longings. We were seekers on a stealth mission to find the pearl of great price we had been searching for all our lives.

I was surprised by the controversy and questions such simple longings and ideas seemed to stir up pertaining to the relationship between spiritual formation, evangelism, and mission. If Christians started paying more attention to discipleship and formation, would they become irrelevant to the world around them? Would they lose their evangelistic zeal because they just wanted to sit around in their growth groups? Would our lives become devoid of any sense of missional engagement with the world beyond us? Would we become so heavenly minded we're no earthly good? How would anything ever get *done*? Instead of holding what seemed like competing priorities in creative tension, false dichotomies began to emerge that resulted in polarity-thinking rather than fruitful synergy. People committed to spiritual formation were seen as a threat to what was by then called "the seeker movement."

Missional churches sprang up that were seen as fundamentally different from communities committed to discipleship and spiritual formation. In some settings, it became slightly embarrassing to admit a desire for more, as though somehow that meant we didn't care about church growth and weren't driven enough to care for the needs of the world.

For all these reasons and more, this little group of us kept our quest on the down low. What responsible Christian wants to be seen as irrelevant when relevance is all the rage? Who wants to appear lacking in evangelistic zeal when seekers are the target audience for what we were selling? Who wants to be accused of being a narcissistic navel-gazer when the needs of the world are so great? And of course, none of us wanted to be viewed as unmotivated slackers who lacked capacity in the high-octane leadership settings we were a part of. Thus, it seemed best to keep quiet about this little community that was gathering to experience spiritual practices we hoped might open us to the More we were seeking.

## TRANSFORMATION, DISCERNMENT, MISSION

We did not plan for a mission to emerge from our stealth operation; honestly, we were in it for ourselves. But it didn't take long for us to wonder if there might be others out there who would like to join us. As we quietly offered up the invitation to others (mostly family and friends at first) and they said yes to the journey, we discovered that a transforming community will, by definition, end up being missional because we have such good news to share. The very nature of transformation is that it leads to an increasing capacity to discern the will of God, which then becomes our mission. "Do not be conformed to this age," Paul says, "but be transformed by the renewing of the mind, *so that* you may discern what is the will of God—what is good and acceptable and perfect" (Romans 12:2, emphasis added).

With that one simple statement Paul establishes a cause-and-effect relationship between our transformation and our ability to discern and do the will of God. In fact, he identifies an ongoing and intentional process of transformation ("I appeal to you therefore, brothers and sisters, . . . to present your bodies as a living sacrifice . . . to God" [Romans 12:1]) as a *prerequisite* to discerning the will of God. Already we were shattering the false dichotomy between formation and mission. We learned *through experience* that rather than being total opposites, our spiritual transformation leads to an increasing capacity to discern God's will, and as we get out there and do the will of God in the world God loves, we become missional.[5]

And the relationship between formation and mission doesn't end there. As we engaged in our mission, we bumped up against our human limitations, which forced us to dig deeper for the spiritual resources that would sustain us in that mission. Being actively engaged in mission catapulted us back into our need for further transformation and the interior resources only a vibrant spiritual life can provide. As you can see from figure 1.1, this is a cyclical process that is never finished; it is dynamic, not static. Progress is made—in our personal transformation *and* in our mission to be Jesus' presence in the world—as we move through this cycle repeatedly, propelled forward by the energy and guidance of the Holy Spirit.

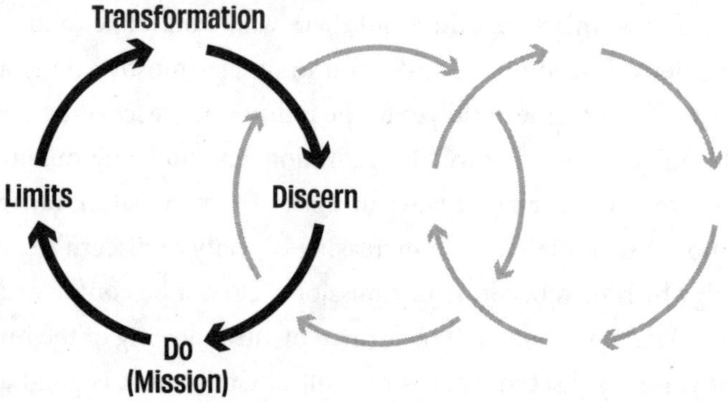


**Figure 1.1.** We enter this process for the first time at salvation but will cycle through it many times in the spiritual life, always being invited further into the transformational journey, which keeps increasing our capacity to discern the will of God. Then as we do the will of God we are drawn deeper into dependence on God for what is needed to effectively carry out the mission God has given us and to be strengthened in the doing of it. Every time we are pushed to our limits, it is another opportunity to rely more deeply on God and discover more of God's unlimited resources. As it turns out, mission cannot be discerned without ongoing transformation, and it cannot be sustained without the inner resources God provides. And our transformation comes to full fruition as we discern and engage our mission.

## WE SPEAK OF WHAT WE KNOW AND TESTIFY TO WHAT WE HAVE SEEN

Over time our explorations led us to begin identifying ourselves as communities of women and men gathered around the presence of Christ for the purpose of spiritual transformation so we could discern and do the will of God—which then became our mission. And that mission was a simple desire for others to experience what we were experiencing as we dared to dream of "little transforming centers everywhere"—intentional communities led by pastors and leaders equipped to cultivate transforming communities in their own settings.

Our mission seemed a little grandiose at first because we knew transforming communities don't happen by accident; they must be led with a great deal of intention and some measure of preparation. So we created a practice-based spiritual formation journey that came to be known as *Transforming Community*—designed to strengthen the souls of pastors and leaders for long-term health and wholeness in their own lives *and* prepare them to lead others in the process of transformation. Our focus on pastors and leaders of intentional communities was intentional because of our conviction that *spiritual transformation is central to the message of the gospel of Jesus and therefore central to the message of his church*, and leaders are positioned especially well to champion this. We have embraced a definition of *church* (big C) that is very broad—that is, the body of Christ on the earth now, along with all who have come before, and all who will come after (otherwise known as the communion of saints). This definition emphasizes our understanding that Christ's body is made up of many members and a variety of expressions, and we want to be very careful about equating the institutionalized church as it exists right now with the organic, ever-growing body of the living Christ.

## A COMMUNITY THAT PRACTICES

Really any group of Christ-followers—especially churches and Christian ministries—can become a transforming community (1) if they are in touch with their desire for deeper levels of transformation, (2) if they allow that desire to shape their intentions and priorities, and (3) if they are intentional about arranging their communal life around key practices that open them to what they say they really want. These practices are not magic, and no human community is perfect, but we can testify that there *are* practices and intentional approaches to transformation that have been means of grace for our community over and over again—when engaged from authentic desire and in a spirit of surrender. They repeatedly foster encounters with God we could not have orchestrated ourselves and have brought about changes that could never be accomplished through hard work and human effort alone.

Whenever we conclude one of our two-year Transforming Community experiences, there is always the question "How can I bring this back to my church or ministry?" This book is an attempt to answer this question by breaking it down into manageable moves that churches and communities can make together to support and catalyze spiritual transformation in the lives of its members *and* in the culture around them. This book is arranged in four parts. Part one explores the theological and biblical foundations for cultivating this kind of community, starting with desire and then moving to intentionality and making concrete decisions that are consistent with those desires.

The rest of the book is organized around the idea of living from the center out in concentric circles of relationship—solitude, community, and mission. Each of these concentric circles contains practices that contribute to the transformational journey in unique ways. Part two focuses on *solitude*—our true life hidden with Christ in God. Part three explores *community* as the relationships that sustain us in the mystery of our faith and God's transforming work in our lives. And part four addresses *mission* as our unique way of being in God for the world, radically available to God for the sake of others. These movements are modeled after the pattern of Jesus' life evident in Luke 6. At the beginning of his ministry, Jesus goes out to the mountain alone to pray (solitude). He emerges from this time of communion with God and calls his disciples "to be with him" (community). Then together they come down from the mountain to engage the multitudes, bringing with them Jesus' healing presence and power (mission).

The conclusion outlines strategies and intentional approaches for moving forward as a transforming community. And the epilogue leaves us with some open questions we all need to be grappling with as we set out on this new adventure. Of course, this book will have its greatest impact as leaders not only take it in personally but also pray for their communities and then process it together with other leaders in their settings; thus, there is a conversation guide available that provides guidance for personal reflection, group sharing, and identifying next steps.

My whole heart and intention in this work is that whatever truth we tell will heal, strengthen, and energize the church in its broadest definition—the body of Christ on the earth now—and that we will find the courage to go all the way out to our growing edges where God is already waiting for us.

# PART 1

# FOUNDATIONS

## *From Desire to Intention*

*One can begin one's quest by attending to the desires of the heart, both personal and communal. The Spirit is revealed in our genuine hopes for ourselves and for the world. How brightly burns the flame of desire for a love affair with God, other people, the world? Do we know that to desire God and seek God is a choice that is always available to us?*

Elizabeth Dreyer

# 2

# ARRANGING OUR LIVES TOGETHER FOR SPIRITUAL TRANSFORMATION

*Because in recent centuries the Western church has developed an individualistic culture, the focus of spiritual formation is often on the self, the inner life, and our personal growth. But we also have a collective soul. Our collective soul has a physical body called the church. What's often missing in spiritual formation paradigms is the health of our collective soul.*

CINDY LEE

---

A PIVOTAL MOMENT in the unfolding of the Transforming Center community took place at a Benedictine retreat center in southern Wisconsin. Still in the embryonic stages of our life together, we went on retreat to deepen our practice of the spiritual disciplines our longings were drawing us into. We also wanted to learn more about the expressions of community that have been known historically as religious orders because that seemed to be more like what we were becoming. We knew Benedictine communities ordered their lives around prayer, study, and work, and this intrigued us because it seemed so balanced; we had only known communities that were fairly lopsided in one direction or another.

While there, we arranged to meet with one of the brothers who had been a member of this community for over fifty years. We wanted to learn from someone who had chosen lifelong stability within one community as the context for his personal transformation and his participation in God's mission. As I recall, it was bright-blue-sky summer day, and after receiving a guided tour of the monastery and grounds, we pulled some rusty metal chairs into a small circle on the front lawn to learn from our host. He talked for a while about a variety of things but then made this penetrating statement: "Pick a community and stick with it; pick a path and stay on it."

Such wisdom, distilled from over fifty years of faithfulness to one community, was all the more impactful because it was offered by someone who had earned the right to say it.

### COUNTING THE COST

This was our first hint about how significant stability is within a community committed to transformation, not to mention the fruitfulness and effectiveness of whatever missional expression emerges from it. Up to that point, we had been a little starry-eyed about what we were attempting to do and as (mostly) Protestants, the idea of staying in one community for fifty years or worshiping in the parish where one lives had never crossed our minds! Clearly, we were more influenced by the consumeristic culture around us—where people shop for a church like they shop for a new car and then trade it in when they're done—than we realized.

Later I would come across Brian Taylor's excellent book *Spirituality for Everyday Living: An Adaptation of the Rule of St. Benedict*, where Taylor, an Episcopalian priest, insightfully unpacks the Benedictine Rule for application to contemporary life. Early in the book he describes three vows underlying one's commitment to a particular community—stability, *conversatio* (conversion), and obedience—pointing out that stability is the first vow because it is the one that makes all the other vows possible. Stability is a vow we make to God in the context of the life we have been given because (counterintuitively) to accept one's life as it is, is to begin to find freedom.

> The grass is not greener "over there": one must work out one's problems with *this* person because if one doesn't, one will have to work it out with *that* person. . . . To have to work it out is to demand growth, as painful as it is, and that is freeing. Faithfulness is a limit that forces us to stop running and encounter God, self, and the other right now, right here.[1]

He goes on to say that commitment to stability makes the second vow of *conversatio* (conversion) possible. This is essentially the vow to do our repenting—our transformation, really—in the context of our everyday existence, with the people and relationships God has given us. Then within the community God has given us, we choose to do what is asked of us there and "obey" the limits and the opportunities of the life that we have chosen or that has been given to us.

I wonder if one of the reasons the church in its current expression is struggling to be a transforming presence in our world is that we have failed to grasp how significant the vow of stability is to the transformational journey.

**PRACTICING STABILITY**

Today, when long-term commitment to a community feels like too much or the demands of transformation in community challenge our self-centeredness or the grass seems greener somewhere else, our most natural human impulse is to pick up stakes and move on. This pattern is in stark contrast to bygone days when being a part of the church that was in one's parish or neighborhood for as long as one lived there was much more the norm.

It seems to me that there is much we miss in community these days, simply because we do not stay long enough to experience the goodness that comes in long-term, committed, stable relationships. It has not always been so. In Benedictine communities, the vow of stability is the first of the vows because, as Episcopal priest Brian Taylor goes on to say,

> Nothing is possible until we give our entire life to the primacy of God's kingdom. If we leave ourselves an escape hatch, we have one foot out the door, and we are not fully committed. If we say to ourselves that we will stay committed as long as commitment stays exciting and devoid of suffering, we are not fully committed. . . . The Benedictine vow is a vow to a community of people rather than to a place. . . . It is a vow by which members of the monastic family bind themselves to each other for life. As long we keep even one opening in the back of our minds, we cannot reap the benefits of a fully committed love relationship. We will always be only partly "there."[2]

Of course this applies to pastors as well as parishioners. In a day when the pastorate is seen more as a career than a commitment, it's no wonder pastors and parishioners alike are watching for signs of who will leave first. People can tell when a pastor sees their current call as a stepping-stone to a "better" position, and pastors are often broadsided by parishioners who leave for another church they feel is "better" or more well suited in some way. To make matters even more complicated, in some church polities the pastor can be sent by a bishop or some other overseer to another congregation at any moment. While this may be a good discipline that prevents human tendencies to become too attached, it does make it hard to know how to practice the kind of stability that opens us to the greatest possibility for transformation. Raising the question of what stability might look like in the context of various church polities might be a worthy conversation.

It will take courageous leaders these days to consider the practice of stability for themselves and then to invite others into it with a pure heart. We are not trying to get people to stay with us as though it were about us. We are inviting them into a level of commitment that will result in their own transformation and ours. It will take a courageous congregation to really listen and consider what this ancient practice might mean for them. But as Taylor points out, the practice of stability holds great promise for transformation, and it may be more important today than ever.

## COMMUNITY AS THE CONTEXT FOR TRANSFORMATION

Spiritual transformation takes place incrementally over time with others in the context of the practices, relationships, and experiences that open us to God's transforming work. Every facet of biblical history and New Testament teaching bears witness to the significance of the community of faith for our transformation. From God's eternal existence as a community of three, to the creation of humankind out of God's own desire for fellowship, to setting us within families, to God calling a group of people to be his own and then guiding them to the Promised Land, to the life of Christ among his disciples, to the apostles' New Testament teachings about the church, the Scriptures situate the human journey of growth, freedom, and transformation within intentional (and in many cases *covenanted*) relationships that contribute to our own good and to the good of all. This is not to create a moral straitjacket but rather to foster the kind of stability in community that makes transformation possible.

One of Jesus' first priorities while he was here on this earth was to call and then cultivate a small community of disciples who were committed to be with him, to learn from him how to be like him so they could be his presence in the world. Jesus' disciples were called first to be *with him,* and by virtue of their commitment to Jesus, they came into relationship with each other. Their relationship with Jesus and their responsiveness to his teaching and leadership was the glue that brought them all together and then held them together amid many dangers, toils, and snares.

Even after his community fell apart during and after his crucifixion, Jesus did not leave them scattered and broken. While it might have been tempting to move on to bigger and better things following the resurrection, Jesus took forty days to systematically reach out to each person in his circle, working patiently to piece them and the community back together before ascending to heaven. Jesus' example reveals a powerful pattern for cultivating transforming communities. First, individuals said yes to Jesus' invitation to be with him and to experience transformation in his presence because his teachings promised them something their hearts had been longing for. Then their commitment to Jesus brought them into relationship with one another as Jesus intentionally cultivated their life together in community. Then and *only then* did he start talking to them about the mission to which he was calling them.

## BEYOND PRIVATE DEVOTION

Somehow spiritual transformation, in many people's minds, has been reduced to the quieter and more individual disciplines like solitude, silence, prayer, *lectio divina*, self-examination, retreat, and so on. These practices are indeed integral to the process of transformation, but community is the larger context in which we work out our salvation (our ongoing process of transformation) with fear and trembling. In community we discover that it is easy to feel pious and humble when we are alone with the Almighty God; it is harder to humble ourselves in the presence of other flawed human beings who inevitably trigger whatever it is that is untransformed in us. Community in all its facets is a *primary* arena for our transformational journey because there our siblings in Christ become agents of grace—and sometimes agents of God's *troubling* grace!—in our lives.[3]

Any approach to spiritual formation that is based solely on our private disciplines is woefully inadequate, biblically inaccurate, and embryonic in its development. Spiritual transformation is not happening only when we are praying, in solitude, or on retreat. Our spiritual transformation (and deformation, for that matter) is taking place in every facet of our lives—in our churches and ministry organizations, in families and friend groups, among neighbors and people who come together to respond to very specific needs in Jesus' name.

All of these expressions of community are arenas in which God can be at work transforming us into the image of Christ if we are intentional about how we engage together.

It's easy to lose sight of the fact that Paul's teachings on spiritual transformation were most often addressed to groups of Christians who were seeking the way of Jesus together. As members of the body of Christ we are given to one another for mutual edification and to spur one another on to love and good deeds. The spiritual gifts bestowed on each of us are not given primarily for our own personal benefit or self-aggrandizement, but as means for building one another up in love so we can "grow up" into Christ who is our Source. There is no true, long-term transformation outside of involvement with some expression of the body of Christ here on the earth now.

The phrase *some expression* is important here. New expressions of Christian community are emerging all over the place and, while they may or may not be typical congregational gatherings, they are expressions of the body of Christ, nonetheless, and need to be received as such. Let's keep in mind that when the author of Hebrews admonished New Testament Christians not to give up meeting together (Hebrews 10:25 NIV), he was referring to gatherings that bear little resemblance to the local churches and denominational structures we know today. We need to be careful not to dismiss gatherings of Christians that may or may not fit into current cultural norms *or* the church as the institution it has become.

## THE GOD WHO IS ALWAYS MAKING ALL THINGS NEW

Dr. Elaine Heath, dean of Duke Divinity School and author of the wonderful little book *God Unbound,* helpfully distinguishes between our own traditions (small *t*) and the great Tradition (capital *T*) of a God who is always making all things new. She challenges us by saying that there are times when we are called to surrender our own specific tradition to the Tradition of following God in the new thing God is doing. We see this in New Testament stories like Acts 15, where the Jerusalem council discerns and responds to the new thing God is doing regarding the conversion of the Gentiles. Or the new thing God reveals through Peter's dream and subsequent interaction with Cornelius in Acts 10, calling him—and the whole church—to a more inclusive stance. Or the new thing Paul describes in Galatians 3:28, where he articulates a kind of equality in the body of Christ that was simply unheard of at the time and that we have yet to fully realize to this day.

Could we be in such a moment right now? Dr. Heath goes on to make this observation:

> Increasing numbers of people within the church feel called to develop faith communities beyond the walls of the church. They serve as emerging leaders of what God is sprouting from the cracks in the crumbling foundation of church as we've known it. . . . Institutions are necessary because they form to promote and protect the core values and purpose of the people—the movement that gives birth to the institution. But over time institutions inevitably become rigid and inwardly focused, entombing the life they were meant to protect. When that happens, innovators within the institutions begin to appear. These pioneers create new expressions of the life that formerly gave birth to the institution.[4]

Adam Russel Taylor, president of *Sojourners*, draws attention to these new expressions as well.

> The Greek word *ekklesia,* which refers to both the universal church and to local groups of believers, is found over 100 times in the New Testament. Acts 2:42-47 offers one of the most poignant and timeless images of what the church should be: a space (not necessarily a physical building) where people are able to worship, engage in fellowship, service, outreach, prayer, and more. As we move into the 21st century, the Christian movement may increasingly resemble these early believers who are known

> as followers of the way of Jesus, rather than as members of a particular church.[5]

I wonder if we are open to this.

**SPIRITUAL BUT NOT RELIGIOUS**

Recently I have been wading uncomfortably through a book titled *A Churchless Faith: Faith Journeys Beyond the Churches* by Alan Jamieson that describes in painful detail the journeys of many "dones"—those who consider themselves Christians who are still on a serious spiritual journey but who are "done" with the organized church and have no intention of returning. He acknowledges that his title *A Churchless Faith* is both a catchphrase and a misnomer. It is a catchphrase to identify a group of people who see themselves as people of faith, but who are also completely alienated from the institutionalized church. But it is also a misnomer, he says, because "all followers of Christ (Christians, from the Greek *christianoi* = 'Christ people') are, by definition, part of the 'church'—the house or community of the Lord (from Greek *Kyriake* = belonging to *Kyrios*, Lord). That is the church universal, the church made up of all those who belong to Christ."[6]

The designation "a churchless faith" is intended to push us to consider that the groups formed by what he calls "church leavers" are offering new ways of being the local church. Whether we are people of faith who have given up on church or not, we all need to be gathering with other fellow pilgrims somehow as part of our commitment to the ongoing process of spiritual transformation. As unlikely as it might seem, could it be that those who describe themselves as "spiritual but not religious" are early innovators (otherwise known as prophets) who are drawing attention to the fact that God is calling forth a new thing through their holy discontent about the church as it currently exists? That's the side of history I want to be on.

The etymology of the word *community* simply means "to come together in unity." People come together in unity around many things—to raise money for a new playground in an impoverished neighborhood, build a new Habitat for Humanity home, provide mutual support for the journey of recovery, fight climate change, and so on. I am suggesting that *a transforming community is a group of people who "come together in unity" around their shared desire to experience deeper levels of transformation*, and it can take many forms. It can be a traditional church, a nontraditional church (like a house church), a religious order, or a ministry organization, but what matters is that they have set their intention to journey together with Christ for the purpose of spiritual transformation.

Human beings do not transform each other. Left to ourselves, even the most wonderful human beings often hurt each other, even when we don't intend to. Our interactions with one another can be very damaging, especially when we form ourselves into groups. We need help, so it's a good thing Jesus is the transforming element in any transforming community. Transforming community is not primarily about warm, fuzzy feelings. It's not about liking each other at the level of personality or having a lot in common. It is not primarily about backyard barbeques, church picnics, or Bible studies. It is not about expecting others to meet our needs or alleviate our pain or provide us with extraordinary social gatherings or doing lots of Christian activities together. It is not something we as human beings can create at all.

German theologian Dietrich Bonhoeffer puts it this way: "Christian community is not an ideal we have to realize, but rather a reality created by God in Christ in which we may participate."[7] This means that what we *can* do is find ways to *participate* in this great reality we call the body of Christ, the community of Jesus, the family of God. This should be a tremendous relief to all of us because it means that creating community is not in any of our job descriptions! (If you ever hear yourself or someone else say, "We are going to create community," that should be a red flag. The work of creating community has already been completed in Christ.)

**THE MANY FACETS OF COMMUNITY**

There are several terms I will use somewhat interchangeably in this work to describe the kind of community Jesus came to initiate among us, each with its own nuance. *Christian community* tends to be about belief—what we believe about God and Jesus and other aspects of faith that we capture in creeds and statements of faith. *Spiritual community* carries with it an emphasis on and an attentiveness to the presence of the Holy Spirit as the one who initiates, animates, and guides the community's life. *Transforming community* encompasses both elements but adds an additional layer, highlighting our commitment to ordering our life around transformation in Christ's presence through the Holy Spirit.

So, in transforming community, we "come together in unity" first and foremost around our *shared desire for deeper levels of transformation in Christ's presence* and our shared intention to prioritize this above all else. We come together based on *shared belonging to God and one another in and through Jesus Christ.* As Bonhoeffer goes on to point out, the more genuine our community becomes, the more everything else between us (including our natural affinities *and* our differences) will recede in significance. They will not disappear, but they will not be as significant as that which draws us together. He goes so far as to say that in the body of Christ we do not relate to one another directly; we relate to one another in and through the person of Christ.

Transforming communities come together based on a *shared desire to seek God and to do the will of God.* In fact, Jesus identified this as the defining characteristic of his community in Mark 3:34-35 when he said, "Here are my mother and my brothers! Whoever does the will of God is my brother and sister and mother." As Rose Mary Doughtery puts it,

> In this passage, Jesus is suggesting that the bond of spiritual community is a common wanting to do the will of God. Those who gather with him in this seeking are his family. They are the ones

> who nourish his life of authenticity with God. . . . The primary question for discernment in such a community is "Do you seek God?" and then, "What does that seeking mean for your life?"[8]

Individuals in transforming communities come together in unity around a *shared willingness to be available to God for each other* as we seek to discern and respond to the will of God. There is a world of difference between the kind of community that helps us seek God and the busy, program-driven places most of us call church! To be present to God for one another and radically available to God as agents of God's grace in the world may call into question a lot of our other plans and priorities.

How does the movement from desire to intention really work? Oak Hills Church is one example of a community that took the deep dive into their desire for something more and eventually reorganized their life together around the promise and priority of spiritual transformation.

### ONE CHURCH'S JOURNEY

Established in 1984 by founding pastor Kent Carlson, Oak Hills Church jumped aboard the seeker movement in the 1990s and became what Kent would come to describe as "an attractional model church."[9] They grew quickly during those years of seeker- and success-oriented drivenness, developing the tagline: Oak Hills Church—Be Surprised! With that came the Sunday's-always-coming pressure to be more surprising, creative, and compelling than the week before. Eventually, however, they began to sense that something wasn't quite right and that there were some unhealthy ramifications of the way they were doing church. As Kent describes it,

> One of the undeniable truths of the large entrepreneurial, attractional model church is that it requires constant feeding. When we structure a church around attracting people to cutting-edge, entertaining, interesting, inspirational, and always-growing

> services and ministries, there is simply no room for letting up. Once we have communicated to the masses that if they come to our church, they'll be surprised, then we have this never-ending burden to surprise people every week. There is no resting. If there is a particularly wonderful experience one weekend, we are driven to do better the next.[10]

Amid these outward signs of success, there was a troubling sense that what they were experiencing was not necessarily good for their spiritual formation. When there was time to pay attention to their souls, they acknowledged a growing hunger for a more substantive life with God. One particularly disturbing realization had to do with how consumerism was impacting the church, bringing to light a sharp contrast between the conflicting values of external success and authentic spiritual formation. They began to understand that "attracting people to church based on their consumer demands is in direct and irredeemable contrast with inviting people, in Jesus' words, to lose their lives in order to find them. It slowly began to dawn on us that our method of attracting people was forming them in ways contrary to the way of Christ."[11]

As these issues were floating to the surface of their collective awareness their spiritual formation pastor, Mike Lueken, enrolled in a two-week doctor of ministry class led by author and professor Dallas Willard. This experience rocked his world and unsettled his vision of what life in the kingdom, and thus life in the church, was really all about. "The contrast between the transformative power of kingdom life and the high-pressure, frenetic, crazy-paced life we were living"[12] became the source of constant conversation among them until shortly thereafter, at a retreat for senior staff and lay leaders, it all came to a head. As they reflected honestly and openly about their life and ministry together, they admitted that their current church structure and focus was working *against* Jesus' invitation to authentic transformation. They acknowledged that to be faithful to the gospel of Jesus, consumerism needed to be named not as a force to be harnessed but rather as an anti-biblical value system that had to be prophetically challenged.

A surprising moment that seemed to catalyze the group's ability to be open and achieve clarity was Kent's confession about how much he had been motivated by personal ambition; he acknowledged that being senior pastor of a large, successful church fed something in him. As he spoke, things got really quiet, and someone called attention to the fact that perhaps this was a holy moment. Someone else suggested they pray—which they did. Over the next few days as they tried to characterize what God was saying to them in it all, it seemed clear that as a church they were

> being called to have authentic encounters with Jesus that would result in transformation and a contagious expression of our faith. There was a pervasive sense among all of us that to be faithful to what had occurred [among us], our church would have to change rather dramatically. We were not being called to a gentle tweaking of some church programs. This was going to be a major overhaul.[13]

A transforming community was being born.

### WHAT DO YOU WANT ME TO DO FOR YOU?

Becoming a transforming community starts with someone's longing for more. It could be a sense that something is not quite right or that something is missing. It could be a hunger for God that cannot be ignored or an encounter with God that makes one unwilling to settle for less any longer. Someone has to be brave enough to speak the unspeakable, and it works best if that person is the leader because it paves the way for others to be honest as well. Mike and Kent's willingness to notice and then express the longings, desires, and questions that were present in their own souls became the genesis of changes that eventually began to reverberate in the church as a whole. Their willingness to be honest about what was going on in their own souls eventually freed others to do the same.

We often assume that sweeping changes in churches and organizations begin with vision-casting by a charismatic leader or a brilliant strategic planning session, but the beginnings of transforming community are typically more intimate and more humble than that. Often such change begins with longings that stir way down deep, underneath the surface busyness of our lives—even the Christian busyness we've created. It ambushes us when we get in touch with what the pearl of great price is for us, and suddenly we find ourselves willing to rearrange everything to welcome it into our lives. It is that way for individuals and for whole communities.

Oftentimes when Jesus sought to move conversations with spiritual seekers forward, he would ask some version of the question "What do you seek?" or "What do you want me to do for you?" Through encounters that began with this very question, blind Bartimaeus received his sight (Mark 10:46-52), James and John (and their mother!) grappled with mixed motives (Mark 10:35-40; Matthew 20:23), John's disciples followed Jesus to his home and spent time getting to know him (John 1:35-42), and the paralytic at the pool of Bethsaida picked up his mat and walked (John 5:1-9)! These conversations, initiated by Jesus himself, opened a whole new set of opportunities and choices.[14]

## TRANSFORMING LEADERS, TRANSFORMING COMMUNITIES

It is unwise to force this conversation or try to make something happen that is just not happening. But what we can do is to stay in touch with our own desires and then be ready to "go there" as the Spirit moves and when the time is right. We can be alert to moments when someone starts to be a little more transparent than usual about their spiritual desires; rather than becoming defensive or dismissing them, we can breathe deeply and open our hearts to really listen, affirming that the desire itself indicates God is already at work in their lives. We can trust the process and express confidence that the longing for more—in our individual lives and in our life together—emerges from an authentic place within. We can slow the conversation down to wait and listen for the whispers and the groans that are too deep for words.

Of course, it works best when leaders go first in taking the deep dive into the churning waters of their deepest desires, their most honest questions, and their awareness of how God is working with them amid their longing. Hanging out in the depths of our own souls and being honest about what is going on there fosters the kind of humility, lack of defensiveness, and acceptance of ambiguity we will need to allow others to do the same. Being able to tolerate the discomfort they feel in the face of their own urgent longings and unanswerable questions is the only thing that prepares leaders for sitting non-anxiously and nondefensively with others as they express such questions.

While the impetus to grapple with the centrality of spiritual transformation to kingdom living can come from the margins, it is easiest and most effective when it comes from the leadership center and works its way out. When these questions and longings are not emerging at least in part from the leadership center they may be experienced as a threat to the powers that be. Unless senior leaders are extraordinarily nondefensive and secure in themselves, the expression of such longing by community members can be experienced as a critique or even as a personal affront to the leader. The defensiveness that results can make things harder than they need to be. This is especially true in communities where any change to vision, mission, or emphasis is expected to come from the leaders.

It will also be helpful if such changes can be introduced in concert with high-level lay leaders (vestry, session, consistory, boards) who have been consistent and influential leaders over time. In any church or ministry there are leaders who have and always will exercise real influence over the direction the community will take. In many cases they are there longer than the pastors and CEOs who come and go. It is best (read: most authentic) when this kind of change in priorities comes from *inside the leadership*—inside what's happening between them and God—rather than being a "church growth" technique. Sometimes leaders go to a conference and get all riled up about some new idea and then come back and try to turn things around too quickly. Eventually the whole thing capsizes, and everywhere you look there are bodies floating in the water.

A much better approach is to trust the slow work of God as it incubates within your own life and the lives of other leaders and key influencers. What often happens first is that the pastor's preaching and teaching starts to change. He or she becomes more comfortable talking about longing (their own and others), affirming the role of desire in the spiritual life, describing what they are experiencing as they explore new spiritual practices, and inviting others into their journey. Those listening might notice that there is something more authentic and more grounded about the way they share or a difference in the way they lead. They may notice that their leaders are more open, honest, vulnerable, and less defensive, better able to listen and receive different points of view with a greater emphasis on discerning God's will together than on top-down decision-making.

Of course, the best possible scenario is when the leaders' longing for more is experienced simultaneously with the congregations' longing for more. In fact, this is often how God works. When the longing for more is coming from multiple directions simultaneously, it can be an indication that God is up to something, and we can trust that good things will come. In many cases aligning a church's mission and emphasis around spiritual transformation may require a major overhaul (as it did for Oak Hills Church), affecting not only the life of an individual church but also (potentially) challenging the way an entire denomination functions. A major overhaul is hard to accomplish without the passion and clarity of the leadership *in spontaneous combustion* with the longings God is stirring up in the hearts of the community.

## THE PARADOX OF LEADERSHIP

As it turns out, transforming community is birthed within a paradox: Even though it's a group thing, it actually begins with you—the leader. Somewhere deep inside yourself you will need to experience your own desperate need and desire and be willing to sell everything *you* have in order to get it. Somehow, by God's grace, you must reorient *your* life and priorities to seek deeper levels of intimacy with God, allowing that to result in your own spiritual transformation first. This is a slow work of God and cannot be rushed.

Tremendous harm can come to communities when *leaders* are not consistently arranging their own lives for spiritual transformation. Shepherds (pastors and spiritual leaders) who are not receiving their soul's nourishment from God may start to feed on the sheep—the very flock they are supposed to be caring for. The result is a leader or leaders who are trying to get their basic human needs for identity, love, approval, and belonging met by the community rather than seeking to have these needs satisfied in their relationship with God.

Many leaders are not even aware of their own unmet needs, let alone their unconscious patterns for trying to get others to meet them—even in a ministry setting. The result is leaders whose profound emptiness results in success-oriented drivenness that drives them and everyone around them. Or whose need for love and approval results in performance and perfectionism that they constantly inflict on themselves and others. Or whose sense of self is so fragile that they can't live without a steady stream of applause and approval from others.

If our legitimate needs for unconditional love, inner fullness, basic self-worth, and a sense of "being okay" are unmet due to a lack of intimacy with God, spiritual starvation can set in, and the shepherd eventually begins to devour the sheep. Henri Nouwen shares this stark truth: "In order to be of service to others, we have to die to them."[15] While this might seem like a radical statement, Nouwen is saying that we must die to measuring ourselves by others' expectations and needing those we serve for our own survival. We can love the sheep and serve them and be committed to them. We can be vulnerable with them and receive the gifts that God is giving to us through them. But our ability to survive spiritually and emotionally must come from the richness of our own intimacy with God, which can only be cultivated in a balanced rhythm of solitude and community. This kind of growth into our own health and wholeness is essential to being able to lead others in transforming community without coercion and manipulation.

In the beginning all of this may feel so tender and so private that you are hardly able to speak of it for fear of violating it somehow. But eventually you will discover that what is most personal is most universal and there are others who want exactly what you have been wanting. There may even be some who were on the brink of leaving the community for lack of this very thing—or maybe they already have and now you can see more clearly why they did. Slowly you discover there are others who are willing to rearrange their lives for what they say they really want. You find that as you talk about your longings, they are willing to talk about theirs and something new begins to emerge that is authentic and pure.

At this point, there is no need for bells and whistles, strategic plans, and grand announcements. Now is the time for quiet recognition, for simply coming together around shared desire and willingness, savoring God's presence in your midst. Eventually and in God's time, you can meet the desires people are expressing with vision that corresponds to those desires. You can build solid biblical, theological, and spiritual foundations to undergird the journey ahead and you can make plans for organizing the community's life to receive what God wants to give. But for now, trust that when the impetus for change comes first from leaders who are simply inviting people to the More in a winsome way, chances are the community will respond well. The longing for change and transformation that is so close to the surface these days means it is more possible than ever for groups to coalesce around their shared desire for authentic transformation in Christ's presence.

3

# BELIEFS THAT SHAPE THE SOUL

## *Biblical and Theological Foundations*

*We cannot think our way into a new way of being, but we can live our way into a new way of thinking.*

Richard Rohr

---

**For some communities,** the presence of desire will be enough to embark on the journey of ordering our lives for what we say we really want. For others, clear biblical and theological perspectives will need to be unpacked systematically by trusted leaders, so spiritual transformation comes to be viewed not as an add-on but rather as one of the basic reasons for the community's existence. After those powerful retreat sessions and the conversations that followed, the leaders of Oak Hills Church recognized the need to put biblical and theological foundations in place that would undergird the changes they were going through.

> Our first order of business was to reshape the theological and conceptual foundation of our church. There was no way to avoid this if we were going to make the radical cultural shift we felt God calling us to make. We went back to the basics and essentially started over. We did it in our teaching. We did it in conversations with our staff. We did it at the elder board. And we did it in various meetings we had with individuals and ministry teams.

> What is the Good News?
>
> What are we called to do in response to it?
>
> What is the purpose of the church?
>
> How does the church relate to the consumer-driven culture?
>
> We spent several years sorting through these kinds of questions [knowing that] new programs would never bring about the radical culture shift. We needed a new foundation.[1]

## CENTRAL TO THE MESSAGE OF THE GOSPEL, CENTRAL TO THE MISSION OF THE CHURCH

How much theological work is needed in your setting requires careful discernment, but what is most important in the cultivation of a transforming community is for the community to grow together in its understanding that *spiritual transformation is central to the message of the gospel and therefore central to the mission of the church.* This shared conviction will result quite naturally in a shared commitment to championing it across all aspects of the community's life.

Beliefs in and of themselves do not change us, but beliefs *can* provide a vision for what is possible; as those beliefs deepen into faith, we can entrust ourselves to what it is we say we believe. Belief that deepens into faith is what shapes us into a new kind of people. I am not suggesting that you bore people to death with long and laborious preaching series that no one knows how to go home and apply; however, transforming communities need enough biblical and theological perspectives to enable them to lean in and trust the process. At the very least, those with significant leadership and influence need to understand what we're doing, why we're doing it, and how we're doing it so they can seed the biblical rationale into the community's life at different points along the way.

*Spiritual transformation is the process of Christ being formed in us for the glory of God, for the abundance of our own lives, and for the sake of others.*[2] Following are some of the most basic biblical and theological categories leaders need to understand, teach, and be ready to communicate about in spontaneous conversations as well as more formal occasions.

**CHRIST FORMED IN US**

Spiritual formation is going on all the time—the only question is whether it is *trans*formation or *de*formation! As Robert Mulholland writes,

> Every thought we hold, every decision we make, every action we take, every emotion we allow to shape our behavior, every response we make to the world around us, every relationship we enter into, every reaction we have toward the things that surround us and impinge upon our lives—all of these things, little by little, are shaping us into some kind of being. We are being shaped into either the wholeness of the image of Christ or a horribly destructive caricature of that image—destructive not only to ourselves but also to others, for we inflict our brokenness upon them. . . . We become either agents of God's healing and liberating grace or carriers of sickness in the world.[3]

Steve Porter asserts that "spiritual formation . . . is simply the Protestant doctrine of sanctification *in a new key*. The theological category of 'sanctification' has traditionally referred to the process of the believer being made holy, which is 'to be conformed to the image of Christ.'"[4] Regardless of what word we use, Paul is very clear that "this is the will of God, your sanctification." As you begin using the language of spiritual transformation, one of the first things people might ask is, "But aren't we already doing that? We have a discipleship program. Isn't that what you're talking about here?" This is an important question and deserves a thoughtful answer. Even though these two words are virtually synonymous, there is a special emphasis contained in each. In the Gospels discipleship emphasizes the immediacy of Jesus' presence and his example here on earth. For the first disciples it was the opportunity to literally be with Jesus to learn from Jesus how to be like Jesus. In the Epistles there is more of an emphasis on the dynamic work of the Spirit mediating the presence of Jesus as we follow our risen and ascended Lord.

I asked Dallas Willard once about whether he used the words *spiritual formation* and *discipleship* interchangeably. He said,

> Not when I'm being careful. They are, of course, closely related, but not the same. Discipleship is, roughly, experiences and practices/activities we go through to achieve, hopefully, the formation of the inner self (heart), will, and spirit into the character of Christ's inner self. "Discipleship" *can* be practiced in such a *way* that spiritual formation in Christ does not occur.[5]

One doesn't have to look very far to see the truth of this. Judas followed Jesus very closely as a disciple but betrayed him in the end. His discipleship did not result in spiritual transformation. The same is true for Peter. He was one of the three closest disciples of Jesus and yet when push came to shove, he became an obstruction to the spiritual purpose of Jesus' life to the extent that Jesus had to push back with "Get behind me, Satan! You are a hindrance to me, for you are setting your mind not on divine things but on human things" (Matthew 16:23). Even with Jesus himself to disciple them, real transformation was still lacking.

It may also be important to note that the word *disciple* does not appear after the Gospels. After the Holy Spirit comes, new language emerges in Scripture to describe the ultimate goal of the Christian life: to be conformed to the image of Christ, transformed into the image of Christ (Romans 8:29; 12:2; 2 Corinthians 3:18; Galatians 4:19), or to "become participants of the divine nature" (2 Peter 1:4). Ideally our discipleship leads to Christ being formed in us, but this cannot be assumed.

This may be more than most people want to know, but it is helpful for leaders to at least understand these distinctions!

### FOR THE GLORY OF GOD

Human beings who are being transformed into the image of Christ glorify God (2 Corinthians 3:18). Full stop. End of sentence. Just as a tree glorifies God by being a tree and growing up toward the sky and just like a flower glorifies God by being a flower and blooming brightly in the spring, a human being glorifies God by being the best human being they can be—a person who accurately reflects the *imago Dei*, the very nature and image of God.

Once we have grasped a biblical understanding of what spiritual transformation is, we might wonder how anything could be more important to the mission of the church than whether or not Christ is being formed in us, whether we are being *transformed* into the image of Christ rather than being *deformed* into the destructive caricature Mulholland describes. Since the presence of sin has obscured the image of God in each of us (even though it is always still there), the only way for a human being to fully glorify God is to enter into the process of allowing that lost essence to be redeemed and restored through the process of Christ being formed in us. Spiritual transformation in the lives of redeemed people is a testimony to the power of the gospel; conversely, when redeemed people are not experiencing transformation, our lives actually become a testimony to the contrary.

As if God's glory is not reason enough, our transformation results in abundance in our own lives as we are increasingly able to align ourselves with the will of God—which is the best thing that can happen to us under any circumstances. Paul even goes so far as to say that finding ways to surrender to God for God's transforming work in our lives ("to present your bodies as a living sacrifice") is an act of worship. This is one very concrete way in which God's will is done in our lives as it is in heaven. No wonder Paul makes such a strong statement about his own ministry priorities: to "present everyone mature in Christ. For this I toil and strive with all the energy that he powerfully inspires within me" (Colossians 1:28-29).

**BY THE RENEWING OF YOUR MINDS**

Another way Scripture describes Christian formation is Paul's phrase "the renewing of the mind" in Romans 12:2, or the process by which we can "let the same mind be in [us] that was in Christ Jesus" (Philippians 2:5).[6] Since it is God's will that we actively resist being conformed to this world and seek instead to be transformed by the renewing of our minds, it is important that we grasp exactly what Scripture means when it refers to the mind. For this, we must return to the original language.

Too often we assume that the word "mind," when used in Scripture, refers to the intellect. From there we have concluded that being a Christian and behaving "Christianly" has to do with believing the right thing. This could not be further from the truth. We have all known brilliant teachers and theologians who have had the right theology and could explain it all very convincingly but somehow haven't been changed by it; they are still selfish or arrogant or unable to love and fully engage those around them. Sometimes they even use their knowledge and intelligence to bully others. The reason this can even happen is fairly simple: Spiritual transformation is not primarily about having the right belief systems in place—although that may be a good place to begin. For it to be real and efficacious, spiritual transformation must impact us at every level of our being. Paul's choice of words bears this out.

Greek is a much more nuanced language than English, and the Greek word *nous* (translated "mind" in Romans 12:2) includes, but goes far beyond, intellectual or cognitive knowing. It denotes the seat of reflective consciousness—the thought patterns from which our behaviors originate. The mind encompasses both how a person perceives and understands the world as well as the patterns of feeling, judging, and determining that shape our actions and responses in the world. It is these thought patterns and the attitudes and behaviors that emerge from them that need to be transformed.

Psychologically, the mind functions in large part to protect the self, to figure things out on its own terms according to the relationships and experiences that have shaped it over time. It works hard to control and manage reality and has its own plans for remedying the human situation outside of Christ and abandonment to his divine will. Thus, any approach to transformation that seeks to bring about real change must go beyond grasping information at the cognitive level to full, experiential knowledge of God that affects our deepest inner orientations and trust structures, our false-self patterns, and any other obstacles that prevent us from fully surrendering to God. *This* is what the Holy Spirit of God must penetrate in order to change us.

Yes, transformation begins with clear teaching that illuminates the path to true change; in fact, we need good information because without it grave mistakes can be made. But teaching is only the beginning. Authentic change and transformation require guidance for engaging in the behaviors, relationships, practices, and experiences that enable us to internalize truth in ways that change how we respond in the world. Or, as Cindy Lee writes in her book *Unforming,* "I use the word *postures* instead of *practices* because it emphasizes that the spiritual life is not a list of helpful activities to do but our ways of being in the world. Postures help us not withdraw from the real world but actually enter into all its complexities."[7]

One of the reasons people in your congregation might resist positioning spiritual transformation as a priority rather than an elective is that they really do not want change at the level we are describing here, and they might even be afraid of it. When this is the case, their resistance is not just a "spiritual" issue; it might also be developmental. To discern this, we must rely on the Spirit's wisdom and timing to fully understand what's going on and how to approach it.

## THE WORK OF THE SPIRIT

Spiritual transformation is something of a paradox: It is natural, and it is supernatural. It is natural for Christ-followers to grow and change just as it is natural for human beings to grow from infancy to childhood to adolescence to adulthood. If something is alive and the conditions are right, it will grow, whether it is a baby, a flower, a puppy, or bacteria in your refrigerator! We do not need to obsess about these things; we just need to create the right conditions for this very natural process to unfold.

Similarly, if the seed of the Christ life has been planted within us at salvation and the conditions are right, we will grow spiritually. The Scriptures are clear that we have already been given everything we need for life and godliness (2 Peter 1:3) so we don't need to obsess about our spiritual growth or anyone else's. We just need to find ways to create the conditions in which this growth can take place.

The paradox is this: Even though birth and growth are natural phenomena, both in the physical world and in the spiritual world, there is also something about the process that is supernatural. It is a God thing—something only God can do through divine intervention.

A biblical approach to spiritual transformation is profoundly trinitarian in that it acknowledges and relies on the activity of the third person of the Trinity. The Holy Spirit of Jesus has been given as our advocate, teacher, and counselor to lead us into truth as we are able to bear it (John 15–16) and to communicate to us the depths of God (1 Corinthians 2:9-16). We can find ways to be open to this process of transformation as it is guided by the Spirit, but we cannot control it or make it happen ourselves. The wind of the Spirit blows where it will (John 3:8).

Paul alludes to the paradox of the natural and the supernatural through his use of two metaphors. The first is the process by which an embryo is formed in its mother's womb: "I am in labor until Christ be formed *(morphoō)* in you." Even though human beings have their part to play in conceiving and giving birth to children—and even though we think we understand certain facts about it—there is something that remains a mystery and a miracle. It is something God does. Every single time.

The other metaphor Paul alludes to is the process of metamorphosis found in Romans 12:2 when he says, "Be transformed [*metamorphoō*] by the renewing of the mind." The Greek word *metamorphoō* refers to the process by which a caterpillar enters into the darkness of the cocoon in order to emerge, eventually, changed almost beyond recognition. Through the process of metamorphosis, the caterpillar transcends its previous existence to take on a completely different form with a completely different set of capacities. The caterpillar's transformation seems to have little to do with cognitive understanding about the process of metamorphosis; something more primal and God-ordained is at work.

And so it is with the process of spiritual transformation. Even though it is the most natural thing in all the world for the seed of the Christ life to take root and grow starting at salvation, there is something about spiritual transformation that is pure gift. Only God, working through the Holy Spirit, can bring it about. Kent Carlson describes what this means for Oak Hills Church: "These days [we] are a community that is trying, throughout every aspect of church life, to invite people to cooperate with the spirit of God in our transformation into Christlikeness. . . . Our language, culture, passion and programs have been reoriented around the challenge and adventure of spiritual formation."[8]

### EMBRACING MYSTERY

The role of the Holy Spirit in our transformation (along with Paul's chosen metaphors) places the process of spiritual transformation squarely in the category we call *mystery*—something that exists outside the range of normal human understanding and human activity. It is something that can only be fully comprehended through divine revelation and brought about by divine activity.

Some personalities are more comfortable with mystery than others, and we are wise to be sensitive about this while at the same time gently pointing out that really everything we affirm as central to our Christian faith is somewhere in Scripture referred to as a mystery. We are servants and stewards of God's mysteries (1 Corinthians 4:1), the mystery of God (1 Corinthians 2:1); the mystery of God's will (Ephesians 1:9); the mystery of Christ (Ephesians 3:4); the mystery of the gospel (Ephesians 6:19); the mystery of marriage, which is applied to Christ and the church (Ephesians 5:31-32); the mystery of Christ in you, the hope of glory (Colossians 1:27); God's mystery, which is Christ himself (Colossians 2:2); and the mystery of the faith (1 Timothy 3:9), just to name a few.

We may need to take time with this because if we are not comfortable with mystery, we are not comfortable with the very gospel we preach. When we enter into a more intentional process of spiritual transformation, we know we will become more like Christ, but we cannot predict exactly what the person of Christ lived in and through us will look like or where it will take us. This not knowing can create anxiety in individuals and in the system, depending on how attached we are to being in control. And for us as leaders, giving up control can be particularly challenging because it goes against traditional models for leadership. Just being aware of these challenges can help your group notice when this kind of anxiety might be at work so you can limit it rather than letting it completely derail you. A good question to ask in the face of such anxiety is "What are we afraid of—really?"

The journey of transformation requires some measure of willingness to relinquish control and give ourselves to a process that we cannot fully understand, control, or predict. The wise leader understands that there may be psychological dynamics at play (such as developmental stuckness stemming from a lack of agency in childhood, trauma, or abuse) and always the spiritual challenges of allowing God to be God in our lives. "Our constant struggle with the issue of control is a crucial part of our spiritual pilgrimage, . . . but in the final analysis, there is nothing we can do to transform ourselves into persons who love and serve as Jesus did except make ourselves available for God to do that work of transforming grace in our lives."[9] How do we do this?

## THE ROLE OF SPIRITUAL DISCIPLINES

While we cannot transform ourselves into the image of Christ, we *can* create the conditions in which spiritual transformation can take place. This is where spiritual practices come in. Spiritual practices are not ways to make brownie points with God or to prove our spiritual superiority to others. They are not a self-help program by which we take control of our journey and change ourselves. Rather, spiritual disciplines are concrete activities we engage in in order to make ourselves available for the work that only God can do. This is what Paul is referring to when he appeals to the Christians in Rome to "present your bodies as a living sacrifice, holy and acceptable to God, which is your reasonable act of worship" (Romans 12:1). He is saying that we can be intentional about creating the conditions for transformation by engaging disciplines that help us surrender ourselves to God—not just in theory but in reality.

Richard Foster puts it this way: "[Spiritual] disciplines are the main way we offer our bodies up to God as a living sacrifice. We are doing what we can do with our bodies, our minds, our hearts. God then takes this simple offering of ourselves and does with it what we cannot do, producing within us deeply ingrained habits of love and peace and joy in the Holy Spirit."[10]

## FOR THE SAKE OF OTHERS

Spiritual transformation is a valuable end in itself in that it brings glory to God, and it is a means to other ends in that it enables us to be the presence of Christ to others and to discern loving action in the world. The litmus test of mature spirituality is an increasing capacity to love

God and to love others as Jesus did (Mark 12:30-31; 1 Corinthians 13; 1 John 4:7). Passages like Isaiah 58:6-14 and Micah 6:8 make strong connections between a real relationship with God and our service to others. In fact, the biblical writers identify a particular kind of hypocrisy that is present when we claim to know God but fail to involve ourselves in the needs of the world that God loves.

One of the major outcomes of our spiritual transformation is an increasing capacity to discern what God-guided action in the world looks like for us. Ephesians 2:10 talks about the good works for which we have been created, which indicates so clearly that none of us as individuals and no single community can meet every need that's out there, although some of us do seem to try. This verse instructs us to discern the good works that we specifically have been created for and to do those. That's all.

Such God-guided activities include (but are not limited to) sharing our faith, generosity, reconciliation and peacemaking (interpersonally and across lines of race, gender, socioeconomic status, and people groups); working for justice; engaging compassionately with the poor; basic kindness; and really anything we do in Jesus' name for the betterment of life in the human community. It is so relieving to know that in the face of unending need, we are invited to discern what God is calling us uniquely to be and do in response to those needs, trusting that in and through the body of Christ as a whole, the needs of our world will be met and God's will will be done on earth as in heaven.

It's not easy to live in the tension between all that needs to be done in the world and our human limitations, and one characteristic of a mature spirituality is that we are able to live humbly and creatively in that tension.

> A genuinely Christian spirituality is not only rooted in a vital, growing relationship with God at the center of one's being but is also incarnated in the reality of the social, economic and political contexts in which one lives. Such spirituality is relevant,

> revolutionary, transforming. . . . There must be a creative tension between our spiritual pilgrimage and the world in which it is lived out. If we attempt to undo this difficult tension, we move either into an "unworldly" spirituality that isolates us from the world or into a "worldly" spirituality that isolates us from the radical demands of a vital relationship with God.[11]

In the next chapter we will take a closer look at what precisely is being formed in us in the transformational process.

# 4

# CHRIST FORMED IN US

## *Love in a Cruciform Shape*

*"What does it mean to be a Christian in this time?" is thus an urgent question. Yet the answer is simple: We have a cross at the center of our faith, and we need to start acting like it.*

Kelly Brown Douglas

---

**One of the things** that bothers me about the way Christians often talk about matters of faith and practice is our tendency to create false dichotomies between being and doing, prayer and action, formation and mission.[1] It can sound something like this—at least in our own heads:

- "He's a contemplative so that means all he does is sit around and pray all day."
- "She's an activist, so that means she doesn't pray enough."
- "He's a mystic, which means he bases everything on experience and has sloppy theology—or no theology at all!"
- "If we focus too much on discipleship and spiritual formation, we will neglect evangelism and engaging with the needs of the world."
- "Soul stuff is soft stuff. Let the contemplatives sit around and gaze at their navels while the activists fly over their heads and get the job done!" (I heard a pastor say this from the platform at a leadership conference once!)

Of course, these stereotypes are stated here in the extreme, which is why most of us would never say such things out loud, but these biases, along with their related concerns, are at work nonetheless. One of the reasons we give in to stereotypical thinking is that there is a grain of truth in every stereotype; this means there is something real to be reckoned with regarding these concerns. Activists fear that encouraging more focus on prayer and the inner life will lead people to become self-focused, narcissistic, and unable to get anything done. Contemplative-types might fear that the activists don't pray enough, that they are shallow and disconnected from the reality of God within. Theologically minded folks might have legitimate concerns about orthodoxy in connection with mystical experiences, while mystics find those with theological concerns to be missing the point entirely. Then, because we're afraid of falling into the excesses of one polarity or the other, we subtly (or not-so-subtly) dismiss those who seem to be wired differently than we are or seem to prioritize things differently than we do. The result is that we diminish aspects of the spiritual life that must be held together in tension if our spirituality is to be healthy.

The truth is that our spiritual transformation is for the glory of God, for the abundance of our own lives, and *for the sake of others* or it is not *Christian* formation at all. Our tendency to create false dichotomies is, quite simply, what the human mind does to make sense of the complexity of our world and to keep our thoughts organized. It's an unconscious process that works something like this: When confronted with aspects of the human experience that seem incongruous or maybe even contradictory, the mind works hard to keep things sorted by filing them away into different categories. Then, without even being conscious of it, we elevate one as being good/better and denigrate the other as being not as good or even bad, placing them in competition or at odds with each other, rather than holding them together in fruitful synergy. The result is false dichotomies that get created between prayer and action, formation and mission, mind and spirit, love of God and love of self, love of self and love for others, and many other facets of the spiritual life that seem different but belong together. As long as this process remains unconscious, we are caught in it without being able to examine it; we miss out on the hidden wholeness that is the fullest expression of our human existence.

## BEYOND FALSE DICHOTOMIES

Fortunately, the very definition of spiritual transformation takes us beyond false dichotomies to a more unified perspective. Spiritual transformation is a lifelong process of growth toward wholeness in Christ measured by an increasing capacity to love God, to love ourselves as God loves us, and to love others as God loves them. All three of these loves are contained within the Great Commandment: "You will love the Lord your God with all your heart, soul, mind, and strength (in other words, with your whole self), and love your neighbor as yourself." To be on an authentic journey of spiritual transformation is to live within the holy tension of balancing all three.

There is no such thing as a generic spiritual journey; each person's journey is taken within the context and culture in which they live, so each life carries its own unique tensions. There is our personal context of family, friends, work, neighborhood, geographical location, and so on, and there is also the historic moment to which God has brought us—maybe for such a time as this. All of these contexts make up the "world" we are to love and engage in Jesus' name. If Jesus loved the world so much that he laid down his life for it, then our transformation in Christ will guide *us* to be present in the world that Jesus loves, bringing his heart with us.

As we live creatively within our own tensions, without giving in to one polarity or the other, we begin to discover how aspects of the human experience that may at times feel like opposites actually do belong together and can be lived in balance over time. It's a bit like riding a bike. To ride a bike, you must find your balance between the left side and right side of the bike; if you are consistently tipping to one side or the other, you're not riding well yet—and you're probably spending at least some time on the ground with scraped knees. It's why, when first learning to ride, we often feel tense and uncertain, we wobble, we grip the handlebars tightly while working hard not to tip to one side or the other. We're not having fun yet. But *with practice* one gets better at balancing until it comes naturally, and we're able to enjoy the ride!

Similarly, in the process of seeking to live a balanced and fruitful life, we discover that it *is* possible

- to love God and love neighbor,
- to engage in solitude as strategic withdrawal that results in empowered engagement with the world,
- to experience prayer that leads to action and action that leads to prayer, and
- to discern the will of God and do the will of God, and then discern some more.

It is in the experience of this back-and-forth movement, and maybe even taking a few tumbles, that the idea of either-or naturally begins to fall away. We find that such bifurcated thinking simply doesn't make sense anymore because moving between both the left and the right in a balanced way *is* the very act of riding a bike. In the same way as we come to know the balance involved in riding a bike, we begin to know experientially that seemingly opposite aspects of the spiritual experience fit together; we begin to experience integration and wholeness and how life-giving that can be.

## BEYOND THE SMALL SELF

A life lived within this powerful pulse is different from a life motivated by mere human activism. Richard Rohr writes,

> Your necessary *no* to injustice and all forms of un-love will actually become more clear and more urgent in silence, but now your work has a chance of being God's pure healing instead

> of your impure anger and agenda. You can always feel the difference in people who are working for causes; so many works of social justice have been undone by people who do all the fighting from their small or angry selves.[2]

There is a difference between being angry and being called. It's not that we're never angry about the sin, the injustice, and the abuses we see all around us; anger is a powerful energy that can motivate us to get out there and fix what's broken. It's just that anger by itself, without submission to the radical demands of love, will probably do more harm than good.

Dr. Martin Luther King Jr. took great pains in his leadership of the early civil rights movement to identify love, unarmed love even, as "the most durable power in the world. This creative force, so beautifully exemplified in the life of our Christ, is the most potent instrument available in [human]kind's quest for peace and security."[3] Elsewhere he referred to this powerful dynamic as *soul force* that not only brings justice for those who have been oppressed, "it does something to the hearts and souls of those committed to it. It gives them new self-respect. It calls up resources of strength and courage that they did not know they had."[4]

The formation of this kind of "love in action" and the discipline it involves is an inside job; no one falls into it by accident because it's too against the grain. According to Henri Nouwen, "The inward journey precedes the journey outward, and the chronology is important. Spiritually, we need to know ourselves and God in order to know other people. We need to love ourselves and God in order to love each other. Communion with God precedes community with others and ministry in the world."[5] If we get these two journeys out of order, it is likely we will find ourselves running at the world with weapons in hand, powered by human energy and activism rather than being drawn by God to engage in God-initiated, God-guided, God-sustained action in the world—action that is motivated by love.

A transforming community, then, by its very definition, is missional. Our transformation in Christ results in an increasing capacity to discern the will of God, which then becomes our mission. This is more than just getting out there and doing stuff; it is being who we were made to be. "For we are what he has made us, created in Christ Jesus for good works, which God prepared beforehand so that we may walk in them" (Ephesians 2:10).

## CONFORMED TO THE IMAGE OF CHRIST, CONFORMED TO THE CROSS OF CHRIST

For a community to even consider arranging its life together around the promise and priority of spiritual transformation, we must know *something* about the outcome of our efforts. What exactly is being formed in us in the transformational process? How do we measure the return on our investment?

A great place to start is to look at the outcome of Jesus' life and to seriously consider the fact that *conformity to the image of Christ is conformity to the cross of Christ.* Here I must acknowledge the profound influence of Dr. Robert Mulholland who, in the last decade of his life, began joining us in our Transforming Community experiences to teach four sessions focused entirely on the last phrase of his definition of spiritual formation: *for the sake of others.* In pointing to Jesus as the One who gave himself totally, completely, absolutely, and unconditionally for others, he taught us that the process of Christ being formed in us means love being formed in us *in a cruciform shape.*

Granted, there are other ways of talking about the essence of who Jesus is and the outcome of his life. Phrases like "sacrificial love," "redemptive love," "restorative love," and "reconciling love" are all in use today, capturing slightly different nuances of this seminal concept. But there is something truly incisive in the phrase "cruciform love" and, one could argue, all that is contained in these other phrases can be summed up in the idea of cruciformity. (Go back over those phrases and see if you agree!)

So, what does the cruciform shape of Jesus' life tell us about the outcomes of our own transformational process? Kelly Brown Davis frames it this way:

> The cross demands that we join in God's eternal mission to create a loving and just world. . . . This divine mission must become our human mission. We are, therefore, called by the cross into a human/divine partnership to cultivate a world and society where the sacredness of all God's creation is respected and where all people—without exception—can live freely and fully into the abundance of life that God promises.[6]

Amen and amen! What does the centrality of the cross have to say about God, about us, and about the outcomes of the transformational journey?

## WHAT THE CROSS DOES (AND DOESN'T) SAY ABOUT GOD

First, God was not taken by surprise when Adam and Eve rejected the truth God had given them. When Adam and Eve gave in to the temptation to doubt God's goodness, God was not forced to retrofit a plan for an event he did not see coming. No, when God chose to imbue humankind with free will at creation, in his omniscience he knew full well that he would be rejected; otherwise, the relationship would have been forced rather than consensual, which would not have been love at all. Cruciform love was *embedded* in God's choice to create humankind; God knew the risk and God took it. *Even when we were dead in our trespasses and sins (in other words, actively rejecting God), God was in Christ reconciling all things to himself* (2 Corinthians 5:19). Throughout human history, God is always moving toward us, risking it all for love.

We tend to peel God off when we think of the cross, as though Jesus and God were somehow separate and distinct in that moment, but that is not theologically accurate. To be precise, it was God-in-Christ who hung on that cross, freely laying down his life for the world he created and loved. As Bob Mulholland taught us so many times, the crucifixion was not *something God did;* it was a revelation of *who God is*—a powerful manifestation of the God who comes and is always coming, always finding ways to move toward us with love, healing, and repair. The cross is the revelation of a God who risks vulnerability and solidarity with the human beings he created.

This is a bit like the risk parents take when we have children. When preparing to welcome a tiny bundle of joy, we as parents are not consciously thinking that that child could reject us somewhere on down that road. But, as much as we might prefer not to think about it, that possibility is embedded in the choice to receive the blessing of children. If such rejection happens (God forbid) at any point, the mature parent doesn't close their heart and walk away, disowning their child forever. Even if "tough love" is needed, loving parents have the capacity to set needed boundaries and consequences while continuing to keep their hearts open to a change of heart on the part of that child. Boundaries are not the same thing as rejection; in fact, sometimes the setting of boundaries is what prepares the way for good sense to win the day as the child encounters those boundaries.

The parable of the prodigal son illustrates this well. The father in this parable represents God as a loving parent who maintains an open heart while enduring complete and utter rejection by his younger son. The father allows his son to make the painful choice to take his inheritance and leave; he does not chase after him to cajole him or use coercive tactics to convince him to come home. But the father also does not close his heart or give up on love. Instead, he watches eagerly for his son to come walking up the driveway, always keeping the possibility of relationship open from his side. Of course, the elder brother, who was much less practiced with the risks and rigors of mature love, resisted this kind of reconciliation while the father continues to demonstrate that it is in his very nature to risk it all for love.

This parable of the loving father and his prodigal son, taken together with the reality of the cross, reveals a God who is ever and always the loving parent who is actively maintaining God's relationship with us from his side.

## RETHINKING THE ATONEMENT

Part of transformational leadership for some of us may be to rethink what the cross really means and how our theology of the cross shapes us. The cross is like a multifaceted diamond; every time you turn it, something different sparkles and draws your attention. If you have always interpreted the cross in one way (as penal substitutionary atonement, for instance), it may surprise you to discover that there are many theories about the atonement and unfortunately, some of them cast God in a harsher light than is actually indicated by the crucifixion itself. If God was in Christ reconciling all things to himself on the cross, he couldn't also be the harsh father who required his "only begotten son" to die a cruel death so his other children could live. No loving parent would make a choice like that.

Ron Rolheiser's perspective on the cross is helpful:

> The cross of Christ is the most revolutionary moral event ever in human history and its implications are still slowly unfolding within human consciousness. . . . Some of the deeper spiritual and moral elements that are contained in the cross are like medicine in a time-release capsule. They are dissolving slowly within history, and we are gradually absorbing their meaning. Simply put, it is taking us many centuries to understand more fully what is contained in the revelation of the cross.[7]

What if we were to open up to the idea that Jesus' death was not so much a father punishing his oldest son for the sins of his other children but rather a choice God made to be one with us—*at-one-ment,* as Richard Rohr parses the word.[8] What if we believed that the atonement had more to do with God coming toward us and seeking to be with us, rather than God needing any sort of "payment" to love us or save us? How transforming would that be? Viewed through this lens, the cross demonstrates *a love that is always moving toward us through nonviolent and noncoercive means.* Rather than exercising the kind of power that comes from cruel punishments, authoritarianism, and heavy-handedness, God-in-Christ chose weakness and vulnerability to draw us to himself. It is more like the power of a baby to draw people to itself precisely in and through its vulnerability. Rolheiser writes,

> God's power is the power of *exousia*, a baby that lies helpless, muted, patient, beckoning for someone to take care of it. It's this power that lies at the deepest base of things and will, in the end, gently, have the final say. It's also the only power upon which love and community can be created because it, and it alone, ultimately softens rather than breaks the heart. And it's a power that invites us in.[9]

## POWER *FOR* AND POWER *WITH*

From the incarnation (God coming in the vulnerability of a helpless baby) to the crucifixion (God inhabiting the vulnerability of a man who lived and died as part of an oppressed race), Jesus is the most complete expression or icon of the very essence of who God is. "God's vulnerability, which the cross invites us into, is power for community with God and with each other."[10] This means that when, by God's grace, we risk showing up in the world vulnerably for the sake of others, transformation is happening. We are becoming partakers in the divine nature. Conversely, when we are unwilling to take the risks inherent in loving, when our focus is primarily on self—maintaining our own safety and security, affection and approval, power and control on our own terms—we're not yet fully clued in to the rigors of spiritual transformation.

In a culture where authoritarian leadership relies on "powering up" and "lording it over" as primary tactics, it will be uncomfortable at times to allow this kind of love and power to be formed in us, and to work from there out into the world. There will be questions as to how it all works; we need our community to help us with this. Since the vulnerability of the cross is foolishness to this world, transforming communities will, of necessity, be settings in which cruciform love as a primary outcome of our spiritual transformation is taught and modeled, supported and practiced. Spiritual formation will move against the grain of the culture of self-actualization and other prevailing perspectives that tend to create God in our own image. The image of Christ *is* the ultimate reality of human wholeness, and it is cruciform love that is the essence of its nature.

There is a dying involved in our growth toward wholeness in Christ, but it is a cross upon which we lose the false self in all its bondage and brokenness so we can receive new life in Christ in all its freedom, healing, and wholeness. The vulnerability of the cross *is* foolishness to those who are perishing because it is the abandonment of our self-referenced way of being, but to us who are being saved it is the power of God—the power that comes through surrendering ourselves more fully to God and being radically available to God for the sake of others.

## NO VICTIMS HERE

This is probably a good place to point out that Jesus makes sure we understand that he was not a victim in the crucifixion. In John 10 where he describes himself as the good shepherd who lays his life down for the sheep, he makes it clear that the choice to lay down his life was all his. He says clearly, "I lay down my life in order to take it up again. No one takes it from me, but I lay it down of my own accord. I have power to lay it down, and I have power to take it up again" (John 10:17-18). There is an odd kind of redundancy in this statement, almost like Jesus wants to make sure we don't miss the point. The point is that Jesus' life and death on the cross modeled power used for the good of others, not victimhood that robs us or others of legitimate power and agency. Jesus exercised agency and personal power when he laid down his life freely at the right time; this means there may (and probably will) be a point at which we face a similar choice as part of our own spiritual journey. But let's be clear: God continues to honor our free will, and we always have a choice about how we will respond to the invitation to cruciform love.

One of the ways we know Jesus' statement about his own agency is true is that there were many other moments during his time here on earth when people sought to arrest or kill him, and he would simply pass through the crowd (Luke 4:30) or in some other way escape from their hands (John 10:40). Why did he do this? Because he knew "his hour had not yet come" (John 8:20). Timing is everything, as the adage goes, and Jesus had a strong sense of it. When he knew it *was* time, Jesus stopped melting through crowds and making his great escapes. When the time was right, he *chose*—voluntarily and of his own free will—to stay put, to wait openly, vulnerable and unarmed as the soldiers came to arrest him in the Garden of Gethsemane. With unarmed love, he surrendered to what was his to do, setting his face resolutely toward Jerusalem where arrest and death were certain.

In this, he models a powerful integration of psychological health (strong sense of self and agency, able to express emotion in the context of relational intimacy, able to be honest about what he was feeling) and spiritual attentiveness (in touch with deeper purpose and able to make meaning, maintain honesty with God in prayer, and act on a strong sense of conviction, etc.).

Jesus' clarity about the fact that he had the power to lay down his life of his own volition and then take it up again in response to the will of God, means Jesus was not a victim in the crucifixion—and neither are we when the cruciform love of Christ is being formed in us. While we may, at times, feel that we do not have all the choices we would like to have in life, in God there is always a choice about whether we are willing to lay down what is false within us or set aside that which no longer serves God's purposes so we can participate in some larger thing God is doing. God will never force this on us *and* there will always be real invitations and opportunities to deepen our understanding and experience of the cruciform life through our responses to those invitations.

This is important reassurance for anyone who has experienced victimhood in their life with other human beings—women who have experienced discrimination or violence, children who have been mistreated or abused, those who have been oppressed and excluded by the majority culture, anyone who has experienced being a victim of harsh treatment beyond their control. God is not asking us to be revictimized. Part of the spiritual journey, even for those who have experienced oppression or victimization, will be to recognize the difference between being forced and having real agency.

God invites us to take up our power and use it for good and then *at the right time* God may ask us to lay down our power—freely and of our own accord—when there is some greater purpose that can be accomplished through it. This is what we see modeled for us in the cruciform shape of Jesus' life. I have had a couple of experiences in my life that were in this category; they were smaller deaths than Jesus' crucifixion, to be sure, but they were significant to me in that they required me to go against what would have come more naturally to my own human impulses. Fortunately, with the help of spiritual direction, I was able to discern what kind of moment I was in, knowing I had the right to stand up and fight if I wanted to. But I also knew I had a choice to lay down my "right" for a greater good. By then, thankfully, I had claimed enough of a sense of self and personal agency that I knew I could lay it down without losing anything of ultimate value.

These choices were heart-rending all the same, and it took time to experience any kind of resurrection; however, knowing what kind of moment I was in spiritually made all the difference in being able to look back and know that the right parts of me died so that other parts could live.

## AT ONE WITH THE CRUCIFORM GOD

Jesus lived a fully empowered life while here on this earth; that is, he was empowered to do whatever love called for in any given moment. Sometimes Jesus did what people asked him to do and sometimes he didn't. He did not heal everyone who needed healing, and he slept in the bow of the boat when his disciples thought he should be doing something about the storm swirling around them. He withdrew to pray when he needed to, and he did not entrust himself to people who were not trustworthy (John 2:24). Sometimes he confronted the religious leaders of his day and sometimes he laid low and melted through the crowds to avoid violent confrontations. In these and many other ways, Jesus modeled a life of being thoroughly self-possessed so he could complete the works for which his father had sent him (John 5:36).

There are some nuances here that we must seek to understand, not just at the level of the mind but also as we "feel it out" in the crucible of our own transforming walk with Jesus. Fr. Ronald Rolheiser frames this as the three stages or struggles of discipleship in a way that is very helpful in navigating this rugged terrain of the soul:

- essential discipleship—the struggle to get our lives together
- mature discipleship—the struggle to give our lives away
- radical discipleship—the struggle to give our deaths away[11]

The cruciform life encompasses all three of these movements as we see them modeled in Jesus.

> Jesus gave his life for us through his activity; he gave his death for us through his passivity. . . . Up until his arrest, the Gospels describe Jesus as active, as doing things, in charge, preaching, teaching, performing miracles, consoling people. Then, after his arrest, all the verbs become passive: he is led away, manhandled by the authorities, whipped, helped in carrying his cross, and ultimately nailed to the cross. After his arrest, like a patient in palliative care, he no longer does anything: others do it for him and to him, . . . and in the manner that he endured that passivity, he gave his death for us.[12]

That is what is meant by the English word "passion"; it takes its root in the Latin *passio,* meaning "passivity," and that is the primary connotation when we talk about Jesus' passion.

To know where we are in the stages of our followership can be helpful in discerning what a particular moment calls for. The cruciform life moves through different phases and expressions as we grow in our ability to surrender to the process of being transformed into the image of Christ. And as we do, we become more than imitators of Christ; we become participants in the divine nature (2 Peter 1:4), able to discern at any point how we are being called uniquely to be in God for the world.

## LIVING IN CIRCLES

Our spiritual transformation unfolds in concentric circles of relationship—our relationship with God, with the community of faith, and with the world God loves. It all begins in *solitude*—that place at the center of our being where God is always present drawing us to himself. In God we find our truest identity along with the inner resources to live the life and calling God has given us.

The next circle is *community*, where we are drawn into relationship with our siblings in Christ who are also cultivating intimacy with God and experiencing themselves to be the beloved of God. This community supports and sustains us in the mystery of our faith because, "left to ourselves, we do not have the resources to maintain the disciplines that God uses as means of grace to transform us to wholeness in the image of Christ. . . . We can no more be conformed to the image of Christ outside of corporate spirituality than a coal can continue to burn bright outside the fire."[13]

The outer circle represents our engagement with the world beyond the community of faith—the world God loves and that Jesus gave his life for. Here we discover our *mission*, our unique way of being "in God for the world," radically available to God for what God wants to do in us and through us for others.

PART 2

# SOLITUDE

## *Our Life Hidden with Christ in God*

*Without solitude it is virtually impossible to live a spiritual life.*

Henri Nouwen

# 5

# LIVING FROM THE CENTER OUT

## *Solitude at the Heart of Community*

*Through the discipline of solitude we discover space for God in our innermost being. Through the discipline of community we discover a place for God in our life together. Both disciplines belong together precisely because the space within us and the space among us are the same space.*

HENRI NOUWEN

---

**IN GENERAL, OUR SPIRITUAL TRANSFORMATION** begins at the center (solitude) and moves out from there to the community of faith and then to the world beyond, always coming back to the center (solitude) in a rhythmic and balanced way over time. In this way we experience the spiritual life more as undulating rhythms than a static reality. Figure 5.1 illustrates this dynamic movement across the concentric circles and also identifies some of the unique practices contained within each circle, practices that keep us open to God's transforming presence and work in our lives.

The practices listed in figure 5.1 are meant to be a sampling, not an exhaustive list. Feel free to add additional practices you know to be transformative and to change the nomenclature to correspond more closely with your own tradition and practice. Seeing the circles and the practices within them laid out in this way can help us:

- look at our own lives and organize our spiritual practices in a balanced way,
- lead our community in envisioning a life together that is lived from the center out, and
- assess which circles and practices are well-represented in our community's life and those that may need more attention.

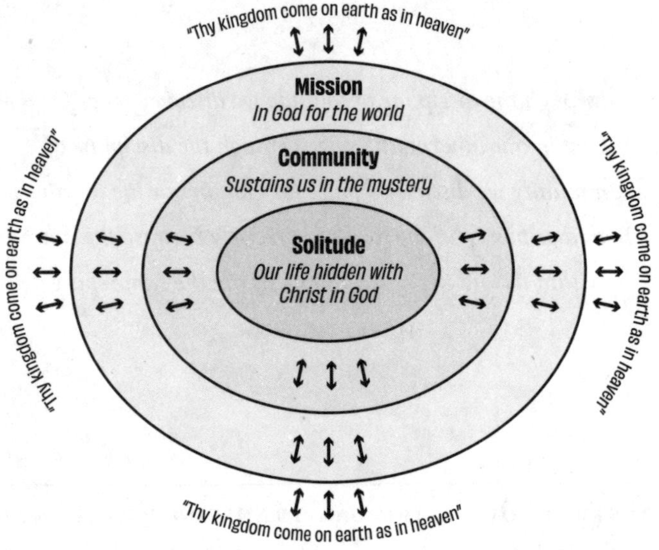


**Solitude**
Our life hidden with Christ in God
***Practices:***
Attending to desire
Silence
Prayer
Scripture
Self-examination
Confession
Journaling
Retreat
Honoring the body
Discernment
Private worship

**Community**
Sustains us in the mystery
***Practices:***
Eucharist/Communion
Spiritual friendship
Spiritual direction
Preaching/teaching
Equality
Sabbath
Communal discernment
Corporate prayer and worship
Forgiveness
Tarrying/lament
Building one another up in love through spiritual gifts

**Mission**
In God for the world
***Practices:***
Good works for which I've been created
Faith sharing (proclaiming the good news)
Generosity
Reconciliation and peacemaking
Justice
Compassion
Working for betterment of human community

**Figure 5.1.** The dynamic movement of spiritual transformation

## ENCOUNTERING GOD IN SOLITUDE AND SILENCE

Paradoxically, transforming community does not begin with community; it begins with God—the One who created us, forms us, calls us, redeems us, saves us, preserves us, and loves us with an everlasting love. Many communities function as though people's spiritual lives begin and end with community, which is a grave mistake. In reality, human beings cannot fix, fill, satisfy, or transform each other—despite our best attempts, and the sooner we accept this, the better. As individuals in the community cultivate this relationship of belovedness and belonging, they are then able to live from that solid center out into the world; from a secure base they can enter freely into relationship with others who are also finding their true life hidden with Christ in God, rather than demanding from others what they cannot give.

Solitude is the intentional practice of being with God and God alone. Especially when coupled with silence, solitude creates space to give God our full and undivided attention and to offer God greater access to our souls. Here, at the center of our being, God is present to us directly through the Holy Spirit, who witnesses with our spirits about who we really are and draws us into communion with God as our loving Parent (Romans 8:15-16). As we cultivate life at the center, we discover our true life "hidden with Christ in God" (Colossians 3:3), and more and more that identity becomes the bedrock of our being. While our physical life in this transient world can be threatened in any number of ways, we grow in confidence that our true life and identity are held securely and cannot ultimately be taken from us. Increasingly, this union and communion with God becomes the source and supply of our life and existence.

If we misunderstand or misrepresent the progression from solitude to community, we run the risk of cultivating a community whose members expect each other to meet the needs only God can meet, who lash out at the community (or leave) when the community disappoints them, and who eventually burn out as they carry out their ministry and mission from a place of emptiness rather than fullness. In solitude we connect with the Source of our life and receive the inner resources needed for that life. When we return to the center, we come home to ourselves in God and are reminded of who we are and to whom we belong, grounding ourselves in our truest identity once again.

## THE DANGERS OF COMMUNITY WITHOUT SOLITUDE

Writing in the crucible of Nazi Germany, German theologian Dietrich Bonhoeffer makes the startling and counterintuitive statement that "whoever cannot be alone should beware of community. Such people will only do harm to themselves and to the community."[1] What Bonhoeffer is saying here is that human beings cannot do for each other what only God can do, and any community whose individual members are not practicing solitude and silence are at great risk.

Catholic priest and spiritual author Henri Nouwen, who was rather famous for championing the importance of solitude as the heart of the spiritual life, wrestled hard to actually live out this concept. One of the most consistent themes in his writings is his gut-wrenching honesty about his voracious needs for love, intimacy, and self-esteem and how he tried to get those needs met in his friendships and relationships in community. His book *The Inner Voice of Love* chronicles one of the most disastrous of these attempts that eventually led to an emotional breakdown and required an intervention from his community. His healing process involved stepping away from his community so he could be held and guided into an experience of listening to the inner voice of God calling him the beloved rather than continuing to overburden his community with his inordinate demands.

Nouwen's courageous struggle and his willingness to put it out there is a powerful example of the potential danger to communities when we are not clear on the need for both solitude and community; when communities are not being guided to practice solitude in fruitful ways, the harm that can be done is incalculable.

## STARTING WITH SILENCE

Once we have set time aside to be with God, we have choices about what we will do with that time—choices based on what we want and what we need in that relationship and choices based on how God might be drawing us. In previous works I have offered more personal step-by-step guidance for entering into the practices that take place at the center—in solitude.[2] My intention here is slightly different; it's more to give a "lay of the land" for how we can frame solitude for our communities and what can be offered as teaching and guidance. The goal is that people can find guidance for their journey into solitude and silence *with us*, rather than needing to look elsewhere. Ideally (and this is important!) those who are teaching and leading in these areas are doing so from the deep well of their own experiences, which is where their inner authority will come from.

One of the main things that was missing in my early devotional training was teaching and experience with silence. There really is no substitute for silence because it helps us withdraw not only from our life in the company of others but also from our addiction to noise, words, and activity. Starting our solitude times with silence allows the inner chaos to settle and helps us get in touch with what is truest within us so we can say something true to God, which is a more authentic beginning to praying with words.

Silence also creates an inner environment in which the Scriptures can penetrate more deeply, and we are better able to distinguish the one true Voice from all the other voices that clamor for our attention. A metaphor I find helpful is the image of a pond that is either very choppy or very still. When the surface of the pond is choppy, you can throw a rock in it and not even really see where it went in, let alone any impact it might have made. On the other hand, when the surface is very still, you can throw a rock in and see the impact as ripples that emanate from where it entered the water. Most of us enter solitude with a lot of surface chop going on in our souls. When we begin with silence, all of that settles down and we can see and hear and be more responsive to God's word to us and feel the tender love God has for us.

While at first it might seem like all we are experiencing is our own inner chaos in the silence, over time this practice of silencing external noise and distraction leads to inner stillness—the ability to "be still, and know that I am God" (Psalm 46:10). This is the beginning of our transformation. As we become more intentional about cultivating a transforming community, we need to teach people to incorporate some silence into their times of solitude and lead them in some shared experiences.

## SHARING SILENCE

Learning to share silence together is a practice that can have a profound impact on our life in community.

Gunilla Norris writes that "sharing silence with others is a profound act of trust, love, and courtesy. It is a mutual gift, a necessity, a helping hand, a path, and a discipline. . . . By such courtesy we are deeply transformed."[3] I experienced this in one of my earliest opportunities to share silence with others. It took place during a thirty-six-hour "silent sabbath" that was carved out in the middle of a ten-day residency in the spiritual direction training program I was a part of. I had known from the very beginning that this was going to be part of the training, but as the time got closer, I realized I was very nervous about it. The time frame for the silent part was longer than anything I had tried before and I was afraid of being bored, missing my family, not liking the food, not sleeping, not hearing from God, or (worse!) hearing from God—you name it, I was afraid of it.

Since this was before the days of cell phones and computers, the only way to be in contact with the outside world was to use the pay phone in a public hallway, so if I "cheated" by breaking silence and making a phone call, everyone would know it. And since I had flown in and taken ground transportation to the retreat center, there was no way to leave. I knew that once we began, I would be pretty well stuck, with no way out, and I have never liked the feeling of being hemmed in. I will admit that there were points when the thirty-six hours felt very long, but what I remember most clearly about that time is that I fell in love with the people with whom I was sharing solitude. There were about twenty-five of us, and we had gotten to know each other to some extent over meals and by visiting together in small groups. For me, it was just enough contact to be aware of who I wanted to get to know better and who I wanted to avoid. As an introvert, I had found mealtimes to be slightly exhausting, what with the awkwardness about who to sit with and the prospect of trying to start up a conversation with people who were complete strangers. But when we shared meals in silence, we could be together beyond the words, beyond all the social striving, beyond the limits of personality. We were in solidarity around something deeper—our shared desire and intention to seek God—which could now be felt, rather than merely talked about.

The most impactful moment in all of this came during one of the meals when the man sitting across from me started to sob. My knee-jerk reaction was to try and figure out if there was anything I could do for him. Everything in me screamed to do *something*! But then I remembered our commitment to holding silence together, which meant that all I could do was just *be there*—in love, in prayer, in solidarity. And believe me, I felt all the feels. I felt uncomfortable. I felt relieved. It felt right. And it felt full. I never did learn what happened for him during that meal, but the details didn't matter. What mattered is that I didn't do anything to interrupt what was happening between him and God. What mattered was the growth that took place in my own awareness that God was with him and in my ability to trust that God was caring for him better than I could. What mattered is that I did not get hooked by my normal impulse to rush in and try to figure out how I could "help."

I can only imagine how freeing it was for him to be able to be in that moment with God, rather than being subjected to all that.

## CENTERING DOWN—TOGETHER

In reflecting on that experience, it occurred to me that words are often expressions of our personalities, and it is often personalities (ours and theirs) that we are liking, not liking, and reacting to. But when we are not using our words with one another, personalities are not so much in evidence; we can actually sense more of the essence of a person and relate to that. Pray into that. Sharing silence is a way of being together that is not so exhausting and in which there is the potential for a deeper solidarity that is not so dependent on the externals of liking each other, finding affinity, agreeing on things, or figuring out social interactions. Many of us have no idea how exhausted we are from constantly relating socially at the level of personality. Sharing silence together is a blessed kind of rest indeed.

In communities ordered for transformation, our commitment to solitude, coupled with the practice of some shared silence, can go a long way in ensuring that each person is bringing a more authentic self to the community, a self that is grounded in God.

> Solitude greeting solitude: that's what community is all about. Community is not the place where we are no longer alone but the place where we respect, protect, and reverently greet one another's aloneness. . . . Our solitude roots us in our own hearts. Instead of making us yearn for company that will offer us immediate satisfaction, solitude makes us claim our center and empowers us to call others to claim theirs. Our various solitudes are like strong, straight pillars that hold up the roof of our communal house.[4]

Centering prayer is one way to talk about incorporating silence into people's lives—alone and with others. Fr. Thomas Keating, who articulated the method of centering prayer, describes the effects of this practice on community:

> Once we begin the spiritual journey, there is no longer merely private prayer. Our prayer becomes a participation in the groanings of the Spirit for all the intentions and needs of the human family. This means that during the periods of Centering Prayer we enter into a sense of oneness with everyone else who is experiencing grace, and with the whole human family. At times we may actually feel this bonding. This bonding is the heart and soul of a Christian community.[5]

I can't help but wonder, Who would we be if we centered solitude and silence and taught people how to practice it as the very heart of our life together? What difference would it make if the practice of centering ourselves in God through silence was built into our communal practices? Maybe we would experience something like what Quaker Thomas Kelly describes in his book *A Testament of Devotion*: "Life from the Center is a life of unhurried peace and power. It is simple. It is serene. It is amazing. It is triumphant. It is radiant. It takes no time, but it occupies all our time. And it makes our life programs new and overcoming. We need not get frantic. [God] is at the helm. And when our little day is done, we lie down quietly in peace, for all is well."[6]

### PRAYER, JOURNALING, AND FASTING

Prayer encompasses all the ways we *communicate* and *commune* with God, so in some ways it is rather artificial to distinguish it from other spiritual practices; the reality is that all of life can be a prayer. That said, it can be helpful to describe communication as prayer that is oriented more toward words, while communion is moving beyond words to simply being *with God with what is*—beyond words, thoughts, and concepts. Moving beyond words can also be a way of resting in God rather than always working for God—an aspect of our spirituality that many of us would do well to cultivate.

Journaling can be an aid to prayer with words, providing a record of our conversations with God. Of course, journaling is not anything that's mandated in Scripture, but it is modeled there. I've always thought of the Psalms as David's journals where he poured out his heart to God in written form and often added music to turn them into songs—a very intimate experience of communication and communion indeed! Incorporating art and beauty through the use of icons and other religious art and symbols can also bring depth, focus, and intimacy to our prayer lives. It is not hard to begin envisioning different kinds of prayer experiences that could be incorporated into corporate worship and prayer, as well as special classes and guided experiences—all for the purpose of your church or community becoming a major source of spiritual guidance for the transformational journey. Fasting (or abstinence, to be more precise) can also be a powerful aid to prayer because it engages the body in creating space for us to connect physical hunger with our spiritual longings in an embodied way. When fasting, we can use the time saved in meal prep and cleanup for added prayer, allowing the pangs of hunger to bring our attention to spiritual hunger, focus the mind on what is most essential, and pray from that place.[7]

Different forms of prayer give shape to our quest for intimacy with God; they are not merely techniques. In transforming community, people should expect to be schooled and resourced in all sorts of different ways to pray, not just the ones that come from our own tradition.

## HEARING GOD IN SCRIPTURE

Most good Christians are committed to learning about God through Bible study and other kinds of theological training—and that's all good! However, a transforming community is committed to moving beyond information to transformation in our engagement with Scripture. Especially in Western culture where mastery of the different texts we read and using them to our own ends is so embedded in our educational process, it is hard to envision how we can give up our unconscious attempts to control the text and instead allow them to be a tool God can use at God's initiative in our lives according to what he knows we need. I am a firm believer in the church's responsibility to foster biblical literacy as part of "present[ing] everyone mature in Christ" (Colossians 1:28), but we cannot stop there. We also need approaches to Scripture that create space for God to take the initiative and address us on God's own terms for us. Such approaches include using a common lectionary, *lectio divina* (an ancient form of contemplative Bible reading that incorporates the rhythm of silence and Word), and finding ourselves in the story of Scripture *(lectio continua).* Providing corporate experiences with these practices also serves to teach people how they can incorporate them into their times of solitude as ways of giving up control and being open to God's surprises.

## SELF-EXAMINATION LEADING TO SELF-KNOWLEDGE

The practice of self-examination is one that fills many of us with a sense of dread because it feels so . . . well, negative. A lot of that has to do with the fact that it has been taught in such a dour and punishing way in many religious settings. This is something we can and should correct in transforming community. Psalm 139:23-24 is perhaps the most well-known Scripture that encapsulates this practice—"Search me, O God, and know my heart; test me and know my thoughts. See if there is any wicked way in me, and lead me in the way everlasting"—but it is the entire psalm taken together that describes self-examination in its fullness.

The psalm begins by (somewhat ironically) affirming that God has already "searched me and known me," suggesting that the point of self-examination is not so much about giving God permission to learn something he doesn't already know (because God already knows everything); it is more about inviting God *to help me know me,* to reveal to me the truth about who I really am and what's driving my behaviors. But the self-examination process is so much more than digging around introspectively trying to identify all the ways I have sinned recently. A truly biblical approach is more balanced than that because it begins with *awakening to God's unconditional loving presence* as the ultimate, orienting reality of our lives (Psalm 139:1-12). In the first movement of this process, we come to an increasing assurance that there is nothing we can do to fall out of God's love.

From there we *awaken to ourselves as we really are* in light of God's presence, starting with celebrating the goodness of our created self and a deep affirmation that we are "fearfully and wonderfully made" (Psalm 139:13-18). Unfortunately, very few people have been taught in church that self-examination involves celebrating the goodness of our own created being! And yet, this psalm is so clear that it is only in the context of knowing how secure we are in God's love and being firmly grounded in the fact that we are part of God's good creation that we can move profitably to acknowledging the darker side of who we are or the parts that simply confuse us (vv. 19-22). Then and only then can we feel safe enough with God to ask him to reveal to us what's what and lead us in a more life-giving way (vv. 23-24).

Historically, this practice is called *the examen*, which includes both the examen of consciousness (heightened awareness of God's presence) and the examen of conscience (heightened awareness of ourselves in light of God's presence).[8]

## CELEBRATION AND CONFESSION

Self-examination leads to greater self-knowledge, which culminates in being able to celebrate our created self as part of the goodness of God's creation as well as repent and confess the ways we have fallen short.

It is impossible to overstate how important it is that leaders strive to keep these two in balance in the way they teach and lead. The God-guided practice of self-examination is the deep heart of the transformational journey because it gives us the opportunity to see ourselves as God sees us—through the eyes of our loving Parent who keeps us as the apple of his eye. Given the biblical warnings against pride, it may be hard for some to imagine that celebrating the goodness of ourselves as part of God's good creation could be a spiritual practice, but it is! Then there are also those times when God shows us how we have fallen short. When this is the case, there is no need to give into debilitating shame, although we probably will experience some godly grief that leads to repentance. When, by God's grace, we are able to recognize sin or negative behavior, the next step is to name it for what it is and ask God for the insight to see what is happening inside us so we can confess not just the behavior but the underlying pattern that produced the behavior. Then we, too, can ask for God's wisdom and strength to live differently going forward, just as David asked God to "lead me in the way everlasting," or life-giving way (Psalm 139:24).

The outcome of this process is not so we walk around feeling defeated. Rather, the culmination of the whole process is the unburdening that comes as we confess our sins, receive the gift of God's forgiveness, and take hold of the opportunity to begin again. All of this reminds me of the old adage: "God loves us just as we are, but he also loves us too much to leave us as we are."

## CONFESSION IN COMMUNITY

Self-knowledge and confession take place first between us and God, but it is also preparation for engaging in communal and interpersonal expressions. In most liturgical traditions, there is a place for some kind of corporate confession somewhere in the community's life and worship. Here is a familiar one:

> Most merciful God,
> we confess that we have sinned against you
> in thought, word, and deed,
> by what we have done,
> and by what we have left undone.
> We have not loved you with our whole heart;
> we have not loved our neighbors as ourselves.
> We are truly sorry and we humbly repent.
> For the sake of your son Jesus Christ,

have mercy on us and forgive us,
that we may delight in your will,
and walk in your ways,
to the glory of your name.
Amen.

I love this prayer because it does such a good job of covering the landscape; I just wish we would pray it more slowly and make use of it as a tool for self-examination. What if we did it this way?

Most merciful God,
we confess that we have sinned against you
in thought, word, and deed,
by what we have done,
and by what we have left undone.

[Pause. Reflecting on the last week, ask God to show you how you might have sinned by what you have done and what you have left undone. Is there any thought, word, or deed that is troubling to you because you suspect it might have fallen short in some way?]

We have not loved you with our whole heart;

[Pause. Ask God to reveal a moment when you were less than wholehearted in your love for God.]

we have not loved our neighbors as ourselves.

[Pause. Ask God to bring to mind a moment when you failed to love and care for someone as you love and care for yourself.]

We are truly sorry and we humbly repent.

[Pause to experience the godly grief that leads to repentance—to grasp at a heart level the significance of what you are confessing.]

For the sake of your son Jesus Christ,
have mercy on us and forgive us,

[Pause to receive God's forgiveness and to experience the unburdening that comes.]

that we may delight in your will, and walk in your ways,

[Does anything come to mind that you could do differently next time that would be more in line with God's will?]

to the glory of your name.
Amen.

The guidance for this could be given verbally by the pastor who is leading the prayer, or it could be written into the liturgy as a reflection and journaling prompt. Of course, doing it this way will take more time—maybe even fifteen minutes—but this will make it a transformative experience rather than just a perfunctory reading. If you are willing to create this space, you could have pastors or prayer ministers positioned around the room and invite people to come forward and receive absolution. I know some communities where time is built in for people to leave their seats and find the person they need to confess to (if they are present) and make their confession to that person right then and there. There is strong biblical precedent for this (see Matthew 5:23-24), and I suggest offering Communion immediately following. This movement from solitude to community is what transforming community looks like! In fact, Bonhoeffer writes that "in confession there is a breakthrough to community."[9]

## SOLITUDE AND DISCERNMENT

Discernment is an increasing capacity to recognize and respond to the presence and activity of God, both in the ordinary moments of our lives and in the major decisions of our lives; a regular practice of solitude and silence contributes mightily to this. In solitude and silence, we are becoming more attuned to the still, small voice of God that is distinct from all the rest; then, when we face significant decisions in our lives, we can increase our time in solitude for more focused listening, just as Jesus did. Immediately following Jesus' baptism the Spirit drove him into the wilderness to be tested by the evil one for the purpose of clarifying and purifying precisely how he would carry out God's purposes. Before choosing his disciples, he went up to the mountain and prayed to his Father all night. When he was experiencing feelings of dread about his impending crucifixion and wondering if there could possibly be another way, he left even his closest friends behind to wrestle with God in solitude before emerging and setting his face resolutely toward Jerusalem. When we as mere humans are facing important decisions, we should probably consider taking more time in solitude as well!

Discernment is a many-layered thing in Scripture. It is a mark of Christian maturity (Romans 12:2). It is a spiritual gift given to some in the body of Christ to help the rest of us learn how to do it (1 Corinthians 12:10). It is a habit by which we become increasingly familiar with the voice of our good shepherd so we can join him into the abundant life he has for us (John 10:1-10). It is a personal spiritual practice we can utilize when we have important decisions to make (1 Corinthians 2:14-16). And it is a communal practice leaders can engage in together to discern how God is leading in their communal life (Acts 15).[10] Since discernment is a major outcome of the transformational journey, a significant aspect of our spiritual leadership is to train people for discernment at all of these levels, providing teaching and guidance for how to do it, and highlighting solitude and silence as a significant part of the practice.

## ALONE TOGETHER

One of the most memorable experiences I have had leading others into solitude and silence happened in a most unlikely place—a megachurch in the suburbs of Chicago. I had been on staff there for a while, and part of my job was to provide resources and opportunities for ongoing spiritual formation among our staff. Together with amazing colleagues, we had developed classes, retreats, and experiences designed to create space for attending to the inner life amid the intense demands of church life and global ministry. It was good and fulfilling work. Eventually, though, we had a sense that, in addition to the teaching and experiences we were offering in smaller elective settings that staff could choose from, it was important for us to drive a bigger stake in the ground about the importance of solitude and silence, in particular. We felt the whole staff needed to engage in and experience something *together* that could become a sort of touchstone for our shared life and practice.

The only problem was that we were a staff of around five hundred people, and finding a retreat center that would accommodate us was not realistic, so we had to get creative. We decided to utilize our own campus, but that meant making significant preparations. It took intention and careful planning to think about shutting down all ministry activity, operations, the call center, and more for a day so everyone could participate. We identified the atrium in the center of the main building as the best place to create a retreat-like environment where people would gather for some initial teaching and guidance before being sent into solitude. The building and grounds crew got busy carving out new walking paths and placing benches all around the property so people could be outside. The elders, management team, and department heads were briefed about the plan so they could be present and supportive of their teams in carving out this time. We arranged for lunch to be brought in so we could share a silent lunch and prepared handouts that gave concrete guidance for the blocks of time we would spend in silence. And we made plans for how we would debrief the whole experience afterward.

When the day came (I think it was a Tuesday), five hundred hard-working, high-capacity pastors, ministry leaders, operations staff, and administrative support staff came to a hard stop and entered into what was, for many, their first experience with solitude and silence in the context of our community's life. We shut down the campus. We gathered for teaching and guidance. And everyone entered into what, for me, was one of the most amazing days I have ever been a part of.

I still cannot fully describe what happened that day—how grateful people were, the unity we shared that was beyond words, how amazed we all were that we had invested at that level in our spiritual practices as leaders in community.

Over the years I have led retreats of all sizes, and all have been amazing in their own way because of God's faithfulness to show up whenever we create space for him. It's not so much the size of this particular group that I'm highlighting but more the set of challenges facing us that could have convinced us that something on this scale was impossible. Now I can say with confidence that where there's a will (and a little bit of creativity) there's a way—whether you are a group of ten or five hundred. Each community will have its own challenges and opportunities, but my point here is that we found our way to do a thing that really mattered for our transformation in community. And you can too.

# 6

# WITH GOD IN OUR BODIES

*Incarnational spirituality is any spirituality that is enfleshed and lived, not simply believed or practiced. It is a spirituality that orients us toward life as it is lived here and now in our embodied existence.*

DAVID BENNER

---

WHEN WAS THE LAST TIME you heard a sermon highlighting the goodness and spiritual significance of our bodies? My guess is that it's been a while or maybe never. This is unfortunate because as human beings, we are not disembodied spirits; we are each a unified whole—body, mind, soul, and spirit—seeking to bring everything we are to our relationship with the Divine.

Many of us have regrettably inherited what Stephanie Paulsell identifies as "an ambiguous legacy" regarding our bodies.[1] On the one hand, we live in a secular culture that glorifies perfect bodies, while at the same time many of us have been shaped within religious cultures that dismiss and denigrate the body. This has produced yet another false dualism between body and spirit that fails to honor bodies as part of God's good creation and neglects to acknowledge our bodies as temples designed for worship and encounter with God. That's the bad news.

The good news is that in transforming community, we can heal this false dichotomy—for the glory of the God who made us, for the abundance of our own lives in our bodies, and for the sake of others as we seek to honor and respect them in their bodies. In fact, I have come to see our intentionality around honoring bodies as a defining characteristic of transforming communities because it is a point of much needed integration in our life with God. As Stephanie Paulsell writes, "The Christian practice of honoring the body is born of the confidence that our bodies are made in the image of God's own goodness. As the place where the divine presence dwells, our bodies are worthy of care and blessing. . . . It is through our bodies that we participate in God's activity in the world."[2]

## AN UNSETTLING AWARENESS

I have not always lived this way, and ironically, it was in the process of trying to stay faithful to my *spiritual* journey that I first began to face my profound ambivalence about life in a body.[3] At the ripe old age of thirty I began acknowledging how out of touch I was with life in my body and that (sadly) I was routinely pushing my body beyond its human limits—in God's service, of course. I had to face the fact that, rather than caring for my body, I had been driving it like a truck and using it for my own ends, to the point that it was now protesting. Teachings about mortifying the body and sacrificing one's health and well-being to unremitting service only contributed to the unhealth.

Beyond that, I was quite out of touch with any sense that life in my body was a gift from God to be treasured or that it had anything to do with my spirituality. Intent on trying to be so "spiritual," I had relegated the body to a lesser category that warranted little attention. I figured as long as the warning lights weren't going on I could ignore it. It didn't help that the surrounding culture idolized perfect bodies, valuing people based on their physical appearance and sexual appeal. These "secular" values made me all the more hesitant to pay attention to my body. I did not want to fall into the excesses of a culture that placed an inordinate value on physical features rather than the beauty and dignity of the human soul reaching toward God.

As I reflect on my early religious training, I realize I never heard one sermon or any other teaching on caring for and attending to my body as an important part of discipleship—except for messages directed at the youth on sexual abstinence before marriage. Imagine my astonishment when a good spiritual director started her work with me by helping me pay attention to life in my body. It took years to unravel it all, which has been an important part of my personal journey and our journey in transforming community. We are not merely souls or spirits; by God's design, we are embodied beings, and our bodies are temples of the Holy Spirit.

Stephanie Paulsell talks about our unsettledness this way:

> Christianity has long struggled with uneasiness about the body, even as it affirms the goodness of the body in its bedrock beliefs. Many people have experienced religious traditions not as repositories of wisdom about how to honor the body but as repressive institutions that deny the goodness of the body and its pleasures, or as beliefs that nurture animosity toward particular bodies.[4]

Once we understand this legacy and how it developed, we can take steps to move beyond it, first by engaging the biblical witness and ascertaining what Scripture has to say about our bodies and then by exploring spiritual practices that help us receive life in a body as the gift that it is. Transforming communities can—and should—offer guidance for receiving and caring for our bodies as a gift, but too often we haven't. We can be a part of shattering this dualism.

## WHY DID GOD CREATE BODIES?

Once I began to see how this ambiguous legacy had worked its way into my own psyche, I became curious: Why did God create bodies? Several ideas came pretty quickly. First, God created and keeps creating bodies because *God is creative.* This is one of the first things we learn about God in Genesis 1. It is an amazing thing to look at our world and see that every body is different; no two bodies are even remotely the same except in the case of twins and multiples, but even they have their distinctions. And God just keeps on creating! How meaningful it is to ponder that each of us is an expression of God's creative work by being the bodies we are.

Second, God created bodies *so we can glorify God in our bodies* (1 Corinthians 6:20). The body takes on greater significance when we grasp the distinction between glorifying God in our bodies rather than merely glorifying the body. I had only heard 1 Corinthians 6:20 referenced in messages on sexual abstinence, but this verse seems to be saying so much more than that! It introduces the idea that we can glorify God by simply *being* the body we were created to be—in whatever capacity God has given it in any given season. We are not talking about obsessing about having the perfect body as our culture would define it but about being the best body we can be *right now*. This will look different depending on whether we are nineteen, thirty, sixty, or on our death bed; an important aspect of glorifying God in our bodies is accepting where we are now and living in that stage with dignity and trust in our Creator.

Third, God created bodies so that *the power of God can be seen in these earthen vessels*. Sometimes this is hard to fathom because life in our bodies can be so unpredictable, yet they are vessels through which God's power can be revealed in unique ways. We carry the gospel—the ministry that's been entrusted to us—in earthen vessels precisely so God's glory and power can shine through. While this may strike us as being full of paradox, being precisely who and what we have been created to be is a profoundly simple way of glorifying God if we could only grasp it. The second-century theologian Saint Irenaeus says it best: "The glory of God is a human being fully alive!"[5]

### A VARIED AND WIDE-RANGING EXPERIENCE

Knowing that God has chosen to make our bodies his dwelling place opens the door to remarkable opportunities for heightening our awareness of God's presence with us, which is really what the spiritual life is about.

But let's be honest—there *are* challenges. Life in the body is, after all, a varied and wide-ranging experience, and there is no doubt that some experiences are better than others. These varied experiences contribute to the challenge of experiencing our bodies as a gift, but transforming communities can be settings where such experiences are normalized and guidance is given for how to open to God in these places. How healing it can be when, in community, we are able to acknowledge that some of us have had very positive experiences in our bodies while others are still grappling with not-so-positive experiences. For most of us, it's a combination of both.

An important aspect of transforming community is to bring to consciousness the ambiguous legacy so many of us have inherited so we can reflect on those experiences as one step toward healing our relationships with our own and others' bodies. Some may acknowledge this ambivalence and how they have ignored their body until something breaks or acts up. Others may acknowledge fear and how they have been overly caught up in trying to control it and manage its urges. Some may be living with thinly veiled disgust or even hatred of their bodies related to family of origin and how their bodies were treated as they grew and developed. There may have been early experiences with others, perhaps sexual or physical abuse, that convinced them that the body is shameful, dirty, or ugly. The #MeToo and #ChurchToo movements are bringing women (who may have been children at the time) into contact with memories of the negative experiences they have had in their bodies. It is an important part of their journey to grapple with how these experiences have affected them, how they may have hidden it, how entire churches and denominations denied it, and how all of that shapes who they are today. If we do not allow ourselves as communities to acknowledge the hard experiences as well as the more positive ones, we will not be able to care for ourselves or be helpful to others in being with God in our bodies. Transforming communities can be places where we offer experiences of being seen and known, believed, and provided with guidance for healing.

Many people sitting in our pews looking very normal are still marked by these early experiences, having never been invited into a safe space to reflect on them and bring them into the light of God's presence. They have never had the opportunity to speak their stories to another human being and say, "This is what happened to me, and this is how it has shaped me" as part and parcel of bringing a more mature, God-breathed perspective. Transforming community should be a primary context in which these things can be held in the light as one part of the healing journey. In situations involving trauma, professional trauma-based therapy is also a crucial part of the healing process; part of our responsibility as leaders is to be in touch with resources that are available and to courageously point people to this kind of help when that is what's needed. As Robert Mulholland points out, "We need to realize that not only is psychology not a substitute for spirituality, but spirituality is not a substitute for psychology . . . psychological brokenness needs treatment in the same way a broken bone needs to be set and healed."[6]

## BEYOND THE SACRED-SECULAR SPLIT

Another dualism prevalent in many religious settings is the tendency to divide the human person into two elements, physical and spiritual, that we then see as being at war with each other.

Moving beyond this dualism requires shifting to a more integrated approach that sees these elements as being distinguishable from each other but actually belonging together in the way God created us. Then we are in a position to ask, How do I help others redeem their sense of themselves as bodies? Spiritual leadership involves fostering the integration of all parts of ourselves into wholeness in Christ.

There is now an area of study within academia called *body theology* that suggests reflecting on our bodily experience as a place of revelation *from* God and *about* God. It stems from Genesis 1:26, where God says, "Let us make humans in our image, according to our likeness," thereby establishing the body as a primary source of theological reflection, not a secondary one. (*A* primary source, along with Scripture, not *the* primary source.)

*Body theology*—defined as an understanding that the body is a place of revelation about who God is—affirms our nondualistic, Hebraic, incarnational Christian roots. In the Hebraic tradition it is understood that we do not just *have* bodies, we *are* bodies. In the Hebrew language there is no word that refers to the body as separate from the person. In the Hebrew mindset, the body *was* the person, with no differentiation between the physical and other aspects of being.

The Hebrew word *nephesh,* which often gets translated "soul," actually refers to the inner aspect of the body, and all of it together makes up the person. In the Hebrew Scriptures there was only one word for knowing, and it was full, experiential knowing between a subject and an object; there was no language to speak only of cognitive knowing. So, when Scripture says that Adam "knew his wife" (e.g., Genesis 4:1), it does not mean that he had information about her. It means that he knew her at every level; they had come together in full, experiential oneness. The idea of separating cognitive knowing from other kinds of knowing is not a part of our Christian history until we get to Paul and the Greeks. Even so, when Paul refers to the body, he uses the Greek word *sōma*, an all-encompassing word that points to integrated body-selves.

This false dichotomy between the physical world, in which we exist as embodied beings, and the spiritual world points to our need to receive life in our bodies as part of God's creation that God said is very good. We need a sacramental approach to life in which the body is understood to be sacred, set apart for the holy purpose of knowing and experiencing God. Our bodies are temples, and what is a temple? It is a set-apart place for encounter with God, for prayer.

The emphasis on our bodies as temples is so often used to talk about sexual purity that we miss the beautiful purpose and function of a temple. Where do we talk about prayer as part of what happens in these temples? Where do we teach that our bodies are a place set apart for encounter with God? A transforming community could preach and teach a more fully orbed understanding of life in our bodies as it relates to our spirituality.

## FLESH AND BLOOD SPIRITUALITY

All the major themes of Scripture affirm the spiritual significance of the body. At creation God created human beings as bodies and declared these bodies very good. In Deuteronomy 30:11-14 God describes a visceral, in-the-body experience of discerning between life and death so that we can choose life.

The psalmist talks about his desire for God as something he experiences in his body as hunger and thirst. "My flesh faints for you, as in a dry and weary land where there is no water" (Psalm 63:1). David affirms his body and soul together as part of God's created goodness when he says, "I am fearfully and wonderfully made. . . . That I know very well" (Psalm 139:14). David calls us to look at our bodies and celebrate them. We are invited to say to God, "Thank you for all these things I can be and do in my body."

And let's not forget the incarnation, when the Word (the logos) took on flesh and entered fully into the human experience. Jesus' embodiment forever elevates our own experience of life in a body. The being, who existed eternally as the Word (the logos), became flesh.

When Jesus was getting ready to leave his followers and ascend to heaven, he did not simply leave them with something to study or to think about; he instituted the embodied practice of footwashing, a specific way of ministering to each other in their bodies. He said (and I paraphrase), "When you forget what you're about here, when you forget how you're supposed to be relating to each other, remember this footwashing. Remember that I, your teacher, got down on the floor and washed your feet. Remember that this is who you are" (see John 13:12-15).

That same night Jesus introduced what would become the central sacrament of the Christian faith: the eucharistic bread and wine, symbolizing his flesh and blood. In the climactic moment of a Christian worship service, the body—in all its beauty and its earthiness, its messiness and its vulnerability—is held high. "The gifts of God for the people of God!" the minister proclaims. The gift of flesh and blood. In the most sacred moment of our life together as the people of God, bodies are affirmed.

And of course, now that Jesus is no longer physically present with us, our bodies are temples of the Holy Spirit (1 Corinthians 6:19). How wonderful to know that when we don't have a physical temple to go to, we can turn inward and meet God right in our bodies. If you listen to it, your body can tell you how to pray, because that's what it was created for.

Second Corinthians 4 tells us that whatever ministry we have been given—including the ministry of the gospel—is carried in our bodies. There will be other things God has for our resurrected bodies, but this is a unique moment when we are on *this* planet, in *this* physical body, carrying the ministry that God has given to us. And beyond our individual bodies, the church itself is the body of Christ (see Romans 12:4-5; 1 Corinthians 12:12-27)! How interesting that when inspiring the writers of Scripture, the Holy Spirit chose to describe how Jesus is present on the earth now as a physical body.

No matter how we feel about the church on any given day, no matter what conflicts are taking place among us, no matter if the church is a wreck and a mess—this is how Jesus has chosen to be present here. In the words attributed to Teresa of Ávila, "Christ has no body now on earth but yours. No hands but yours, no feet but yours. Yours are the eyes through which compassion is to look out to the world. Yours are the feet with which Christ is to go about doing good. Yours are the hands with which Christ is to bless all people now."

The resurrection of the body (1 Corinthians 15:51-52) tells us that our bodies will not be discarded as detritus but will be changed into a new and imperishable form, and we will spend eternity not as disembodied spirits but as glorious, embodied beings (see 1 Corinthians 15:35-44).

This tells us that God does not give up on bodies; our bodies will be resurrected on the last day. And until then, every day—*this very day*—we have the opportunity to offer ourselves to God as living sacrifices, to offer ourselves to God in our bodies, holy and acceptable, which is our spiritual worship (Romans 12:1).

I pray this brief "walk through the Bible" will inspire you to hold a more sacramental view of the body and that providing guidance for being with God in our bodies will become part of your shared journey as a community. "Until we can be at home in our bodies, we can never truly be at home anywhere."[7]

## SPIRITUAL PRACTICES FOR BEING WITH GOD IN OUR BODIES

Psychologist and spiritual director David Benner makes the crucial point that authentic spirituality must ground us in the God-ordained reality of our lives, including life in our bodies.[8] Following are some ideas for embodied practices leaders can guide and encourage in their communities to help people be with God in their bodies.

***Paying attention to your body.*** Start by simply noticing how things feel in your body. Breathing is one of the simplest ways of getting in touch with God's gift of life in a body. This is not an Eastern practice as some would have us believe. It actually emerges from the early chapters of Genesis where we read that God breathed life into the first human (Genesis 2:7) and continues to give us our breath each and every minute. With each breath God is affirming our life, and if God were to withhold our breath, we would be dead! Breathing can be a source of great gratitude, because not only does breathing give us the gift of being alive, breathing deeply can help calm us in times of stress and can help us move through difficult emotions. We can learn to recognize when our breathing is shallow, indicating we are stressed, so simply taking a moment to stop, pay attention, and then consciously breathe more deeply can help us slow down and get in touch with the Spirit of God deep within.

***Caring for the body.*** Fueling our bodies with the right kinds of food, drinking enough water, exercising, getting regular physicals and medical procedures, releasing places that are tight and sore through body work, stretching our bodies, and working with our breathing through a good yoga practice can all become spiritual practices if we approach them that way. Even being able to do this is a great gift—a privilege, if you will. There are so many in our world for whom these basics are so far out of reach that we really must practice a more global awareness and a deep sense of gratitude if this kind of care for the body is possible for us.

***Receiving God's gift of rest.*** Our bodies were not meant for the adrenaline-fueled, sleep-deprived lives most of us are living. Facing our physical, emotional, mental, and spiritual exhaustion can feel rather daunting, so it can be helpful to think about the increments of time we have to work with—days, weeks, months, quarters, and years. Start with making sure you are getting enough sleep daily. "The Lord gives sleep to those he loves," the psalmist says, so let the Lord love you.

The next one is a bit more challenging—and that is commitment to a weekly sabbath, which is one of God's best gifts to us. Our Creator knows we were not made to work 24-7. The Sabbath is the kingpin of a life well lived in God, a gift from God to our weary bodies, minds, and souls. In my mind, any transforming community needs to also see itself as a sabbath community—one that takes God at his word that this is what we need and plans their communal rhythms around it. It is ideal if the whole community can practice together, with senior leaders leading out and modeling it, writing it into employee policies as well as organizational or congregational rhythms. Then all scheduling is done with the commitment to sabbath firmly in place.

Annual rhythms of rest include taking all of one's vacation time and fully disconnecting from work when you do. Senior pastors and leaders need to be the ones who lead out on this by arranging to be fully unplugged rather than setting any expectation that they will be checking in. Everyone needs to see this example, and many will be inspired to follow it.

Distinct from vacation would be a retreat of some kind at least once a year, anywhere from one day to seven or eight days. This is different from a vacation in that it is extended time for you and God alone. Retreat time is a generous investment in your relationship with God and can be, with its emphasis on rest, deeply replenishing in a different way than a vacation.[9]

***Listening in the body.*** Our bodies have much to tell us if we could only learn to listen. Our bodies often send the first signals that we are overcommitted, stressed, uneasy, or joyful—if we could only figure out how to listen. When we attend to something that causes us pain or dis-ease in the body, we are alerted that something in our lives needs our attention. Elouise Renich Fraser writes about the significant role that listening to her body has played in her personal and theological journey. "My mind tries to talk me into business as usual, but my body isn't fooled. Insomnia, intestinal pain and diarrhea let me know that there's work to be done."[10]

***Praying in the body.*** Since the body is a temple of the Holy Spirit, when we gather as a community we can make intentional efforts to cultivate prayer experiences that incorporate the body. We can encourage people to pay attention to their posture when they pray by offering the following suggestions:

- Settle into a relaxed and comfortable position with back straight and feet on the floor, feeling the chair supporting your body.
- Breathe deeply as a way of releasing tension.
- Open your hands in your lap as a way of saying, "God, I'm letting go of whatever I usually cling to, and I'm ready to receive whatever you want to give me."

The opening of my hands has become my favorite prayer posture—so much so that I now assume this posture without even thinking. It's a way of saying to God *with my body* that I am letting go of what I usually cling to and that I'm open to receiving what God wants to give.

## EMBRACING THE GOD-ORDAINED REALITIES OF LIFE IN OUR BODIES

The God-ordained realities of our lives include ethnicity and race, gender and sexuality, being differently abled, times when it seems like our body has betrayed us, and all the experiences we've had in our bodies that are now held as memories. These are some of the harder things to figure out how to integrate into our spirituality.[11] I will cover just a few of them here to give examples of how transforming communities can approach healthy integration of these in-the-body experiences with the spiritual transformation we are seeking to foster.

***Gender and sex.*** None of us exists in this world apart from being gendered and sexual, even if we experience gender to be fluid rather than binary, have mixed feelings about the gender we are, or do not fit into heteronormative categories. We may be in the process of working this out with God, but our creation as male and female (however we relate to that) is one of the ways God has revealed the diversity of God's self. To be precise, biological sex has to do with the physical characteristics associated with being male and female. One sex or the other on its own could never fully represent who God is.

Gender, on the other hand, is biological sex *plus* the societal and cultural expectations that go along with it. While some people fit quite well into these stereotypical expectations, others have deeply mixed feelings about being the gender they are and the expectations that go along with it. Both women and men who don't fit society's stereotypes experience pain and confusion around gender. All of these are experiences that need to be processed spiritually in a maturing relationship where we are increasingly bringing more and more of ourselves to God, allowing God to tell us who we are. Most of us cannot do this alone; we need the help and support of a community that is intentionally working to bring understanding to these areas, with appropriate connections being made from childhood all the way through adulthood.

***Sexuality.*** Another dualism that is often powerfully at work is splitting off our spirituality from our sexuality. This can cut us off from knowing God and thus from fully knowing and understanding ourselves. The longing for communion and union is one aspect of what it means to be created in God's image: Our spirituality is all about union and communion with God, and our sexuality is all about union and communion with other human beings. This means that sexuality and spirituality are closely aligned within the human person. As we work to fully comprehend the complexity of our humanity, we can learn to embrace the powerful drives within us as part of the created good that we are *and* we can bring this essential part of ourselves openly into our relationship with God as part of our transformational journey. As we awaken fully to the spiritual, social, and sexual dimensions of ourselves in God's presence, we find that they are inseparably intertwined and must be lived together. Transforming communities will provide guidance for this.

***Ethnicity and race.*** Ethnicity is the biological fact of the people group we are a part of and where we came from geographically. Race is now commonly understood as a social construct, a concept created and defined by societal meanings, expectations, and purposes—including economic gain. The experience of injustice and discrimination due to one's race and ethnicity is another in-the-body experience that is challenging to integrate into our spirituality. If someone has been part of a people group that has oppressed others, they will need to come to terms with their part in systemic injustices and all the ways they have benefited from how other people have been treated in their bodies within their historical context. These experiences are part of being bodies on this earth, and these harder topics will naturally come to the fore if we start talking about bodies. We as leaders need to do our own deep work around issues of race and ethnicity so we can be nondefensive and welcoming to these topics and to the people who bring them.

As we realize the significance of grappling with race and ethnicity as part of personal and societal transformation, we can be proactive in creating space and context for real conversations about these issues of such importance to all of us—not because they are the hot topic of the day but because being spiritual beings who are trying to become good humans is such a significant part of the transformational journey. In the Transforming Center, we devote an entire retreat to honoring the body as a spiritual practice in our transforming communities, which means we walk right into conversations about gender and sexuality, race and ethnicity, along with other topics that have to do with life in the body. It is only after we have been together long enough to build trust that we are able to "go there" safely together. This is always a pivotal moment in the life of our communities, another place where we break through to community. Taking the risk of diving into these deeper waters is hard and necessary work and we need to do it *with others* who are willing and able to hold this kind of space for God's healing work.

One pastor described what this was like for him.

> When I came to Transforming Community I was in a lonely place, not in terms of friendship, but in terms of deep spiritual formation and community. . . . I just wasn't going there with people, and transforming community was exactly what I needed as a leader who was in a lonely dark place and needed support and a completely safe environment in which to heal. I had heard that Transforming Community was going to be a safe space, but I had my reservations. As a Black man in his late forties, I'm used to going to predominantly white spaces that don't feel safe. And there was so much going on in our country around race at that time that, honestly, I had built up a lot of trepidation about entering into this space. The only reason I gave it a chance was because my therapist, who was a Black male, had been through a Transforming Community and I was like, "If he's been there, it must be safe." Then, in our fifth retreat we had a conversation about race. And let me tell you, it opened up a conversation that for me was foreign in environments where I was the minority. At that moment I started to feel the walls go down and that's when I knew, "OK, I'm wanted here. I'm not just a commodity.

I'm not the token Black guy for the promotional video. They are really passionate about creating a diverse community, especially among leaders." So yeah, that was my moment.

There are so many observations we can make from this simple witness. First, the fact that this conversation was initiated by the senior leader (in this case, me) told him something very important about what is significant in the life of our community. Of course, I very quickly passed the mic to persons of color for their leadership, but I knew that, even though our communities have become much more diverse over time, I needed to be the one to drive a stake in the ground and say, "This is important. This is what we're doing and where we're going. And here's why." How interesting that this was the precise moment when this pastor started feeling like he belonged, like he was wanted. We had already been meeting for a year with a focus on all sorts of spiritual practices, but for a Black man in a majority White space, this was the moment that changed everything. It drew us all together in ways we had not yet experienced.[12]

## HONORING BODIES IN THE BODY OF CHRIST

Every time we open up the conversation about race, gender, and sexuality in our communities, we are aware of how fraught these subjects are in a culture that is changing so fast it is hard to keep up with the new information, fresh perspectives, and finer nuances that always need to be considered. Every time, there is this sense we are taking a risk that those of us who are together in the room might not be able to "hold" the understanding and sensitivity these tender topics deserve, that we can't possibly do it perfectly. And the truth is, we have never held the conversation the same way twice; each time it is a new effort depending on how we discern the moment we are in.

There have been many times when I've been tempted not to even try, given the risks involved. The risk of not doing it perfectly always feels very daunting, and when you invite people to cocreate the conversation with you, you can't control everything. People could get hurt, feel misunderstood, or respond in ways that are generally clueless. And yet, we have always chosen to take the risk, providing simple guidance and structure for these courageous conversations, trusting God's presence in our midst.

What we have discovered over the years is that it is precisely when we engage around these sensitive issues that we break through to another level of knowing and being known. It is a risk worth taking because we believe it is more honoring to God and to the community to try than not to try. Intentionally fostering understanding, care, healing, and redemption in these tender, human places is one way we can practice honoring bodies as a spiritual practice in community. It helps to be undergirded by the truth that *our differences are not a problem to God.* God built diversity right into his creation as something to be embraced and celebrated as an expression of God's creativity. It is human beings who have made it a problem.

## PAIN, SUFFERING, AND DISAPPOINTMENT IN OUR BODIES

Barbara Brown Taylor wryly observes,

> Deep suffering makes theologians of us all. The questions people ask about God in Sunday school rarely compare with questions we ask while we are in the hospital. This goes for those stuck in the waiting room as well as those in hospital beds. . . . To spend one night in real pain is to discover depths of reality that are roped off while everything is going fine. *Why now? Why me? Why this?*[13]

All these questions and more will present themselves as we stay grounded in the fundamental experience of life in our bodies, even when that experience includes physical suffering and disillusionment.

This is another universal aspect of the human experience that will be present in any community over time: the inevitability of the disappointments, limitations, and physical challenges that go along with life in a body. This may include the experience of being single—a choice for some and a source of desperate desire and disappointment for others. There will be those who are differently abled or neurodivergent, those experiencing frustrating injuries and surgeries, and those who feel betrayed by their bodies due to infertility, chronic pain, battles with serious illness, aging and diminishment, and (for all of us) facing our mortality. These in-the-body experiences raise profound questions. Can I find God here? How do I pray with this experience? Do I even believe in prayer anymore? Can I open this experience up to God and air my disappointments and even my rage and despair? How do I make meaning of this? How do I pray when I am feeling abandoned?

To remain committed to the spiritual journey is to stay present to all of it in God's presence. And part of being a transforming leader is to be able to stay present to all of it with our people, even when we would rather turn away or relegate it to someone else who has expertise in such things. We as leaders can see it as part of our pastoral responsibility to offer guidance for facing whatever bodily circumstances people are in, helping them stay in touch with the reality that their body is still a temple that God has chosen to inhabit and where God wants to meet them—even when they are going through hard things. Facing our mortality, knowing when to let go versus continuing to fight, choosing quality of life over longevity, and trusting God with our very lives is something the medical community is not prepared to help us with.[14] It is something transforming leaders must be prepared to help with in a spiritually grounded way.

## CREATED FOR WHOLENESS

We were created for wholeness, not fragmentation. As David Benner writes, "There is no use pretending that being religious—even Christian—automatically makes you a whole, vital, and growing human being. I am convinced that becoming fully human—more specifically, becoming the unique and whole human being that I am intended to be—is right at center of the Christian spiritual journey."[15]

Transforming communities give guidance and support for embracing all aspects of the human experience—even the painful ones—and finding that, in God, everything belongs. When aspects of our selves that were always meant to exist together are more fully integrated (or re-integrated), the result is a spontaneous combustion of joy, vitality, and peace that goes far beyond the physical dimension. It is a spiritual vitality that can manifest itself even when the physical body is wasting away. In life, in sickness, and in death, how we honor our bodies speaks volumes about how we relate to our Creator and bear witness to the abundant life that Jesus came to bring. Wouldn't it be something if your community was the place where people learned how to experience *that*?

# PART 3

# COMMUNITY

## *Sustaining Us in the Mystery*

*Left to ourselves we do not have the resources to maintain the disciplines that God uses as means of grace to transform us to wholeness in the image of Christ.*

M. Robert Mulholland Jr.

# 7

# CHOOSING TO WALK TOGETHER

*Christian community is not an ideal which we must realize; it is a reality created by God in which we may participate. . . . The more genuine and the deeper our community becomes, the more will everything else between us recede, and the more purely will Jesus Christ and his work become the one and only thing that is vital between us.*

Dietrich Bonhoeffer

---

**Early in the Transforming Center's journey** from offering just one retreat to developing our two-year Transforming Community experience, I remember asking God for a place in Scripture that would give us a picture of what it might look like for a group of people to journey together in a way that was transforming. The little group that gathered for that first retreat had asked if we could keep meeting, and while we had some idea of what that might look like, we needed something concrete and a little more inspiring to rally around. We needed a shared vision that would help us coalesce around what we were trying to be and do.

As the time neared for me to present at our retreat, I hadn't yet found the text I was looking for. As I sat alone in my room, sifting despairingly through the dry bones of all my accumulated notes on Christian community, God drew my attention to the post-resurrection story of the two disciples walking the road from Jerusalem to Emmaus.

It was a familiar story, but I had never looked at it through the lens of transforming community and as I did, the fresh wind of the Spirit my soul had been looking for began to blow. As I sat with it in that moment, I recognized that what the disciples experienced on that road and in the meal they shared was nothing less than the miracle of transformation.

### A WALK TO REMEMBER

It was the third day of what had been a most traumatic weekend. They were riding a roller coaster of emotion: On Friday they had witnessed the violent and humiliating death of their beloved teacher, leader, and friend. On Saturday they had sat together in despair. And now it was Sunday. They had hung around as long as they could, but at some point, it is time to head home.

But just as the disciples started finding their way back to their new normal, some hope had been introduced into the situation. Several of the women disciples had told them about visiting Jesus' tomb and finding it empty! Now they had to at least entertain the idea that perhaps there had been a resurrection, as Jesus had predicted, but it was too soon to tell. They were suspended between loss and possible gain, grief and possible joy, human suffering and perhaps some kind of redemption of that suffering, swinging wildly between dashed hopes and *maybe* daring to hope again.

This walk from Jerusalem to Emmaus was an in-between time for these two disciples, a time for waiting in what Richard Rohr calls "liminal space"—a unique spiritual position where human beings hate to be but where God is always calling them. It is when you have left the tried and true (or it has left you), but you have not yet been able to replace it with anything else. As uncomfortable as it is, this sense of being betwixt and between can signify (as it did for these disciples) a major transition from one spiritual reality to another, one way of being to another. Even though they didn't know it yet, these disciples were on the path to a new reality—knowing and experiencing Jesus as their resurrected Lord. This transition would change everything; they would not, in the end, settle back into the lives they had had before, but rather would be sent out to accomplish the mission Jesus would give them. They would move beyond trusting in their own human programs for safety and security, affection and approval, power and control, to complete and utter surrender to God. They would become something they could never have imagined. That journey would require companions who can walk the road with us.

A transforming community is a group of people who are between the now and the not-yet in some area of their lives and are willing to walk together. The church as a whole is on the road between the now and the not-yet, trying to figure who and what we will be on the other side of the dark times we have been through and are in right now. One of the most striking things about the Emmaus Road encounter is that "while they were discussing all these things" Jesus himself drew near. They were not praying in any kind of formal way, nor were they having a Bible study or a worship service or even a quiet time. It was *while they were discussing the stuff of their lives* that Jesus came near. This conversation was not pretty. What they had just been through and the emotions they were processing were quite dark, and they did not yet have perspective on it all. But there was something about the quality and content of their conversation that caused Jesus to want to come near and be a part of it.

## WHILE THEY WERE DISCUSSING ALL THESE THINGS THAT HAD HAPPENED

Jesus did not join them to make small talk or avoid the hard topics; rather, he went straight to the point and asked, "What are you discussing with each other as you walk along?" knowing full well what they were discussing! While that might seem forward and even a little bit rude to us, Jesus knew they needed to tell their own story, process their emotions, and try to make sense of it all. He also knew he was the one to help them. As they struggled to put what they had been through into words, Jesus stood there with them, allowing space for their sadness, feeling it with them, giving them time to find the right words. He didn't rush them, but he also didn't let them off the hook.

Finally, Cleopas got a little exasperated. He gave up trying to be patient and diplomatic and blurted out, "Are you the only stranger here in Jerusalem who does not know the things that have taken place here in these days?" (Luke 24:18). Jesus could have responded by proving that he knew *exactly* what was going on, but instead he was very restrained and held back what he knew. He played dumb and asked, "What things?" And with that simple question, Jesus kept the space open for them to share their thoughts, experiences, and feelings in the face of the horrors they had experienced. In response to Jesus' question, it all came pouring out—the pain, the disillusionment, the questions, their lost hopes and dreams.

Only after he had listened deeply did Jesus guide them into a brief but significant reflection on Scripture that helped them make sense of things from a spiritual point of view. He helped them find themselves in God's story of redemption so they could see that their pain, which felt so personal, was actually part of something bigger. Furthermore, he used it as an opportunity to describe the essential rhythm of the spiritual life—death, burial, and resurrection—and framed this penetrating question: "Was it not necessary for the Messiah to suffer all these things, and then enter his glory?" This meaning-making was spiritual leadership at its best.

Suffering is hard, and we must never minimize the pain, the suffering, the veil of tears that life on this earth can be. Yet suffering can become the doorway to our deepest transformation, as it did for Jesus. To be guided into finding meaning in our suffering and to be offered spiritual perspectives on the disturbing things that are happening in our world make it worth getting up and going to church! One of the hallmarks of transforming community is the ability to be with the hardest and most complicated aspects of our lives within a shared understanding about the nature of the spiritual life and the role of suffering in it. It is knowing we cannot fix each other, and giving up on every attempt to do so, but it is also a commitment to hold space so Jesus can meet us in our suffering and do for us what no one else can do.

**SOME WOMEN OF OUR GROUP ASTOUNDED US**

I love this little sentence in Luke's Gospel: "Moreover, some women of our group astounded us" (Luke 24:22). It draws attention to the fact that women and men together comprised the transforming community gathered around Jesus and that something new and surprising was taking place among them.[1] At Jesus' initiative (presumably Jesus chose where, how, and to whom he appeared following his resurrection), women were breaking out of stereotypical roles and conducting themselves in a way that astounded their male counterparts, and probably the entire Jewish community.

This might not seem like a big deal to us, but in the Jewish culture of that day, the way women and men were together in the community of Jesus was fairly radical and maybe even a little scandalous! In the synagogues men and women were separated by a curtain, women and girls were not taught the Torah, and they served quietly in the background as the men discussed and argued about spiritual matters. Women were not allowed to speak or ask questions in public gatherings, let alone teach or proclaim anything important. In addition, they were limited in their interactions with men who were not family members.

The fact that Jesus appeared first to women at the tomb, interacting with them intimately and substantively about the resurrection, was quite out of the ordinary. He then charged them with announcing the good news to the rest of the disciples, complete with instructions for their next steps. This was so unusual and such a reversal of typical gender roles that some scholars have suggested this remarkable and very specific detail corroborates historical evidence for the resurrection. No one trying to fabricate a believable resurrection story would have included such a culturally unbelievable detail!

The various Gospel accounts all record that women were the last ones to linger around the cross and the first to arrive at the tomb. They also record that Jesus appeared to them and interacted with them personally on the morning of the resurrection.

While most of the disciples tried to dismiss the women's excited announcement as idle tales (Luke 24:11), Peter found their report convincing enough to at least check on the veracity of their story. And wouldn't you know? The good news these women proclaimed was actually true, making them the first Christian evangelists. (The word *evangelism* means "to proclaim the good news.") They delivered this news with the clarity and conviction that comes from a real encounter with Christ *and* provided leadership for what they were to do next.

Every time Jesus interacted with women or with men and women together, he modeled new relating patterns that began the process of redeeming us all from the oppressive effects of the curse on male-female relationships. That is why we see Jesus talking to an immoral woman about theology, worship, the state of her relationships, and the state of her soul (John 4). It's why we see him pointing out to a group of religious leaders that a woman caught in adultery was no more guilty than the man who participated (John 8:1-11), and why we see him receiving Mary's embodied act of worship with oil and hair as more meaningful than anything that was going on in the synagogues (John 12:1-8). It's why some of his best friends were women—indicated by his visits in their homes (Luke 10:38-42), the give and take in their conversations (John 11:1-44), and the fact that they were last at the cross and first at the tomb (Mark 15:40-47). No wonder his disciples and the religious community were always surprised or befuddled by the choices Jesus made in relation to the women who were around him.

Jesus' presence and relational choices routinely shifted the balance and tone of relationships between men and women, actively redeeming them from the effects of the fall. After Jesus' resurrection things were just plain different. When the disciples returned to Jerusalem to await the Holy Spirit, they were all together in the upper room and "were constantly devoting themselves to prayer, together with certain women, including Mary the mother of Jesus" (Acts 1:14). In Jewish culture it was unheard of that men and women would be together in such an intimate way, but by now these new Christ-followers were more influenced by him than by the surrounding culture! On the day of Pentecost, they were still together as tongues of fire rested on each one of them; they were filled with the Holy Spirit and began speaking in tongues (Acts 2:4). This was just the beginning of a whole new level of partnership and teamwork among men and women in the community of Jesus.

## WOMEN AND MEN IN TRANSFORMING COMMUNITY

The community that was so intimate with Jesus while he was here on this earth gave birth to a whole new reality for men and women in friendship and community. As the early church grew, women worked right alongside the men in spreading the gospel and planting churches. In some cases, women (such as Lydia in Philippi) were the prime movers in getting churches started by hosting them in their homes. Other women taught theology (Priscilla), served as ministers or deacons (Phoebe), prophesied (Phillip's daughters), and simply worked very hard (Romans 16:1-16).

Eventually Paul put words to what was already in evidence in Jesus' relationship with women that got carried into the patterns of the early church: To each is given the manifestation of the Spirit (spiritual gifts) for the common good without regard to gender. This was entirely consistent with Peter's assertion that "God shows no partiality" (Acts 10:34) and that we are all members of the royal priesthood (1 Peter 2:9)—again, with no exclusions related to gender.

By the time Paul got around to describing a biblical vision for oneness and mutuality in the body of Christ (1 Corinthians 12; Ephesians 4), it was more than just a theory—it was the way women and men were already functioning in the community of Jesus. He summed up the new reality Jesus' redeeming presence opened up in this way: "*In Christ Jesus you are all children of God through faith. . . . There is no longer Jew or Greek; there is no longer slave or free; there is no longer male and female, for all of you are one in Christ Jesus*" (Galatians 3:26-28). Now, for the first time, rather than experiencing physical characteristics like race, socioeconomic status, and gender as cause for limitation and discrimination, the body of Christ was becoming a place where followers could experience something wholly different from what the effects of sin had produced.

In communities gathered around the transforming presence of Jesus, women and men of different giftings, ethnicities, social standing, and socioeconomic status are equally privileged to serve, lead, and participate fully in the life of the community. Everywhere you look you see men and women with their sleeves rolled up serving food and taking care of others side by side, in their clerical robes preaching and teaching side by side, in the board room discerning and leading together side by side. How could it be any other way in communities formed around the presence of Christ? But what this means is that we may need to learn new practices that are more influenced by Jesus than by the prevailing culture.

We will need to be intentional about practicing oneness and including each other in every way possible. Rather than seeing our relationship through the lens of "women's issues" and "men's issues," we will simply see human issues that affect us all. We will strive for mutuality, equality, and shared responsibility for all aspects of our life together in the family of God. This could be as simple as making sure that every Sunday there are men serving in the nursery and the children's ministry while an equal number of women and men are on the platform providing leadership in your worship service. It could be as straightforward as counting members of your senior leadership team to make sure there is an equal representation of women and men at all levels. It could be as human as listening carefully to both women and men about what it is like to work and worship in your setting. This is a radical kind of inclusivity that is really not all that complicated.

We will also need to commit ourselves to respecting and honoring the power of sexuality while at the same time refusing to let it be a barrier between us. In the midst of a secular culture where sexuality is often overplayed, a religious culture where sexuality is often repressed and ignored, and both cultures abusing it in their own ways, transforming communities can and should be a place where the gift of our sexuality is received and stewarded with wisdom and care. We can appreciate the good chemistry that is produced when core elements of our humanity are in proximity while at the same time allowing the sparks generated by maleness and femaleness to be harnessed toward building a fire that can warm us all. We do not have to let those sparks fly out of control and burn down the whole forest! Tending the sparks wisely may involve facing our fears about sexuality and getting the help we need to move beyond them so we can love each other well. We can explore healthy connections between our sexuality and our spirituality (as we talked about in chapter six) and open our sexual longings to God, seeking God's wisdom and care in this area of our lives. We can cultivate self-awareness and take responsibility for the healing and transformation of any distortions that exist in our experience of sexuality. And we can move toward one another in Christlike expressions of love, friendship, and partnership—whether we are single or married. Marriage cannot possibly meet all our needs for friendship and community, and singleness doesn't mean we are not intended to experience love and friendship with the other gender. Community is the place where we can all find the fullness God intended for us.

Certainly, there is a fine line between respecting the power of sexuality and refusing to live in fear, but it is the line Jesus himself walked. A striking example of this is Jesus' encounter with the woman who broke an alabaster jar of costly ointment and began to anoint Jesus' feet with the oil and dry them with her hair. Kissing his feet and anointing them with ointment in this way can only be described as a rather sensual moment that made his disciples very uncomfortable. But Jesus was quite comfortable. He stayed present, received her expression of gratitude, and elevated her as an example of hospitality and love. What made this situation "safe" was the person Jesus was, the meaning he placed on it, and how he conducted himself. Being a person who is safe like this is something we can all aspire to, and I pray that we will.

What a worthy goal it would be for men and women in transforming community to model relationships that are more like Jesus' culture-defying example than the cultural distortions for which we have often settled. What a testimony that would be to a world that is lost in a sea of confusion, selfishness, and sin . . . simply because they have never been presented with another option.

### CHOOSING TO STAY TOGETHER

I realize we've gotten a little ahead of ourselves in the Christian story, so now let's get back to the disciples on the road to Emmaus. When the two disciples arrived at their exit, it seemed they would be parting ways with this intriguing stranger; however, there was something about their conversation that was so compelling, so enlivening, so life-changing that they didn't want it to end. So "they urged Jesus strongly to stay."

The word "stay" is used twice in the Emmaus Road story (both times in Luke 4:29) and, in some ways, it was the disciples' invitation for Jesus to stay with them and Jesus' choice to say yes that is the hinge point of the story. Think about it. If the disciples had not urged Jesus to stay, and if Jesus had not agreed, Jesus would not have been revealed to them in the breaking of the bread. This simple meal became an opportunity to look back on the walk they had shared and realize that Jesus *had been with them the whole time,* causing their hearts to burn within them while they walked along. What was this burning? Almost certainly there was a feeling of *Don't I know you from somewhere? Have we met before?*

Further, if it wasn't for what happened at that meal, they might have just gone to bed rather than getting up from the table, running back to Jerusalem, and discovering that there were other disciples who had had encounters with Jesus as well. They wouldn't have been in the room when Jesus appeared, and they would have missed the commissioning that took place before Jesus left them. And here we see that movement from the center out modeled for us once again: These two disciples had a personal encounter with Jesus, they sought out community with others who had also encountered Jesus in the midst of their loss and grief, and then as they came together to share these experiences, Jesus sent them out with a new sense of what their mission would now be.

## FELLOWSHIP OF THE BURNING HEARTS

The ability to recognize Christ's presence in and among us so we can respond faithfully to it is the heart of transforming community. This is another facet of the spiritual practice of *examen;* that is, paying attention to "consolation" and "desolation," as Saint Ignatius has helped us to understand it. In transforming community we help one another pay attention to the moments our hearts burned with awareness of Jesus' presence on the road of our own life. Together we pay attention to experiences of resonance as truth is revealed, of recognizing Jesus' presence at work in the ordinary moments of our lives, of awakening desire to make sense out of our lives from a spiritual point of view, of awareness of times when we sensed God's invitations and yet resisted. All these experiences become fodder for spiritual conversations. We need others who can affirm that yes, indeed, it was Jesus with us on the road helping us to see things more clearly, inviting us forward, and supporting us in responding faithfully to whatever Jesus is guiding us to do and be. And in the process, *we* are transformed from dazed, dejected wanderers on the road of life to confident, joyful bearers of good news who can hardly wait to tell others about what has happened to us in Jesus' presence.

The only way for these kinds of life-changing encounters with Jesus to take place is to find ways to stay together and have a certain kind of conversation, just as Jesus and these two disciples did. Stability is a radical call and commitment in our transient, fast-paced, and technology-driven society where we are still experimenting in our relationships with AI and virtual community—a term which seems like an oxymoron to me! These cultural forces may mean that many people simply do not know what community is or how to envision it and will need, perhaps, more guidance than has been needed in the past.

Once people are familiar with paying attention to consolation and desolation in their personal lives, it is a short distance to making this part of our communal practice. As part of our spiritual leadership, we can encourage this kind of attentiveness as a way of discerning Christ's presence and guidance among us. Where have we encountered Jesus' presence in our community's journey on the road between the now and not-yet? How and when have we recognized it? What is Jesus saying to us in and through such moments of recognition? What is that encounter saying to us about what Jesus is calling us to be and to do?

## PRACTICING JESUS' PRESENCE TOGETHER

There are some underlying commitments we can observe in the Emmaus Road narrative that any community can embrace to welcome the transforming presence of Christ into their shared journey.

***Choose to walk together.*** In a world that has become increasingly harsh and polarizing, it has never been more tempting to retreat into ourselves and choose isolation rather than seeking out a transforming community where we take the essential risk of engaging conversations that move beyond the superficial. The phrase "talking with each other about all these things that had happened" indicates a willingness to take the deep dive beneath the surface to share the joys, the pain, and the process of acknowledging and waiting in the liminal spaces of our lives and communities. No matter how put together people might seem or how bright and shiny the surface of their lives might appear to be, I guarantee you we all have some area of our lives where we are traversing the road between the now and the not-yet. The only question is whether we are willing to "go there" in conversation. Here's an idea. Start (or deepen) a conversation by asking this simple question: "In what area of your life do you feel like you are on your own road between the now and the not-yet?" If people choose to answer honestly, you might be surprised by how quickly you find yourselves swimming in the deep end of the conversational pool.

***Welcome the stranger.*** This might be someone who seems to appear out of nowhere, whose presence feels like an interruption to your "real" community, or who feels like they don't belong in the conversation. Chances are the reason this person feels like a stranger is that they are different from you in some significant way—ethnicity, life experience, theological beliefs, political persuasion, life stage, or personality. And let's not forget that the original idea of welcoming the stranger had to do more precisely with welcoming the alien. "The alien who resides with you shall be to you as the native-born among you; you shall love the alien as yourself, for you were aliens in the land of Egypt: I am the LORD your God" (Leviticus 19:34). Surely there is some application we can make here to our current situation.

One of the most spiritually profitable things a transforming community can be and do is to provide a safe space that holds the rich diversity that exists within the body of Christ. The choice to walk together is not merely for the purpose of experiencing the support and understanding of other like-minded folks—as helpful as that can be. It is also so we can be "joined" by people who are different from us in some way, which is where the real transformation takes place.

***Listen rather than fix.*** Choosing to take a listening stance rather than a fixing stance includes refraining from problem solving, advice giving, or even saying, "I know just how you feel!" because I promise you don't! Rose Mary Dougherty points out, "At times the strength of spiritual community lies in the love of people who refrain from getting caught in the trap of trying to fix everything for us, [who] pray for us and allow us the pain of our wilderness, our wants, so that we can become more deeply grounded in God."[2] That includes us as pastors.

If our communities are going to cultivate this kind of listening, they are going to need to learn it from what we model for them.

***Keep finding your story in God's story***—both our individual stories and our communal stories. Where do we see evidence that we are participating in the bigger thing God is doing? How do we allow that to guide us in what we are becoming? This practice of finding our story in God's story speaks, at least in part, to how we utilize Scripture in transforming community. We utilize Scripture not to convince people to believe like we do but to lead us to the kind of life-altering insight the disciples gained on the Emmaus Road. As Robert Mulholland wisely points out, "The goal of Scripture is that we would know God better—not that we would know Scripture better."[3]

***Choose to stay together.*** Share the ordinary moments and the not so ordinary moments and watch for Jesus' presence there. Over time establish rhythms and patterns of honest conversation that invite Jesus to draw near. Knowing we are committed to each other will go a long way toward cultivating a healthy sibling dynamic in the family of God that enables us to partner meaningfully together.

***Pay attention to the moments "when our hearts burned within us"*** and share them with one another. One way to do this is to make a regular practice of the *examen*: a regular practice of looking back over a short period of time (a day or a week) or even a specific event asking God to bring to your awareness a moment when Jesus was near to you—caring for you, protecting you, guiding you—and you did not recognize it. Experience the gratitude and warmth that comes from recognizing such a moment. You can also ask God to reveal to you a moment when your transforming self was in evidence—when you were able to be fully given over to God and to others in love—or a situation in which you might have fallen short of the Christ-in-you self. Depending on what kind of awareness God brings, you might experience a sense of celebration about God's transforming work in your life or a moment of self-knowledge that leads to repentance and confession, opening the way for a different choice next time. Make it part of your life together to create space for sharing these consolations and desolations in small group settings or even in larger group settings where people turn to one another in dyads and share.

## AND THEN WHAT?

All of these characteristics of transforming community need to be taught and modeled by leaders who preach and teach with vulnerability, model spiritual noticing, cast vision for stability, and by their example "make it okay" to talk about hard things. Then smaller groups can be structured as a place to practice, using a resource like the book *Life Together in Christ: Experiencing Transformation in Community* to provide a structure for companioning one another in this way.[4] Having such a structure will create the safety people need to share at these levels.

As we walk together and share with one another in these intentional ways, Jesus will make his presence known to us, just like he did with the larger group of disciples who were gathered excitedly in Jerusalem, comparing notes about how he had appeared to each of them so personally. He will bring peace to us, as only he can. He will answer *our* questions, fill in the gaps of *our* understanding, and encourage us in *our* unbelief. And soon we, too, will have a story to tell. Pretty soon we will hear Jesus say to *us*, *You are witnesses of these things.*

We will discover it is not only our words but our very lives that "preach" and bear witness to the transformation that can take place in Jesus' presence.

# 8

# TRANSFORMING WORSHIP

## *Opening to God Together*

*Here is my fear for the church: in the midst of all the smoke machines, high-def video loops, and latest worship hits, we may be settling for something less than true transcendence, something less than Spirit-breathed worship, something less than God on God's terms.*

MANUEL LUZ

---

WORSHIP LEADER AND CREATIVE ARTS pastor Manuel Luz opens his book *Honest Worship* by telling the story of the time when his teenage son, Justin, attended a megachurch with a friend. Since this was Justin's first experience with a church like that, Manuel wondered what his impression might be. Sure enough, soon afterward Justin asked, "Why do they need smoke machines in church?"

Luz recounts,

> There is so much I could have said in that moment. I could have contrasted different philosophies of ministry . . . and explained how some view the Sunday service as having components of both worship and evangelism. I could have articulated the differences between entertainment and engagement and how the two, while they may look similar, are very different in intent and outcome. And I could have passionately shared my deeply held convictions on worship theology. . . . But I didn't. Instead, I

simply replied, "Well, technically, you need the smoke machines to be able to see the lasers."[1]

I remember almost falling out of my chair laughing because I had had a similar parental experience while attending a Christmas Eve service at a megachurch. There were trapeze artists coming down from the ceiling on pullies and an angel sitting up in the rafters. Not to mention the light show. I was used to all this because I was on staff at the church and familiar with the philosophy about Christmas Eve services: Since it was the most well-attended service of the year and so many seekers and people who hadn't darkened the door of a church all year would be there, we needed to be at our creative best. I was sure my kids would be thoroughly impressed. But one of our daughters who was in junior high school at the time leaned over and whispered, "I feel like I'm at the Jesse White Tumblers!"

## WORSHIP THAT TRANSFORMS

Imagine my surprise, when after many years of being on staff in contemporary model churches, I participated in liturgical prayer and worship for the first time and felt like I had come home to a place I had never been and yet a place where I truly belonged.

It was a simple evening prayer service signaling the beginning of a spiritual retreat with a few like-minded souls. There were six of us, and one person in our group prepared a simple liturgy using prayers from the Psalms, a reading from the Gospels, and written prayers from the *Book of Common Prayer* and the Methodist hymnal. We set aside a simple prayer space. We entered that space in silence. We lit a candle to signify Christ's presence with us through the Holy Spirit. And then we prayed the prayers provided for us, beginning with these words:

*From the rising of the sun to its setting,*
*Let the name of the Lord be praised.*
*YOU, O LORD, ARE MY LAMP.*
*MY GOD, YOU MAKE MY DARKNESS BRIGHT.*

*Light and peace in Jesus Christ our Lord.*
*THANKS BE TO GOD.*[2]

Some of the prayers were read in unison, some were read responsively—and I just lost myself in the beauty and simplicity of it all. Instead of having to think hard about what to pray, I simply gave myself to the beauty of words that expressed deep longings and powerful praises that were true for me but I could never have found the words to say. Instead of getting caught up in the ego's attempts to say something profound to God (and to the people around me!), I rested from all of that and actually *prayed*. Instead of listening to someone else's interpretation or application of Scripture, I heard Scripture read without comment and listened for what God was saying to me in the silence that followed. Instead of being distracted by "culturally relevant" programming, this small group of us settled into a silence that was so rich and satisfying I lost all track of time until someone nudged me to remind me of the part I was supposed to bring next.

That was over twenty-five years ago now and you may have guessed that this little group eventually became the Transforming Center, and we've been praying that way ever since. Praying at a fixed hour of the day is one of the main ways we open to God's transforming work among us. This affinity for a more liturgical way of praying came as a surprise to me because I had been raised in a church environment that was highly suspicious of what some Christians called *rote prayers*—written prayers we all feared would foster the vain repetitions Jesus warned about. At that point, I was convinced that spontaneous prayers were the only real prayers because they came from the heart; I thought only people who weren't very spiritual or didn't have much to say to God needed to rely on prayers that were written by someone else! But over the years I have discovered another option—and that is to pray the great prayers of the church and really mean them.

Many Protestants departed from liturgical approaches to prayer and worship in protest of the Roman Catholic Church during the

Protestant Reformation, but it turns out that by distancing ourselves from our own origins in this way we lost rich avenues of prayer and worship that are rooted in Scripture and in our historic Christian tradition. Liturgical worship experiences are deeply biblical, expressing spiritual truth in stirring language that has the potential to shape the soul. The Psalms, Old and New Testament prayers (called Canticles), the Lord's Prayer, and the great prayers of the church are offered as aids in expressing the universal experience of the human soul reaching out to God. Turns out, there is no better way to *learn* to pray than to actually pray with the great ones of our faith.

We have not done away with spontaneous prayers by any means, but we have experienced powerful benefits from approaches to prayer and worship in which at least some of the prayers are written out, relieving us of always needing to figure out what to say, which can be completely impossible and exhausting at times. It seems that the farther along one gets in the spiritual life, the harder it is to articulate what's really happening with us spiritually—our spiritual and human longings, the intimacies of our relationship with God, the questions and disillusionments that leave us in wordless silence. When our own words fail us, the words and prayers of Scripture and the prayer books of the church can help us express the inexpressible in ways that are deeply satisfying and open us to encounter with God. During moments when we don't know how to approach God, liturgical prayers can show us the way, helping us to anchor our daily lives in rhythms of prayer, Scripture reading, and silence.

## WHAT IS TRANSFORMING WORSHIP?

Transforming worship is simply worship that has a transforming effect on those who participate.

Rory Noland, my partner in cultivating transforming worship in the Transforming Center over the years, defines transforming worship as "a communal experience that combines classic spiritual practices with a formative encounter with God in Christ through the Holy

Spirit."[3] He goes on to say that "worship is fundamentally a meeting between God and his people, initiated by God himself. Every time we gather, we take God up on his holy invitation to come together with our brothers and sisters in Christ to fellowship with God."[4]

There are two practices that provide the skeletal structure for everything we do in the Transforming Center: solitude and silence plus fixed-hour prayer and worship. I have been a part of planning hundreds of worship services over the years, partnering with Rory and other gifted worship leaders primarily as a spiritual director and liturgist. In that role I am always asking, What does the soul need right here, right now in response to what we are hearing and learning? What might the soul need to express to God right now and what might God want to say to our souls? What prayers, musical and other artistic elements, Scriptures, and practices would create space for God to be active among us? Over the years we have developed a shared sense of some characteristics of transforming worship that transcend any particular worship style and can be applied in any worship setting.[5]

## SOME CHARACTERISTICS

Transforming worship is *highly relational* because it is fundamentally about cultivating moments of encounter with God that change us, both in our private worship as well as in our corporate worship. This kind of worship is not primarily about the up-front performance of a few, nor is it primarily about momentary inspirations and emotional manipulation. It is about participation and encounter. Transforming worship is *highly participatory* in that it is about facilitating an encounter with God that can only happen when people are fully engaged rather than just sitting back and watching other people do the work. The word *liturgy* literally means "the work of the people," so a liturgical approach to worship is not so much about a specific style as it is about level of involvement and how we invite and make it possible for everyone to participate. Such involvement includes reading *and* responding to Scripture, praying spontaneously *and* being formed by the prayers of the church, listening to God in the silent spaces of the heart *and* joining our voices with others in song. This is "work" that is deeply engaging, satisfying, and delightful to our souls.

From Scripture (going all the way back to the Old Testament) we understand that *excellence in worship* is God-honoring and honoring of the souls who show up to participate, so we invest a lot in worship planning even though our services are relatively simple. This is not so much about perfection as it is about the careful thought and planning we give to creating space and providing guidance for these transforming encounters. We pay close attention to every element of the service to support what is happening or needs to happen spiritually in that service, in that season of the church year, or in the context of what's going on in the world around us. Part of our preparation is making sure everyone involved is clear and fully equipped for their parts in the service while at the same time maintaining an openness to the surprising movements of the Holy Spirit and identifying where those moments might be and how we will handle them. Since spiritual transformation is a work of the Spirit, transforming worship means there must be *room* for the Spirit, and usually it is the worship leader and liturgists that must be attuned enough to steward these moments. We are very intentional about always having at least one male and one female liturgist up front, along with ethnic and cultural diversity as well, when possible. Worship is intended to direct our hearts and our minds toward God, so whatever people see up-front needs to be as accurate and fully orbed a picture of who God is as possible.

## PSALMS, HYMNS, AND SONGS OF THE SPIRIT

My own worship journey has carried me from Plymouth Brethren worship services that were almost completely unstructured (so as to be guided by the Spirit) and barely utilized a piano, to contemporary model churches in which the band and the vocalists were rehearsed to perfection and amplified by sound professionals for large amphitheater-type worship spaces, to high church liturgies that take place in ornate chapels with robed celebrants and every element carefully scripted. In the Transforming Center we've landed on appreciating worship experiences that blend different styles and elements together. This is known as *liturgical synthesis*—the successful marriage of two (or more) worship styles that don't usually mix.[6] This could be the "marrying" of evangelical praise and worship to a more traditional eucharistic liturgy (as embodied in the Episcopalian Book of Common Prayer), or it could be the "marrying" of different ethnic styles of worship. In addition to combining styles, this kind of synthesis includes the integration of seemingly opposing theological ideas within the worship service, ecumenical sensitivity and dialogue, along with active and inclusive participation by all the faithful. In other words, people should expect to be challenged theologically sometimes.

Liturgical synthesis is the art and theology of weaving together diverse threads of Christian experience into a rich, coherent, and transformative worship experience. It is not unusual in our worship services to combine moments of more formal ritual with more casual moments or to offer an old hymn or anthem (like "Great Is Thy Faithfulness" or "How Great Thou Art") with a spiritual from the Black church (like "I Want Jesus" or "Precious Lord"), the "Gospel Doxology," a Taizé song, or a contemporary worship song (like "10,000 Reasons" or "Let the Glory of the Lord Rise Among Us") woven together in the same service.

This kind of synthesis is powerful and worth the effort because it means that in every service, there will be moments that are familiar for participants based on what they're used to and moments that feel fresh and offer a bit of a stretch. Even though our worship services are liturgical in that most prayers are written, we have made a conscious effort to include a synthesis of elements from a variety of traditions over the years, sensing this contributes to the spiritual impact of our worship—for those participating and for those of us who are leading!

Singing together—especially when you can hear your own and others' voices harmonizing and blending in a room that has the acoustics for it—is a significant aspect of transforming worship. We are joining our voices in real time to affirm truth together, speak directly to God about our longings, offer our praise, and respond to God's love in an experience of profound attunement. Singing in unison gives us an experience of unity that carries us beyond our normal divisions while harmonizing blends soprano, alto, tenor, and base voices together to generate a fuller sound than any of us could experience alone in our own houses. In the Transforming Center we regularly have song practices where people learn the harmonies so they can sing them out with confidence in the worship service. In such moments, the worship leader functions more like a choir director, and the community gets to experience itself as the choir.

In the past, singing together was simply expected as part of the worship experience, but now we might have to be a little more intentional about making sure it happens. Worship services in which the music is so loud that you can't hear yourself or anyone around you are missed opportunities for "attunement"; we might make conscious choices to temper the volume of the instruments at times or to have the instruments stop playing altogether, inviting and encouraging the voices only to settle into rich harmonies. Another challenge that has developed recently is the virtual worship experiences that became more of a norm during the pandemic. With gratitude for the technology that made it possible for worship to continue even in the face of such frightening realities, we can also acknowledge that singing and responsive readings are hard to replicate online due to the slight delay in timing. Yes, you can have people turn off their audio when singing or responding to avoid this awkwardness, but then each person only hears his or her own voice.

I say, let's be grateful for how technology served us back then, and let the joy of singing together be one of the things that brings us back together now.

> The music we share attunes us to one another. We "fall in step" with others on the paths we travel. We sway with them . . . and are lifted into a new state of mind by the sheer energy of blended voices. A thicket of voices summons us for at least the duration of a song out of the entrenchments that divide us and into an energy field that can be, some moments, transformative.[7]

**ENGAGING THE WHOLE PERSON**

Transforming worship is *holistic* in that it is designed to engage the whole person in interacting with the divine presence. Thus, there is a great deal of intentionality around incorporating

- icons, Christian symbols, beauty, and art (candles, crosses, banners, etc.);
- imaginative prayer experiences to engage the imagination; and
- embodied prayers that guide people into different postures, movements, and gestures (kneeling, making the sign of the cross, raising hands, passing the peace, liturgical dance).

All of these are ways of bringing our whole selves into relationship with God and each other in our worship, opening us to life-transforming encounters. At the same time, it is important to avoid being emotionally manipulative, overly sentimental, or melodramatic—which can be a very fine line to find. One of the ways we try to find and maintain this line is by always using invitational language, assuring people that while the invitation is real, they are always free to respond yes or no. There can be no forcing or social pressure brought to bear in the worship setting, otherwise it can easily become manipulation.

Incorporating time for *silence* is also a vital practice for engaging the whole person in worship. Silence helps people get in touch with their own center, allowing space for God to speak and for us to respond. A key place in a worship service where we might incorporate silence would be immediately following the Scripture reading so that before anyone else interprets or applies it for us, God can speak to us individually in the way only God can. Another place for silence would be after the sermon to let whatever was said sink in; whoever is speaking or preaching could even offer a question for reflection with some time to ponder these things in our hearts. We can also incorporate silence as a way of resting in God in a frenetic culture where rest is so hard to find.

Barbara Holmes describes a tradition from the Black church in which the service begins with a Holy Hush and people are encouraged to center themselves and pray.

> Today, worship services move at such a pace that often there seems to be no space or time for the congregation to unify itself in spirit. In times past, the old folks would tarry, pray, and rest in the presence of one another until the lover of their souls joined them. Those elders who remember these Africana worship practices know that something is missing today. Perhaps *missing* is not the right word. . . . Contemplative practices still exist in the Protestant black church, but they have not been consciously embraced and nurtured as necessary and important aspects of worship. The lack of contemplative abiding time creates a restless longing in the people.[8]

## GATHERED AROUND THE PRESENCE OF CHRIST

Transforming worship is decidedly *not* about celebrity pastors, musical guests and performers, or precise runs-of-show; it is about spiritual guidance into an encounter with the living Christ. It goes without saying but I'll say it anyway: Transforming worship is *Christ-centered.*

One of the main practices that keeps Christian worship Christ-centered is celebrating Communion together, but this is not always as simple as it sounds. In his book *Our One Great Act of Fidelity*, Fr. Ron Rolheiser points out, "Christians argue a lot about the Eucharist: what does it mean? What should it be called? How often should it be celebrated? Who is allowed to participate, consecrate and celebrate?"[9]

Divisions along these lines are the height of irony, given that the word *communion* has the word *union* in it, referring not only to our union with Jesus but also to our union with each other. Rolheiser devotes an entire chapter in his book to the different dimensions of the Eucharist in a way that is helpful and thought provoking. "For some it is a meal, for others it is a sacrifice. For some it is a ritual act, sacred and set apart, for others it is a community gathering, the more mess and kids the better. For some it is a deeply personal prayer, for others it is a communal worship for the world." This goes on for a page and a half and then he concludes by saying,

> In truth the Eucharist is all these things and more. It is like a finely cut diamond twirling in the sun, every turn giving off a different sparkle. It is multivalent, carrying different layers of meaning, some of them in paradoxical tension with others. *There is, even in Scripture, no single theology of the Eucharist, but instead there are various complementary theologies of the Eucharist.*[10]

These differences can be observed even in our architecture. In classic Protestant theology and practice, the Word is central; it is first and foremost what draws us into community, and the Eucharist might or might not follow. In more sacramental expressions of faith (Roman Catholic, Anglican, Lutheran), the Eucharist is given priority, and the Word and all the other sacraments are ultimately in support of attending to the real presence of Christ in the Eucharist. If you walk into a more Protestant expression of church, the pulpit will be front and center, indicating the priority of the written Word and the preached word. When you walk into a Catholic, Episcopal, or Lutheran church, the altar is front and center, indicating the priority of the sacrament, which is the moment that all other moments are leading up to in the worship event.[11]

In my own religious upbringing, Communion was primarily about remembering Jesus' sacrifice for us on the cross, and we did this every week in a special service devoted entirely to what we called the Lord's

Supper. This service was always very serious and somber—almost like a funeral where the purpose is for loved ones to share memories about the deceased—and it was the most important moment of our communal existence. It is in my DNA to have a very healthy respect for the centrality of Communion in a community's life. Since then, I have celebrated the Eucharist in many different ways—everything from partaking weekly as the climactic moment of the service to receiving it daily from a priest in a retreat setting to having it distributed in tiny little to-go containers on the way out of a large church auditorium at the end of the service. (That was a hard one for me and I hope to never experience that again.) Each of these experiences is a turning of the diamond in which another facet is revealed.

Because the sharing of the Eucharist is so central to our life together in Christ, every community is going to have to figure themselves out on this one—maybe even to the extent that we rethink our architecture and how we set up our worship space! I only know this because part of our history is that we have had to figure *ourselves* out! Two instances come to mind. The first one was during an initial planning retreat when we attended a mass together at a Catholic retreat center, thinking it would be a unifying experience. However, when it came time for Holy Communion, the priest made it clear that only confirmed Catholics could come forward to receive it. One of our group who was a devoted Catholic went forward while the rest of us stayed seated, and I will never forget how painful and shocking it was that what was supposed to be a unifying experience only served to highlight our separateness instead. That night, we didn't do much planning; instead, we spent time talking about the meaning of Communion.

The other incident happened when we attempted to celebrate Communion together on our own. It was part of an evening prayer service, and again, we felt that taking Communion together would be an important part of our formation together in Christ. One of the pastors among us served the elements, but he was not an ordained priest and did not consecrate the elements the way other traditions would have required. This was uncomfortable (if not offensive) to the Episcopalians among us; the pastor who was doing his level best to serve us was hurt as well. Given my own background, it had never occurred to me that having someone who was not an ordained priest serve the elements would be offensive. In my very "low church" tradition we placed more of an emphasis on Jesus' Last Supper, which seemed to be very casual and spontaneous. We took quite literally Jesus' heartfelt request to his disciples that when they were together in homes and over meals, they should do this in remembrance of him. It didn't seem like this required much in terms of pomp and circumstance, and since the first "Last Supper" would have taken place long before there were ordained priests, I had always assumed it was okay to have someone who was not a priest serve the elements. I was devastated to realize I was so ill-informed about other traditions that I failed to be attuned to the sensitivities of my siblings in Christ.

We processed this experience together in a loving way, but it was so unsettling that we backed away from doing Communion going forward because we didn't think there was any way to do it without the risk of offending someone. Eventually, Rory and I made the decision that we just couldn't call ourselves a community gathered around the presence of Christ if we weren't sharing Communion together. So, we took the risk of starting to share our story in each of our communities as a way of letting people know we were aware of different traditions and would be celebrating Communion in a variety of ways during our time together. We share how deeply we respect the different understandings and traditions around the Eucharist and encourage anyone who is uncomfortable that they do not have to come forward. Or they could come to the Communion table with arms folded across their chests as an indication that they would rather just receive a blessing. Since then, I don't think we have offended anyone (that I know of), and sharing Communion together is always so unifying that now it's hard to imagine we went so long without it.

Recently I was in a church service where the officiating pastor invited "all who want to know the love of Christ" to come to the table. No limits were placed on participation due to religious beliefs, church membership, confirmation completed, and so on. I know others might vigorously disagree with this way of offering Communion but all I could think was, "That's it! That sounds exactly like something Jesus would say!" I took my place in line with the other worshipers and made my way to the table with more joy than I had experienced in a long time.

In the next chapter we'll be turning to our life together with Scripture—another important aspect of transforming worship.

# 9

# OUR LIFE TOGETHER UNDER THE WORD

*The Holy Scriptures come alive for us in a whole new way precisely when they are read during worship services. We receive a part of that which once took place for our salvation. Forgetting and losing ourselves, we too pass through the Red Sea, through the desert, across the Jordan into promised land. With Israel we fall into doubt and unbelief and through punishment and repentance experience again God's help and faithfulness.*

Dietrich Bonhoeffer

---

Engaging Scripture for spiritual transformation is not just about how we are shaped personally but also about how it shapes whole communities. The worship gathering is one of the most central places where we are shaped by the Word together through reading, responding, and preaching. It is to the whole community gathered in Rome that Paul writes, "Do not be conformed to this age, but be transformed by the renewing of the mind" (Romans 12:2). Here he is referring to the renewing not only of the individual mind but also of the renewing of the corporate (together) mind.

Scripture is one of the most significant tools God uses to make our minds new, and times when a community gathers for worship is one of the best opportunities available for engaging in this kind of renewal together. But what is absolutely key to engaging the Scriptures for spiritual transformation is that we find ways to surrender to God in and through his Word, rather than controlling it for our own ends, pontificating about it to prove we are right on any number of things, or wounding people with our interpretations. According to Romans 12:1, finding ways to offer ourselves to God as a living sacrifice—that is, to surrender ourselves to God—is our spiritual worship, so that points us to another characteristic of transforming worship: It *guides us in a spirit of surrender*, especially as it has to do with "our life together under the Word."[1]

The question is, Are we willing to let the Word of God penetrate the corporate mind in the same way we allow God to shape and renew the individual mind? Are we willing to put rhythms and patterns in place that open us to being engaged intimately by God corporately—that is, when we are together? How can we experience God's Word as being living and active among us?

## SHAPED BY THE WORD IN COMMUNITY

Here are a few ideas—not exhaustive at all but some of the most foundational practices that enable us to place the Scriptures in God's hands as a tool for God to accomplish God's purposes in our lives versus us maintaining such tight control over how we use them.

***Approach the Scriptures relationally.*** For our purposes here, I am going to assume that people are being taught how to study Scripture through traditional Bible study methods, Christian education, and Sunday school classes, along the lines of how Paul instructed Timothy: "Do your best to present yourself to God as one approved by him, a worker who has no need to be ashamed, rightly explaining the word of truth" (2 Timothy 2:15). It is impossible to overstate the importance of biblical literacy in our churches today; with all our emphasis on relevance, many churches and ministries have gotten very lax on this. Seminary and other kinds of training for ministry are usually very good about teaching about Christian history, Bible study methods, and principles of biblical interpretation; it is our job in transforming community to teach people how to move from information to transformation, and that only happens in the back and forth of relationship. Justo Gonzalez calls it "the miracle of dialogue. . . . To read the Bible is to enter into dialogue with it. . . . It is not only the text that speaks to me, but I who speak to the text, demanding its responses in genuine dialogue."[2] Our job is to teach and offer experiences with Scripture that foster this dialogue.

***Utilize methods for engaging Scripture that help us relinquish control.*** It is incredible to observe how human beings try to control everything, including Scripture, for their own ends. This is devastating to any spiritual journey. As Bob Mulholland writes,

> "Graspers" powerfully resist being grasped by God. Controllers are inherently incapable of yielding control to God. Manipulators strongly reject being shaped by God. Information gatherers are structurally closed to being addressed by God. Information takers have extreme difficulty becoming receivers of God's voice. Functionally oriented people have great problems getting still and letting God act in God's own time. Frenetically functional activists find it extremely difficult "be still, and know" that God is God.[3]

As it has to do with Scripture, transforming worship services are an ideal time to teach and model ways of using Scripture that put us in a receptive stance, willing and able to let God be in control of the interaction, letting God initiate with us what God knows we need. This is very different from coming up with our own agendas for what we think people need to know and then delivering on it.

***Teach people how to use Scripture responsibly.*** To approach Scripture responsibly is to understand that it is a story—or, more accurately, a collection of stories—written by multiple authors from multiple points of view. It is "a complex unity" as Bonhoeffer describes it.[4] Because of that, context matters. We must always be asking two questions at once: What was this Scripture saying in the context in which it was written and what does it say to me now? What was for that specific time, and what should be considered a timeless principle that applies now?

Because Scripture is the story of God's presence and activity in human history, we need to ask, What is the arc, the trajectory? What are the overarching themes of God's story? Then we can let Scripture interpret Scripture (including difficult passages) in light of those overarching themes. We need to cultivate respect for the original languages, realizing that original meanings can be lost or obscured in translation, and subjectivity is always present. We can help people clarify the role of tradition by being respectful of the wisdom contained there but also open to what God is doing now. We can notice how we pick and choose what Scriptures to obey and which ones we dismiss, especially in our tradition and life together. We can encourage people to pay attention to what happens when they encounter teachings that are uncomfortable. Is it our pattern to dismiss or ignore them?[5]

Finally, we need to recognize and be deeply respectful of the fact that we all read through the lens of culture and ethnicity. We can't help it, and most of it is done unconsciously until our life in community reveals it. We all approach Scripture for what we need, so that is what we tend to see and find. Being aware of this should keep us very humble in how we hold our views and interpretations of Scripture.

## PRACTICES THAT HELP US RELINQUISH CONTROL

Here are four practices that can help us transcend our control issues. These are not intended to replace Bible study and corporate preaching and teaching intended to cultivate biblical knowledge and literacy. These four practices should be seen as being *in addition* to methods that cultivate biblical literacy appropriate for every stage of spiritual development.

- *Lectio divina*—an ancient practice for reading Scripture that includes multiple readings with deepening questions interspersed with silence so God can bypass our defenses and speak to us.

- Following a common lectionary (*lectio continua*)—a historic practice of following a shared reading plan (typically a three-year plan) that keeps us connected with the life of Christ through the Gospels as well as keeping us grounded in the Christian story. This is a practice surrender and submission because we are not picking and choosing our own readings.
- Finding ourselves in the story—a God-guided practice in which we prayerfully imagine ourselves as various characters in the story being told in Scripture. The Ignatian exercises emphasize this practice.
- Using Psalms as our prayer book in community. Reading the Psalms regularly and systematically (rather than always picking and choosing our favorites) is one way to enroll in the school of prayer, allowing the prayer book Jesus and his disciples used to be our guide.

## THE PREACHING MOMENT

I do not claim to be an expert on preaching and, of course, homiletics is its own field of study. But no discussion of engaging Scripture would be complete without talking about the preaching moment and its place in a community's transformational journey. How does preaching move beyond information, how-tos, and even inspiration to becoming a transformational experience for all involved—including the preacher? How can it become a God-breathed, cocreated moment?

Transformational preaching is a fire in our bones that is sparked by what is happening in our own encounters with God, protected and fanned into flame in the depths of our own souls until it is ready to be offered up for others. I have long been convicted and challenged by Henri Nouwen's perspective that as ministers "our first and foremost task is to faithfully care for the inward fire so that when it is really needed it can offer warmth and life to lost travelers." He describes the temptation to open the door so often that the fire eventually dies, and no one can find strength and warmth. Many of us who preach and teach a lot need to keep an eye on how often we are opening the oven door to make sure we are not letting the heat of our fire dissipate. "Silence is the discipline by which the inner fire of God is tended and kept alive."[6]

Transforming preaching begins, then, with hearing a word from the Lord that has first penetrated our own hearts and is now living and breathing there, changing *us* in some fundamental way. It comes from the soul of us where God's Spirit witnesses with our spirits about things that are true until we are willing to risk speaking that truth out loud in ways that meet the moment. It involves casting a vision for what the kingdom of God looks like in your life and mine, moving beyond broad generalities to hard specifics, and celebrating the hope contained within the good news that is ours—no matter how dark things seem.

The role of preaching in the Black church is a compelling example of preaching that transforms. Dr. Martin Luther King Jr. is one who used the power of his pulpit and his gifts as an orator and preacher to "meet the moment" of racial inequality with his God-given vision of racial justice. His vision for a world that reflected more accurately God's intentions for all God's children was clear, compelling, and concrete. The method he outlined for how to accomplish this vision was a deeply spiritual journey with actual steps that he clearly outlined. He was also in touch with the challenges to seeing that vision become reality, so his preaching task was to continually point people to the inner resources only God can provide. His preaching literally changed minds and changed the world.

Renowned preacher Frank Thomas highlights the role of celebration in the Black church in his book *They Like to Never Quit Praisin' God*—one of my favorite books on preaching. Here he points out,

> In the midst of profound anguish and suffering, the African American preacher sought not to give answers to the problem of suffering and evil in life, but to help people experience the

> assurance of the grace of God. The preacher gave assurance to the people that God was with them, in and through the suffering, and would ultimately liberate them from the suffering.[7]

Thomas writes significantly about the elements of emotional process in the preaching moment. He highlights the dialogical nature of preaching in the Black church in which both preacher and congregant take mutual responsibility for calling forth the Word of God and uplifting the one who is delivering the word. Part of the responsibility of the preacher is to guide the congregation to celebration "until one has received an inner assurance, affirmation, courage, and a feeling of empowerment."[8] If that's not transforming worship, I don't know what is!

I draw major inspiration for transforming preaching from Moses. We mostly think of him as the great leader and liberator of God's people, Israel. But he was also a man with a message, a message given to him by God that needed to be communicated in a very convincing way. There was a lot riding on his ability to be prophetic (that is, speak God's message) in his communication, *and* this was the part of his job he was most uncomfortable with. His resistance was so strong that he and God had a major argument about it. But he was God's choice for the job, entrusted with a vision that really mattered to a lot of people, and God wouldn't let him squirm out of it. Moses risked his life over and over again to say, "The Promised Land is that-a-way. I've been there! I've seen it! Let's go there together."

This kind of preaching is more than Sunday morning inspiration. It's more than just getting our job done. It is an act of spiritual leadership that moves people from here to there. Transforming preaching is more than just the words we say; it is our very presence on the journey with our people, attuned to the voice of God on their behalf and willing to bring a word when God gives it. It's a person who may not be the most gifted in the homiletics class. It might even be a person whose dearest wish is to fade into the background or who may even have a speech impediment. But there is an anointing and, against all odds, we carry it through.

Transforming preaching is forged in the cauldron of our own relationship with God as we have tended the fire in our own soul. It is clear, concrete, and compelling in the way it meets the moment. It helps people experience and celebrate the assurance of grace that is our gospel. And it takes us out to the edge of our own courage in response to the One who calls us and then gives us the word we need. It is at once prophetic and reassuring, risky and anointed. As Barbara Brown Taylor, observes,

> Most preachers I know are afraid of something . . . so my first piece of advice is to figure out what they are afraid of and then what matters more to them than their fear. Fear is a great gagger of preachers. The second piece of advice is to work at least as hard at saying something true to life as something true about God. Being divinely right is not nearly as important as being humanly real. In my own preaching . . . I fail as often as I succeed. . . . If I'm not risking my theological neck in a sermon, then I'm not sure why anyone would listen.[9]

## WHY TRANSFORMING WORSHIP MATTERS

Rory Noland offers a fourfold sequence for worship drawn from the Emmaus Road encounter.[10] I have adapted it a bit to incorporate much of what we have described in this chapter and help us envision how to put the pieces together:

- gathering
- Word
- response
- Communion and celebration around the table
- blessing and sending

Invocation serves as a call to worship, gathering the community together for the express purpose of worship and encounter with the living God. There is interaction with the Word through Scripture reading, silence, the preached word, and prayerful response. All of this culminates in Jesus' invitation to join him at the Communion table in remembrance and celebration. Then strengthened by the assurance of the good news, we are sent and empowered to take the transforming presence of Jesus into the world.

Over time, one of the ways transforming worship works is that *we become what we behold.* As 2 Corinthians 3:18 puts it, "And all of us, with unveiled faces, seeing the glory of the Lord as though reflected in a mirror, are being transformed into the same image from one degree of glory to another, for this comes from the Lord, the Spirit." We all behold a lot of things in a day, and most of them do not contribute to making us who we most want to be. But when we gather for transforming worship, we are saying, "This is what I want to be. This is who I want to be." And somehow, that very act of beholding God's glory and experiencing Jesus' love once again transforms us little by little—from one degree to another. This might be imperceptible to us. On some days it might feel like not much is happening in and through our efforts to make it to worship, but Scripture bears witness to the fact that something *is* happening. We are becoming what we behold. And we can be assured that the journey of transformation itself *is* an act of worship, as we present ourselves to God in such moments, surrendering once again to what God wants to do in us and through us as we are empowered for his service.

10

# WORKING WITH STAGES OF FAITH IN THE FAMILY OF GOD

*The journey of faith, the path to spiritual wholeness, lies in our increasingly faithful response to the One whose purpose shapes our path, whose grace redeems our detours, whose power liberates us from the crippling bondages of our previous journeys, and whose transforming presence meets us at each turn in our road.*

M. Robert Mulholland Jr.

---

**Earlier in this work** I described hitting a wall in my spiritual life. Even though I had done and was doing all the things I was supposed to be doing—attending church, reading my Bible, praying, participating in small groups, serving in any way that was allowed—I still hit a wall. By "wall," I mean I was asking questions for which there seemed to be no answers, experiencing emotions I could manage but not control, feeling empty, and longing for more of God and deeper levels of transformation than I knew how to accomplish on my own. I was stuck, and no one around me seemed to understand, let alone know how to help.

Fortunately, through the help of a good spiritual director who recognized that I was in a particular "place" on the spiritual journey, I did break through that wall, and the rest, as they say, is history. But I did have to go beyond the churches I was a part of at the time to find the help I needed. What I know now is that this was stages of faith stuff and that this kind of experience comes to most all of us who stay on a true faith journey. The trouble is that many communities do not know much about the stages, how to recognize them, or how to resource people who are in them.

One of the most strategic (i.e., thoughtful, intentional, and wise) things we can do in cultivating transforming communities is to go to school on stages of faith and human development so we can resource people at every stage. The family of God needs to be big enough and experienced enough to love and care for God's children at all ages and stages.

### THE JOURNEY OF SURRENDER

The goal of the spiritual life is nothing less than complete surrender—that is, an increasing capacity to trust God with our whole selves and our very lives rather than relying on human-made programs for safety and security, power and control, affection and esteem.[1] Since the process of spiritual transformation takes place primarily at the points of our unlikeness to Christ, it is in that very place that we are called to relinquish ourselves in complete abandonment to God. This includes seeing and naming these places of unlikeness, saying yes to God, and releasing ourselves to God in those places of unlikeness through corresponding spiritual disciplines. The journey of surrender is not something that can be humanly orchestrated. As Richard Rohr writes,

> I don't think we can chart its course ahead of time. Our own private salvation projects seldom do the job. Surrender is something that is done *to* us, more than something we do ourselves. Someone else must determine the timing, the circumstances, the shape of the ordeal. None of us can engineer our own transformation—or it would not be transformation at all but merely cosmetic surgery to make us think well of ourselves.[2]

I'm not sure this is the journey most communities are set up to facilitate. So, in the following pages we summarize the classic stages of faith along with a biblical model that provides a compelling illustration of what the stages look like in the lives of real people. There are many other insightful models that can round out the picture—James Fowler, Janet Hagberg and Robert Guelich, Richard Rohr, just to name a few. The very existence of a plethora of models speaks to the universality of stage theory as the models have been named and described by different authors.

One thing all the models hold in common is the understanding that the stages function on two levels: They describe the overall journey of conversion that begins with awakening to God for the first time (at salvation) and culminates in complete union with God in the afterlife. At the same time, the stages can be experienced as the path of transformation in a particular area of unlikeness to Christ. Mullholland writes, "God calls us out of unlikeness (awakening) and moves us to an increasing relinquishment of that unlikeness (purgation); this leads to a new structure of being and doing (illumination) and eventually culminates in Christlikeness of spirit and behavior at that particular point of our life (union)."[3] This means we can be at different stages in various areas of our lives all at the same time—that is, well along the path to wholeness in one area while in another area we are just beginning to awaken to another part of our lives where we are not fully surrendered.

In addition, all the models acknowledge that there is usually some sort of precipitating event that gets the ball rolling into the more advanced stages of the journey; it could be deep suffering, feeling stuck, experiencing failure, or going through a significant transition that takes us out to our emotional edge. By advanced, we do not mean that one stage is better than another, just as no stage of human development is better than another. All are necessary, and each one builds on the one that came before. All the models acknowledge that the stages are not so much linear in the sense that we arrive at a destination and then we're done. Rather, the stages represent more of a cyclical process in which we cycle through the stages multiple times throughout our lives, propelled forward on the journey toward greater freedom and abandonment to God.

There is so much to learn about stages of faith that this one chapter will only be a beginning, but hopefully it will whet your appetite to learn more and dig into this significant field of study. As you read, you may want to highlight words and phrases that correspond to your own experience. When and where have you experienced aspects of the different stages? What do you remember needing at the different stages? What observations do you have about what your community offers as resources for each stage, as well as noting any gaps?

## UNPACKING THE CLASSIC STAGES OF FAITH

The classic model of the spiritual journey emerges from John of the Cross and Teresa of Ávila and identifies four stages: awakening, purgation, illumination, and union. Some models identify five stages, placing the dark night of the soul between illumination and union, while others include it as part of the movement within the stage of union. Robert Mulholland summarizes the stages very nicely in chapter eight of his book *Invitation to a Journey*, and I have condensed them here with encouragement for you to pick up his book to see more of the work he has done in describing these four stages.

***Awakening.*** The first stage is a twofold experience of encountering God as God really is and encountering ourselves as we really are in the light of God's presence. Isaiah's experience in Isaiah 6 is a biblical example of this. He sees God high and lofty and he responds, "Woe is me! I am lost, for I am a man of unclean lips!" (v. 5). There is a sense of comfort and threat in this encounter: comfort in awakening to the presence of God in this worshipful experience but also threat in recognizing that we are not who we thought we were, and God is something different and more than what we thought God was. All of a sudden, we know we really do not have God in our back pocket; in other words, God is not something or someone we can control. There is a bit of a push-pull phenomenon going on here—something in us feels drawn and another part of us wants to pull back. We know we are on the threshold of something wholly new and different.

***Purgation.*** Awakening initiates the purgation process in which God gradually strips us of those aspects of the self that are not in harmony with who we know God to be.[4] This is signified by the angel touching Isaiah's lips with the hot coal. Purgation is its own deepening process. First there is the renunciation of all blatant inconsistencies with wholeness in Christ—obvious sins like those Paul lists in Galatians 5:19 that even our culture eschews. Then purgation moves to other deliberate sins that may be normal and acceptable in our culture but are clearly not acceptable for kingdom living, like uncontrolled anger or sexual promiscuity. There may also be behaviors that are not inherently bad but may be unloving or unhelpful in a more subtle way, such as, in Paul's day, eating meat that had been sacrificed to idols. Next, purgation causes us to become aware of unconscious sins and omissions—things that we may have tolerated earlier in our lives but now we recognize are a hindrance to our growth or our life in Christ. Aspects of our uses of technology might fit in this category; they are not inherently sinful, but we recognize they contribute to a distracted life.

The final stage of purgation deals with deep-seated attitudes and the inner orientation of our being out of which our behavior patterns flow. Here God is dealing primarily with our "trust structures," especially those deep inner postures of our being that do not rely on God but on self for our sense of well-being. As painful as it is to have these layers of the false self stripped away, it is God's grace guiding us into deeper levels of trust and reliance on God. This is classically known as *detachment,* a consistent posture of actively turning ourselves over to God. This is God dropping the plow and excavating deeper and deeper into the soil of our souls.

***Illumination.*** This stage is characterized by total consecration of ourselves to God in love—at least in the area God has been working on.

This is signified by Isaiah's response, "Here am I; send me" (Isaiah 6:8). Now, rather than experiencing God as being "out there," we experience God to be intimately within. Rather than harboring illusions of control, we have given God absolute control of the relationship. Illumination brings us to a life of deep sensitivity to the Spirit within, increasingly attuned and responsive to the heart of God in all things—within our own hearts and in the world around us. "Illumination is characterized by increasing social concern, not out of obligation but out of a deep sense of God's love poured out in our hearts for others, . . . not as responsibility or duty, but again as a response to love."[5]

***Union.*** This stage is characterized by abandonment to God's grace, which at times gives us experiences of complete oneness with God—being "caught up," as John describes his experience on the island of Patmos. These unitive experiences are a gift of grace, not the fruit of our own efforts. The prayer of quietness as described in Psalm 131:2—"I have calmed and quieted my soul, like a weaned child with its mother"—has become our way of life, at least in the area where we have been seeking greater levels of surrender. What's interesting is that this stage is also where we experience the dark night of the senses in which God removes the normal consolations we used to experience in prayer—experiencing God through our imagination, our emotions, our felt sense of his presence. We go through a period of spiritual emptiness and dryness, through which we must persevere in faith. In this space, the last remaining dependencies on intellectual and emotional experiences are painfully surrendered; we may even doubt our relationship with God, wondering if we have fallen off the spiritual path. This can be a time of real suffering in that we are being purified of our familiar ways of "sensing" God's presence.

The dark night of the spirit comes much later in this stage and is completely at God's initiative. Here the soul experiences profound darkness, not because God has abandoned the soul but because the light of God is so overwhelming. This can be likened to what happens when we stare directly into the sun or another bright light; we experience darkness—not being able to see—simply because we are so close to the light. The dark night of the soul is not due to God's distance; it is due to God's closeness. This is an all-encompassing purification of the higher faculties of the soul in preparation for total union—"the last and narrowest tunnel of the spiritual journey, the eye of the needle through which no remaining vestiges of self-will may pass."[6] It is the final stage of losing "self" (the clinging false self, that is) so that it is no longer we who live but Christ who lives in us and through us. This may result in periods of ecstatic union or total absorption in God, which we could also categorize as mystical experiences.

These experiences are not something we can manufacture; we can only receive them as gifts. We do not cling to such experiences, as the disciples tried to do on the Mount of Transfiguration; rather we receive them as they are given, and we also don't make too big a deal of them because there we are no longer trying to control or manipulate God. Technically, the "dark night of the soul" is the overarching term that encompasses both the dark night of the senses and the dark night of the spirit—both of which are moving us toward the union we seek, even when it doesn't feel like it!

This is a lot like a mature marriage. We are married (in union) to our spouse all the time; experiences of ecstatic union come and go, and we recognize they are not more or less important than the quieter experiences of union, like going for a walk or sitting together without the need for words. Couples who have been married for a long time know the profound goodness of this kind of union.

## THE EXODUS AS A BIBLICAL MODEL FOR STAGES OF FAITH

The spiritual journey is often disruptive to our psychological state, so we need some sort of community that understands what's really going on. We need a community that sustains us in the mysterious work of God in moments that don't make sense from a human point of view but make every bit of sense from a spiritual point of view. The exodus narrative puts flesh on the bones of the classic rendering of the stages of faith, illustrating how a whole community moves through them together.

Reflecting on the story of the exodus through the lens of stages of faith is helpful because it is grounded in a real story about real people who are taking a physical journey to union with God, signified by the Promised Land. The Promised Land was a physical place, but it was also a metaphor for the journey toward finally experiencing the freedom of living on God's terms for them. "The whole congregation of the Israelites journeyed by stages, as the LORD commanded" (Exodus 17:1). The journey to the Promised Land can be seen as an archetype of the journey from salvation to finding our true home in heaven, or it can describe moments when God is calling us to greater freedom in a particular area of our lives that will require leaving familiar territory and our familiar bondages. As we consider the different stages of the Israelite journey, I will overlay the classic stages to demonstrate how these two very different models describe what is fundamentally the same process.

***Pre-awareness/pre-awakening (Exodus 1:1-7).*** In this stage, we are not yet aware that we are in bondage or that we need God to lead us into something more. There might even be good things going on ("The Israelites were fruitful and prolific" [Exodus 1:7]), and much like the Israelites, we are lulled into believing that this is as good as it gets. This stage could be characterized as blissful ignorance, or we may be relying on behaviors that numb our awareness of the price we are paying for the life we are living. This stage can last for a long time because there is something so comforting about the security of the familiar. In pre-awareness/pre-awakening we really don't know there is anything better out there; like the Israelites, our bondage is familiar. It is a way of life that makes sense to us.

***Awareness/awakening (Exodus 1:8-14; 2:23-25).*** But in God's way and time, God begins to move us toward an awareness that there might be something more. Eventually something happens that heightens our awareness of longing and desire, and we may start to feel frustration and even desperation that gets harder and harder to ignore. Awakening takes place at God's initiative as we start to see glimpses of the More. This can be very gradual, or it can be sudden, and oftentimes there is some sort of crisis that moves us toward a turning point.

***Turning point/conversion (Exodus 12:33-42, 50-51).*** Another facet of the awakening process is that things often get worse before they get better. It is something that happens that brings a sense of urgency, a willingness to make a change. Note that the Israelites' awareness grew as their suffering got worse. When they were required to make bricks without straw and couldn't keep up with their quotas, they were beaten mercilessly. This might seem like an unnecessary cruelty, but it is an important part of the process because *it brings them to a turning point* where they are willing to do something decisive about their situation. It is the last straw, the thing that caused them to say, "We just can't do this anymore." Obviously this awareness can be disruptive to life as we know it, and things might get messy and chaotic before they get better. But we know it's time to make a change, whether we do it perfectly or not. For me, this was the moment when I knew I had to leave the church (small *c*) as I had known it in order to seek what I sensed God had for me. For the Israelites, the turning point was things getting so bad they were willing to leave Egypt under Moses' leadership.

This is one of the scariest parts of the journey because you are letting go of what's not working, and you haven't yet arrived at what's next. This is liminal space again, the place where God is always leading God's people—out of bondage and into a greater freedom than we have yet known.

***The roundabout way/illumination (Exodus 13:17-22).*** After the stress of deciding to leave the security of all they had known and following Moses' specific instructions about how they were going to get out of Egypt, the Israelites were ushered into a time of spiritual flourishing characterized by enthusiasm, gratitude, voracious learning, and service. They experienced this first in leaving Egypt triumphantly and then in being protected by God as God led them in "the roundabout way." God knew they were simply not ready to take on the challenges that a more direct route would require them to face. The roundabout way is a time of spiritual flourishing in which God shows up in very tangible ways, assuring us of his presence on the journey. For the Israelites this assurance was in the form of guidance provided by the cloud by day and a pillar of fire by night. For us this stage corresponds to early discipleship when flourishing comes in the form of a sense of certainty about who God is and how God may be found, along with a certain simplicity about what it means to follow God. This part of the journey is very fulfilling as God makes God's self known as a vital and loving presence on the journey. It's not that this stage is a walk in the park, it's just that God is very present, using every difficulty and challenge to teach us things, bolster our faith, and prepare us for the more rigorous parts of the journey. We have a sense we are growing, and because things seem to be going so well, we can be a little judgmental of those who are on a different leg of their journey. We can be very black-and-white in our thinking and a little (or a lot!) legalistic because we're kind of feeling our oats!

***Ambivalence/dark night of the senses (Exodus 13:17–14:30).*** But the challenges do come. Somewhere along this way, we are faced unexpectedly with our first real obstacle, and we're surprised because things had been going so well! For the Israelites, the first obstacle was the Red Sea: As they approached what appeared to be an uncrossable sea, they looked back only to find that the Egyptians had changed their minds and were pursuing them to take them back into slavery. Even with all they had experienced of God's presence with them, their faith faltered. For the first time, they experienced real ambivalence about this journey toward freedom and what it was now requiring of them. They attacked Moses and accused him of bringing them out to the wilderness to die. They were convinced that God had abandoned them, and they longed to go back to Egypt where at least there was a bit more security.

This ambivalence is a predictable part of any true spiritual journey, and it is helpful for people to know this so they don't get down on themselves. There may even be enough of a sense of fear and threat that we contemplate going back into bondage, because at least that was familiar. Sue Monk Kidd describes this in a way that resonates deeply with my own journey.

> There is a natural diapause in the human journey of transformation—a time when we hold onto the self we know. It seems that at the moment of our greatest possibility, a desperate clinging rises up in us. . . . In the words of Daniel Day Williams, "We fear [that the self we know] is all we have. Even its sufferings are familiar, and we clutch them because their very familiarity is comforting. . . . Yet so long as we aim at the maintenance of this present self, as we now conceive it, we cannot enter the larger selfhood which is pressing for life."[7]

Mature leaders can normalize this experience by helping people understand that ambivalence is a common response to the challenges of the journey, encouraging them to stay with it rather than running back to what feels more secure. He or she can help them to "be still and wait for the deliverance of the Lord," just as Moses did. This is the dark night of the senses when our previous ways of knowing and experiencing God are not working anymore and we need to persevere in faith. It's like a marriage, when you're past the honeymoon phase; if you stay faithful to it, you enter a deeper kind of intimacy that is not so dependent on emotions.

***Immersion/wilderness (Exodus 15–20; 33–34; 40; Deuteronomy 1–11; 34).*** In this stage, we are consumed with the work of the journey and trying to figure things out. Most of the exodus story is about the wilderness part of the journey and how God was preparing them for the freedom they would eventually enter into. Here they experience

God's protection as they face conflict, they learn to trust God for their deliverance and their day-to-day sustenance, they learn important lessons about confession and cleansing, and God instructs them and shapes them into a community that can actually function together. It was also a time of purification in which the generation of those who had doubted God had to die off. This mirrors the dark night of the soul, in which the higher faculties of the soul—intellect, memory, and will—are purified and stripped away in preparation for union, that is, the Promised Land.

This stage can feel rather turbulent and chaotic as we are consumed with our own inner wrestling, which we may, at first, seek to address with voluminous reading, study, and seeking advice. Eventually we are able to settle down and just be where God has us. There is something exhilarating about it as we can see and feel that we are becoming more whole. This is liminal space and there are few who can accompany us here. Usually, spiritual directors are the most prepared to accompany people through this part of their journey. The journey may feel very lonely at this point, but God does break into our reality in startling ways to assure us that we are on the right path and moving in the right direction. No one does this stage perfectly; we *will* make mistakes because it is uncharted territory for us, but best of all, God is with us.

***Internalization/union (Promised Land/book of Joshua).*** This stage is represented by the Israelites crossing the Jordan and entering the freedom of the Promised Land. While this part of the journey is very gradual—almost imperceptible at times—the process of moving toward freedom has been internalized; it is now something that is a part of you rather than being something "out there" that you are trying to attain. You are living in the freedom that, up to this point, you could only imagine. In this stage the focus shifts from self to others who may still be living in unfreedom; the pain you have been through results in compassion rather than judgment. Our inner security now comes through union with God, allowing a truer sense of calling (versus the drivenness of the false self) to emerge. We are now unencumbered by the limitations of the past because we have come to peace with it. This comes from having wrestled with God and come out on the other side with deep trust that enables complete surrender—at least in the aspect of the false self God has been working on.

The last vestiges of the false self with all of its clinging have been stripped away. We accept the fact that there may be additional skirmishes along the way—additional places of unfreedom that need to be worked through by moving through the stages once again—but more and more our overall experience is characterized by peace and the inner freedom that comes from being given over to God and love. No wonder tradition sometimes calls this experience of union *spiritual marriage.*

## WHAT DIFFERENCE DOES IT MAKE?

There is so much more to be uncovered in this narrative that I hope you will take the time to read the story of the exodus through the lens of stages of faith. Pay attention to how it deepens your understanding of the dynamics of your own spiritual journey and how we can better support one another on that journey. Any community that aspires to be a *transforming* community needs to understand and be able to work with all the stages of faith. And we need to be prepared to resource people at all stages of their journey—not just the easy ones or the ones we're good at.

There are many benefits to making sure the leaders in your community understand stages of faith. First of all, a shared understanding of stages of faith can help us figure out how to more effectively support people at all phases of their journey, invite them into whatever next step would be right for them, and then resource them as they do. Without this foundational piece, our approach to transformation will be somewhat haphazard and full of gaps, or it will be a cookie-cutter approach where we expect the same offerings to meet everyone's need.

Understanding stages of faith can also provide a diagnostic tool for identifying more clearly what we already offer related to each stage (every community has things it does well), along with identifying those stages we don't support and resource quite as well. We can look at the different aspects of our life together through the lens of stages of faith and identify how each one contributes to the formation process. And we can find support for staying together when there are differences in what we need and want from the community. Knowing that we're all on the same journey but, perhaps, at different stages on that journey can help us persevere with others right where they are and right where we are.

Stop for a moment and reflect on a conflict that has taken place in your community recently or an ongoing difference of opinion that you have not been able to resolve. It could be issues having to do with changes in vision and mission, worship, programming, or related to Covid. Now that you are familiar with stages of faith, can you see how people being at differing places on their faith journey might play into the stuckness your community is experiencing? Attending to what people who are in different stages might need could help get things unstuck. But here's the challenge:

> According to stage theory, we can understand all the stages through which we have been, and we can grasp intellectually the one immediately ahead of us. But we cannot fully comprehend the day-to-day existence of people whose home stage is two stages further along on the journey. We can read the words that describe these people, but living with them, working with them, or being in a meeting with them leaves us perplexed and perhaps frustrated.[8]

This is a tough truth because you cannot force yourself or others to be where they are not. It takes patience, compassion, and long-suffering to walk with a community of people who are in a variety of different places on the journey, but that is our job. May God help us!

I wonder if we can catch the vision for communities that not only understand these movements of the spiritual life but also know how to help and support each person as they move through them. After all, it is expected that families can hold all the stages human beings go through in their developmental process. As parents, it is our *job* to welcome the newborn, keep toddlers safe, provide guidance for adolescents, and care for aging parents. Likewise, a transforming community is expected to invite, hold, and support all the developmental stages of the spiritual life, providing appropriate resources for each one. In the end, perhaps it is best not to obsess about the stages but rather to understand them, to resource folks as best we can, and then to trust their journeys to God, as Pierre Teilhard de Chardin calls us to do.

**Patient Trust**

*Above all, trust in the slow work of God.*
*We are, quite naturally, impatient in everything*
*to reach the end without delay. . . .*
*We are impatient of being on the way to something*
*unknown, something new.*
*And yet it is the law of all progress*
*that it is made by passing through*
*some stages of instability—*
*and that it may take a very long time. . . .*

*Only God can say what this new spirit*
*gradually forming within you will be.*
*Give our Lord the benefit of believing*
*that his hand is leading you,*
*And accepting the anxiety of feeling yourself*
*in suspense and incomplete.*

—Pierre Teilhard de Chardin[9]

# PART 4

# MISSION

## *In God for the World*

*A genuinely Christian spirituality is not only rooted in a vital, growing relationship with God at the heart of one's being, but is also incarnated in the reality of the social, economic and political context one lives in. Such spirituality is relevant, revolutionary, transforming.*

M. Robert Mulholland Jr.

# 11

# PARTAKERS OF THE DIVINE NATURE

## *Participating in God's Generosity*

*Our growth toward wholeness in Christ is for the sake others within the body of Christ, that we might nurture one another into the wholeness of Christ. . . . [It] is also for the sake of others beyond the body of Christ, that the redeeming, healing, transforming love of God might be made known in a broken and hurting world.*

M. Robert Mulholland

---

**In his teaching** at the Transforming Center Bob Mulholland taught us the difference between being in the world for God and being in God for the world. (You may need to read that twice!) To Bob's way of thinking, being in the world for God is doing God's work in our own way, according to our timetable, when and how it works for us. To be in God for the world, on the other hand, is to be radically available to God for others without the need to be so self-referenced and controlling. To undergird this point, he offered us his own highly nuanced translation of Philippians 2:3-5: "Do nothing from self-referenced strife or empty conceit, but in humility regard others without self-referenced-ness. Let each of you look not only to your own interests, but also to the interests of others. Have the same inner orientation of being that was in Christ Jesus."[1]

The first time we heard this distinction, those of us who were listening were rather taken aback. We had never thought about it in exactly that way before, and yet we recognized the truth of it immediately. Most of us were Christian leader–types who had spent a lifetime trying to do good, but in that moment we couldn't deny that most of it had been about our preconceived ideas of what needed to be done, our vision and our plans for getting it done, our schedule, our control, our predetermined outcomes. . . . Lord, have mercy! I remember us sitting there in stunned silence as the scales fell from our eyes.

## A NEW ORIENTATION

A major outcome of our transformational journey and a marker of Christian maturity is that we come to know ourselves as being "in God" and our identity being firmly rooted there. Because our lives are held there securely, we are released from the constant impulse to control, manipulate, and force our own agenda on others—no matter how worthy that agenda may seem to be. Knowing God's got us and that God is the source of all we need, we are free to be generous with ourselves and our resources just as God has been generous toward us. We find ourselves quite naturally participating in the generosity and openness of God's nature.

On the other hand, when we are *not* finding ourselves in God, it means we are seeking our identity somewhere else—in some identity we have cultivated to keep ourselves feeling safe in the world. *That* identity is very fragile because it is humanly orchestrated, causing us to be self-protective, defensive and hard-edged, possessive, always trying to get what we need and want on our own terms. This attachment to the false security of a self-made identity makes it impossible to be radically available to God for others, which is to be free from self-referenced concern and able to *let God be God for others on God's own terms for them.*

Thomas Merton expresses it this way:

> One's great need is now no longer to be loved, understood, accepted and pardoned, but to understand, to love, to pardon and

> to accept others just as they are, in order to help them transcend themselves in love. But basically, the discipline involved here is that of crucifixion which eliminates a superficial and selfish kind of experience and opens to us the freedom of life that is not dominated by egoism, vanity, willfulness, passion, aggressiveness, jealousy, greed.[2]

**BEYOND IMITATION TO DIVINE UNION**

I am not sure why we as Christians have settled for the idea of imitation rather than union, copying versus inner transformation. Imitation, by its very definition, signifies trying to be something or someone we are not. It means we are working hard to pattern ourselves after something or someone *outside* of ourselves—which is nothing more than acting or performing. This brings to mind the agonies of adolescence when everyone is trying frantically to be like everyone else or copy the person who is deemed to be the coolest. But Paul's use of the word *metamorphoō* in Romans 12:2 signals something different from mere imitation. As discussed earlier, this highly nuanced Greek word means "to transform," "to change form," "to transfigure," referring to the mysterious process by which a caterpillar goes into the chrysalis and emerges as a beautiful butterfly.

Of course, we all love the hopeful metaphor of the caterpillar-turned-butterfly, but most of us underestimate the rigors of the process. Metamorphosis is a dramatic reorganization of the caterpillar's being in which the old body actually disintegrates and a new body is formed! The caterpillar body breaks down as its muscles and organs dissolve through the release of special enzymes—much like what takes place in the digestive process—leaving behind only the most life-supporting cells. What's needed for the caterpillar to become a butterfly is contained within these cells that are left.[3] But who knows if the caterpillar knows anything about that? And who knows what it's like to be the caterpillar in this in-between state!

What we do know is that through this process of dissolution, the caterpillar is rebuilt into a butterfly with a new set of capacities, now able to fly above the earth rather than being limited to crawling around on its belly. When the butterfly emerges from the cocoon, it is not imitating anything or anyone; it is simply being what it now is, naturally living out the possibilities and capacities of a completely reorganized inner being. Transformation is to change the very essence of something, while transfiguration is to change the shape or the outward manifestation of something so that it is observable by others. Both are present in this metaphor for our own transformation. This "change in form and nature" is a far cry from copying someone else—even if it's someone as worthy as Jesus.

It may be helpful to note that imitation is Paul's language (1 Corinthians 11:1—"Be imitators of me, as I am of Christ"), but that is not Jesus' language. His language is always so much more intimate, like when he prays for us in John 17:21: "As you, Father, are in me and I am in you, may they also be in us." This also seems to be closer to what the apostle Peter is getting at in 2 Peter 1:4 when he writes, "Thus he has given us, through these things, his precious and very great promises, so that through them you may . . . *become participants of the divine nature*" (emphasis added).[4] This is what the Eastern Orthodox tradition describes as deification, divinization, or *theosis,* which clarifies that "Christianity is not merely a philosophical theory or a moral code; it involves a direct sharing in divine life and glory, a transforming union with God face to face."[5]

The doctrine of *theosis* does not imply that human beings become God. Rather, the apostle Peter seems to be describing an experience of *union* with God in which God's very nature is formed in us and flows through us in increasingly natural and unimpeded ways—"the Holy Spirit is intimately united with our inmost self so that the Spirit's presence in us makes our 'I' the 'I' of God."[6] The very purpose of Jesus' life here on earth was to incarnate the love of God that is at once generous, compassionate, redemptive, restorative, sacrificial, and reconciling. Through transforming union with God, we too can participate in and become conduits for the multifaceted love that is God's very nature. Now, rather than pretending, we are participating in that love!

The difference between being in the world for God and being in God for the world is subtle yet real; it takes practice to learn the difference and then to discern how to live out that difference as we bring ourselves to our world. Such experiential learning takes place as we engage in specific practices that form God's love in us, bringing goodness to others while at the same time creating space for God to continue God's transforming work in us. Some (like generosity, forbearance, and forgiveness) are more personal in nature while others (like justice, compassion, and using power for good) are more public. Both the personal and the public practices are needed as we learn and discern how to be in God for the world within our social and cultural context. If we engage in these practices with any sort of sincerity, we will find ourselves changing in deep and fundamental ways because we are participating in the very essence of God's goodness. We begin with the spirit and practice of generosity.

## GOD SO LOVED THE WORLD THAT HE GAVE

Since it is in God's very nature to be generous, one of the most obvious ways we can participate in the divine nature is by allowing the generosity of God's nature to be formed in us. God so loved the world that he gave—generously, personally, radically, not holding anything back that would be for our good.

Generosity is a many-layered thing spiritually speaking. For many Christians, our perspectives on generosity have often been shaped (or misshaped) within the context of tithing, fundraising campaigns, and the never-ending call of urgent needs. But generosity is first and foremost a *spirit* that can apply to anything that is ours to share—time, money, material possessions, spiritual gifts, professional expertise, love, attention, and on and on. A generous spirit can result in financial generosity, to be sure, but that's not all. We all know people (maybe even ourselves!) who would rather write a check to avoid getting involved and giving of *ourselves*. There is an odd sort of stinginess inherent in that approach, rather than a spirit of generosity.

Not all giving is transforming; some giving can actually be deforming. The story of Ananias and Sapphira (Acts 5:1-11) is a case in point. To fully understand this cautionary tale, we need to back up to Acts 4:32. Here we find a description of the community of Jesus at its healthiest, indicated by—you've got it—generosity. The Scriptures describe such a frenzy of generous giving that there was not a needy person among them.

> Now the whole group of those who believed were of one heart and soul, and no one claimed private ownership of any possessions, but everything they owned was held in common. . . . There was not a needy person among them, for as many as owned lands or houses sold them and brought the proceeds of what was sold. They laid it at the apostles' feet, and it was distributed to each as any had need. There was a Levite, a native of Cyprus, Joseph, to whom the apostles gave the name Barnabas (which means "son of encouragement"). He sold a field that belonged to him, then brought the money and laid it at the apostles' feet. (Acts 4:32-37)

Generosity was flowing freely, and it was evidence of God's grace upon this community of new believers. There was probably even a little bit of peer pressure going on because this was something that would have been very cool to be a part of. Enter Ananias and Sapphira. Apparently, they had not gotten the message that they were free to share as much or as little with their community as they wished. Wanting to appear more generous than they actually were, they sold a piece of land and gave a portion of the proceeds to the community while making it seem like they were giving all of it. When pressed, they out-and-out lied about it. Turns out their giving was not an expression of generosity; it was a tool for image management, and when they brought their gift, Peter called them on it. He reminded them that they were free to do whatever they wanted with their resources and that there was no coercion here. But they were *not* free to lie to God and to the community, and for this they were struck dead.

Of course, this outcome seems harsh to our way of thinking, and I must admit that if I had been one of the apostles (or in my current role as a not-for-profit leader) I might have taken what they were willing to give thinking, *Well, cool, at least they're giving something. We'll take it!* But God's ways are not our ways, and the point we don't want to miss here is how seriously God takes the heart of the matter, not just the outward action. The way Ananias and Sapphira did their giving was deforming, not transforming, because it was not coming from a place of generosity. It was coming from a distorted desire to be seen as something more than they were, and it formed in them a kind of dishonesty and deceit that could not be tolerated in this fledgling community. Their giving was in service of that which was false within them.

This cautionary tale begs the question: How can we practice generosity in such a way that it blesses others and furthers God's purposes in the world, while at the same time furthering God's transforming work in us? Since the work God is doing *in* us is as important (if not more important) than the work God is doing *through* us, it's helpful to develop some sense of what makes for transformational giving. Here are a few principles about transformational giving that might be helpful.

***Transformational giving reflects what we truly value***, not what we feel obligated to. Jesus says in Matthew 6:21, "Where your treasure is, there your heart will be also." This suggests that there is and should be a strong connection between what we treasure most deeply (as we are being shaped by kingdom values) and where we choose to invest our resources of time, physical capacities, material possessions, prayer, attention, and focus. When Jesus' love for his world is being formed in our hearts, we can trust our hearts to guide our giving. It makes sense, then, to check in with ourselves every so often to make sure that our investment on these levels really does reflect what is important to us. Our hearts follow our giving, and our giving should follow our hearts.

***Transformational giving helps clarify where we are putting our hope and our faith.*** I read an article several years ago titled "God Doesn't Love Your 401(k) and Other Hard Truths" by Jonathan Wilson-Hartgrove. The title was so provocative I almost didn't need to read the article! I wondered, *Is that really true?* Investing in a 401(k) had always seemed like good financial practice to me, but what if it was true that God doesn't love my 401(k)? And why not? Isn't saving a good thing, or are we supposed to just trust God with our future without doing any saving and investing? Does having a 401(k) (or some other vehicle for saving) somehow mean I don't trust God for my long-term security?

I'm not the first person to ask these questions. In my family, we discussed these kinds of questions quite a bit given that we were living pretty much at poverty level because of how little my dad got paid as a pastor. Finances were always a fraught subject, to be sure. But back to Wilson-Hartgrove's article. The title, being something of an overstatement, was, of course, meant to be provocative, and it certainly got my attention. And he did have a point. "The greatest obstacle to faith in our time may be that most of us are too invested in securing our own futures to trust Jesus for the good life—the generous life—he wants to give us now."[7]

Wherever you land conceptually on the question of whether God cares about your 401(k), giving that is truly transformational keeps questions about where we are ultimately placing our trust at the forefront of our minds, hearts, and prayers. And well it should. For our giving to be truly transformational it should always be challenging us to keep considering where we are putting our faith. The Old Testament story about the widow of Zarephath (1 Kings 17:8-24) illustrates this.

Due to a famine in the land this widow, along with her young son, was on the brink of starvation. She had just enough flour and oil to make one more meal before (she believed) she and her son would simply wait to die. God, in the meantime, instructed Elijah (who was living through the same famine) to go to her and ask for the last little bit of food she had, which seemed rather cruel—both to Elijah and the widow. But Elijah did what God told him, the widow complied, and then there was this miracle in which the widow's meager supply of flour and oil never ran out. So, what is really going on in this story? Well, it's certainly not about getting Elijah fed; God had many ways to do that. Since God had previously sent ravens to feed Elijah, he clearly had options! It seems to me that what God was doing here was more about the widow than it was about Elijah. By inviting her to share generously from the little she had, God was calling her out to the edge of her faith, orchestrating an experience that would take her trust in God to a whole new level—the level where she knew beyond a shadow of a doubt whom she was relying on for her safety, security, and survival. Forever after, she would know that it was not her savings account or her investments that would save her, nor would it be her effectiveness in carefully parceling out what little she had or refusing to share at all. What she knew now that perhaps she had not known before is that it would be God's provision that guaranteed her survival, and God's provision would not fail. That is a significant step in one's faith journey!

Giving can be transformational for others as it meets their need, but it also becomes transformational for us when it takes us to the edge of our faith and God meets us there as he met the widow of Zarephath. Transformational giving offers us the chance to know this for ourselves.

***Transformational giving requires something of us.*** It is personal and sacrificial. When Jesus commented on giving, it was never about amounts; it was always about the level of personal sacrifice involved. In Luke 7 when a woman broke open an alabaster box of expensive ointment and used it to anoint Jesus' feet, he held up her action as an example of deep love and generosity in contrast to the minimal hospitality offered by the disciples. Part of the reason Jesus elevated her offering is that this gift clearly cost her something, and that is what made it noteworthy. Likewise, when Jesus witnessed a poor widow putting two copper coins into the offering and contrasted the self-sacrificial nature of her gift with the giving of the rich, who give what they can easily afford, his assessment was, "Truly I tell you, this poor widow has put in more than all of them, for all of them have contributed out of their abundance, but she out of her poverty has put in all she had to live on" (Luke 21:3-4). In Jesus' view, poor people were consistently better at giving than rich people.

Jesus' words are sobering for those who are rich in the things of this world and encouraging for those who are not. One has to wonder, *When was the last time I gave in such a way that it cost me something—even my morning Starbucks?* As David said, "I will not . . . offer burnt offerings that cost me nothing" (1 Chronicles 21:24).

***Transformational giving is humbling.*** On one level, we know that God doesn't need our money. The Holy One can rally ravens, donkeys, worms, and angels to accomplish God's purposes. But God knows that *we* need the opportunity to participate in something greater than ourselves and our own self-referenced goals. There is something within each and every one of us that has a need to contribute to something that carries us beyond our myopic concerns for safety, survival, and personal comfort. We are given the opportunity to be generous because generosity is good for us—so much better than living as selfish clods.

Transformational giving is humbling when we acknowledge that we are giving back to God what God has given to us. In the Old Testament and in the New, we are cautioned against any sort of pride due to material wealth and what we can give, or for expecting or bestowing any sort of special treatment on that basis. In Deuteronomy 8:17-18, God explicitly warns against becoming prideful in our prosperity and forgetting where our wealth comes from: "Do not say to yourself, 'My power and the might of my own hand have gotten me this wealth.' But remember the LORD your God, for it is he who gives you power to get wealth." King David models this attitude when making offerings for the building of the temple. "O LORD our God, all this abundance that we have provided for building you a house for your holy name comes from your hand and is all your own" (1 Chronicles 29:16). This passage has everything—generosity, humility, leadership, and celebration that a whole community was able to give freely and joyfully to something they cared about together.

Given that Paul was so deeply schooled in Jewish history and the teachings of the Old Testament, one can only assume that David's example provided the backdrop for his instruction to the New Testament community of Christ-followers: "As for those who in the present age are rich, command them not to be haughty or to set their hopes on the uncertainty of riches but rather on God, who richly provides us with everything for our enjoyment" (1 Timothy 6:17).

We can't deal with our arrogance and pride by gritting our teeth and trying harder. And there is certainly a big difference between trying to be humble and actually *being* humble. True generosity (as opposed to perfunctory giving) can be a great leveler, spawning real humility, if it keeps us in touch with the reality that whatever we have to give comes from God and we are simply stewards of it. If our giving is not humbling us in one way or another, we are probably missing something.

***Transformational giving is participation in the divine nature.*** If you've been wondering what it could possibly mean to participate in God's nature, the practice of generous giving—of oneself and all God has given us to steward—is one concrete way to do so. God so loved the world that he gave . . . generously, personally, and radically. It is in God's very nature to give his very best and not hold anything back, so to cultivate a generous spirit and respond generously to the needs around us make us conduits for God's goodness to flow. What an exciting possibility! And it's just not all that complicated.

## A WORD ABOUT TITHING

Too often we preach, teach, and encourage generosity almost solely in the context of tithing to the church, making special gifts to a capital campaign, or stepping up in times of urgent need. These are important moments for emphasizing generosity in our communities, to be sure;

however, a strong case can be made that generosity in all its facets should be taught and modeled regularly in a variety of contexts as a fundamental spiritual practice that forms Christ in us. To accomplish this, we may need to be a little bit more nuanced and accurate in our teaching about tithing.

One of the reasons people tune out when preachers and pastors talk about giving is that we make too much of the concept of tithing—that is, giving 10 percent of one's income to the church, which of course means the church you are attending where they are preaching. To the savvy listener, this may seem a tad self-serving and a little bit awkward, not to mention rather legalistic. New Testament theologian Scot McKnight shares a perspective on tithing that is worth considering:

> The Bible I read taught *tithing*, but the Bible does not insist that all of one's tithe must go to the local church. Truth be told, the New Testament doesn't even bring up the tithe. In the Bible, the tithe is a combination of spiritual support (for the temple) and social service (for the poor). Moses says tithes are to be given not only to the Levites (roughly the temple servants) but also the alien, to the fatherless, and to the widow. The churches I was attending had nothing to do with immigrants, did little to help orphans, and so far as I knew did little to strengthen widows. What was more, the tithe we were hearing about was something to give to our local church for buildings, maintenance, pastoral salaries, missionaries and the like. . . . I was learning that we sometimes live out the Bible, rightly or wrongly, by morphing one thing into another, that is, by taking a tithe for temple assistants and also for the poor and turning it into a tithe for the local church.[8]

What are we to make of all this? For one thing, I wonder if more authentic generosity might be unleashed in our communities if we were a little less legalistic in our approach. What if we framed the practice of generosity as being less about legalism and more about the spirit behind it all? What if we made it less about percentages and more about passion? Less about bolstering institutions and more about committing our resources wherever the wind of the Spirit is blowing? I think we can do better, and we must!

## LET'S GET THE GENEROSITY PARTY STARTED!

Only God knows what will constitute generous giving for each of us versus giving that is perfunctory, obligatory, or (God forbid!) the very least you can get away with and still be considered a good Christian. One of the things that is so striking about David's spiritual leadership is how he led in generosity and how he made a major celebration out of it. In 1 Chronicles 29 we see that he led by example and told them about his own giving (vv. 1-5). Then he created space for other leaders to follow suit—very publicly (vv. 6-7). Then whoever had something to bring gave it to the house of God (v. 8). And then they took a minute to rejoice "because these had given willingly, for with single mind they had offered freely to the Lord; King David also rejoiced greatly" (v. 9). Then David used this as an opportunity for worship, thanking God for the *privilege* of being able to give. He turned it into a pastoral moment by offering a prayer for the people who had just given.

> O Lord our God, all this abundance . . . comes from your hand and is all your own. I know, my God, that you search the heart and take pleasure in uprightness; in the uprightness of my heart I have freely offered all these things, and now I have seen your people who are present here offering freely and joyously to you. O Lord, . . . keep forever such purposes and thoughts in the hearts of your people, and direct their hearts toward you. (1 Chronicles 29:16-18)

And then then they partied! (That's my translation of verse 22: "They ate and drank before the Lord on that day with great joy.")

What strikes me is how public all this was and how much pastoral leadership in the context of community played a role in it. These days, I can't help wondering: What are we missing out on when giving takes place automatically and out of sight? By offering automatic debit in order to make "tithing" more convenient (for the giver) and more regular (for the churches and institutions who are relying on the gifts), are we missing out on a ritual that enables those who give to feel connected to God in and through their giving and robbing children of the opportunity to see generosity in action? Is there any way we could make generosity feel more like a party we all want to go to rather than an obligation we're trying to discharge in the most convenient way possible?

I will be the first to admit that I don't like talking about money and usually find it all to be more than a bit awkward. But I also know that generosity is a key element of participating in the divine nature; it enables us to partner with God in his work in the world, *and* it's another good reason to have a party!

# 12

# PRACTICING FORBEARANCE AND FORGIVENESS

*As God's chosen ones, holy and beloved, . . . bear with one another and, if anyone has a complaint against another, forgive each other; just as the Lord has forgiven you, so you also must forgive.*

Colossians 3:12-13

---

I'll never forget the day Bob Mullholland dropped the word *forbearance* into his teaching on spiritual transformation for the sake of others, identifying it as a significant aspect of being "in God for the world." It's not like we weren't familiar with the word, it's just that we didn't really know what it meant or how to practice it, so I think we had just skipped over it. In Scripture readings, it was a word you sort of slid by on your way to forgiveness, and since it had sort of an old-fashioned ring to it, we rarely even heard it used anymore. But, oh, how things have changed! Now I would say that, thanks to Bob and his teaching, this has become one of the most transforming practices in my relationships—and what I mean by that is that it has changed me in terms of how I am with people, and it has changed my relationships in terms of what those relationships can hold. Since then, we talk about it regularly in our community, seeking to apply it to the troubled times we are in. It is consoling to even know of a biblical approach to having hard conversations in life-transforming ways.

Now, there is no doubt in my mind that to *forbear* or to *bear with* one another has the potential to be one of the most significant elements of transforming community, especially in the divisive times we are living in now. So, buckle your seatbelts as we reclaim this incredibly important word as both an attitude and a practice that opens us to transformation in community.

## BEYOND JUST TOLERATING EACH OTHER

The idea of bearing with one another figures so prominently in Paul's teachings about what it means to be a functioning and (dare I say) *transforming* community, that I'm not sure how we've lost track of it. He writes to the Ephesians, "I, therefore, the prisoner in the Lord, *beg you* to walk in a manner worthy of the calling to which you have been called, with all humility and gentleness, with patience, bearing with one another in love, making every effort to maintain the unity of the Spirit in the bond of peace" (Ephesians 4:1-3, emphasis added). Notice the sense of urgency Paul seems to have here as he pleads with them to bear with one another in love, using the words *humility, gentleness*, and *patience* to describe what "bearing with" looks like. And he connects all of this with our calling!

*We* usually connect the idea of calling with things we do, but Paul is saying, no, living a life worthy of your calling has to do with the inner attitudes that produce our outward behaviors, and forbearance is how he gathers it all up. When Paul writes to the Colossians about forbearance, it is just as important but with a slightly different emphasis. In this letter, he writes that forbearance has to do with practicing our belovedness. "As God's chosen ones, holy and beloved, clothe yourselves with compassion, kindness, humility, meekness, and patience. Bear with one another and, if anyone has a complaint against another, forgive each other; just as the Lord has forgiven you, so you also must forgive" (Colossians 3:12-13). In both instances, Paul is trying to help these communities understand what it will take to preserve their life together, and forbearance is right in the middle of it—as an attitude, a posture, and a concrete practice.

To *forbear with* or to *practice forbearance* carries with it that idea of restraining oneself, being still under provocation, and refraining from demanding something—especially when it takes effort and self-control to endure immaturity or wrongdoing patiently. Clearly, this is a very challenging practice, and that's probably why we don't hear much about it anymore! But Bob made the whole thing a lot more doable when he taught us that to bear with another person is to meet them where they are, to be available to God for them so God can be God in their lives *on God's own terms for them*. In this posture of restraint, we trust God for any work that might be needed in their lives rather than taking matters into our own hands. At the same time, we are radically available to God for whatever God might have us be or do on their behalf

I had never heard forbearance put this way before and was convinced that it just wasn't in my personality, given how attached I can be to my thoughts and opinions! And yet, it made so much sense. As I was getting more accustomed to letting God be God in my own life *on God's terms for me,* I could now envision letting God be God in other people's lives *on God's terms for them* rather than on *my* terms for them. This is a major internal shift for most of us who are Christian leaders. Part of Christian leadership has always been about thinking you know what's best for other people and bringing it on. Most of us rather like taking on the role of God in other people's lives, believing we know what's best for them. I think most of us really like going around believing we're right all the time and foisting that on people, whether they ask for it or not. Life feels a lot more manageable that way. But forbearance the way Bob described it is a radically different stance for most of us, intent as we are on evangelizing, moralizing, and trying to change cultures and worlds more to our liking and way of thinking. (Think colonization, aspects of the missionary movement, forcing Indigenous people to live on reservations, and so on.)

But how do we make the shift needed *inside ourselves* to forbear with one another rather than always trying to convince everyone that we are right or forcing them to be where we want them to be on our timetable? Paul offers this very challenging question that can help us make this shift: "Who are you to pass judgment on slaves of another? It is before their own lord that they stand or fall. And they will be upheld [or "stand they will"], for the Lord is able to make them stand. . . . So then, each one of us will be held accountable" (Romans 14:4, 12).

## FORBEARANCE AND THE CRUCIFORM LIFE

A number of years ago a young pastor joined one of our transforming communities. He was sweet and sincere—always sat in the front row, asked thoughtful questions, and engaged fully in all the rhythms and practices we offered the group. I thought we were tracking along quite nicely until we came to the retreat where we tackled issues of gender, race, sexuality, and so on. One of the sessions in this retreat was about partnership and equality among women and men in the community of Jesus. During a break he approached me to inform me that if I came to his church, I would not be allowed to preach or serve as an elder. I can't remember now why he felt the need to tell me that—maybe he wanted to make sure I understood that there were other points of view on the matter. I was in disbelief as it seemed completely incongruent with the relationship we had as teacher and student.

My first reaction was a powerful urge to straighten up my back and tell him how insulting it was that a young man the age of my own children would think he could tell me what I could and couldn't do in any church! I could feel the familiar fire rage through my body, and since I had been studying the Bible for longer than he had been alive, I wanted very badly to take him on and *crush* his position from a biblical point of view. This was an all-out war between my old self and my transforming self, and fortunately Bob's teaching on forbearance saved me. Very swiftly and strongly I felt God's hand on me, hemming me in, letting me know that indulging in such a response would not help anything and would reveal me to be less than the person I aspire to be. By God's grace, it was so clear that forbearance was the needed response that I went against all my natural instincts and just obeyed.

I consciously decided to let God be God in this young man's life, trusting God to guide his spiritual formation journey. I breathed deeply, brought my shoulders down from up around my ears, opened the heart space in the middle of my chest, and decided to just be *with* him—right where he was. While I did calmly (I hope) hold my ground on communicating my experiences as a woman and my convictions based on years of studying Scripture, I knew that arguing the point or trying to prove anything was simply not the focus. Being present and keeping my heart open were what mattered most. Humility (in this case, not needing to prove that I'm right), patience (with someone who was in a different place on their journey), gentleness (no one grows in tender places by being treated harshly), and compassion (for whatever it was that was going on inside him that made it necessary for him to say what he said) came into play as well. It was all about staying in God and staying in love. I knew that beyond a shadow of a doubt and was grateful I had been working with forbearance long enough to instantly recognize this as a moment to practice. And the choice to forbear rather than force my perspectives on him any further enabled us to stay on the journey of transformation together.

This is the outcome of "bearing with" rather than bullying, forbearing rather than forcing someone to be who I want them to be. Is this not an expression of cruciform love—laying down my "life," my need to prove something, my right to defend myself, my attempt to convince someone of something, my insistence that they must be a certain way in order to be with me? I think it is.

To be clear, this instruction from Paul is given to people in the context of Christian community, although it can apply to those beyond the community as well. Forbearance does not apply in the same way to despotic presidents, corrupt law enforcement, abusive leaders, or any kind of criminal or abusive behaviors. There are some things that must be confronted, and these require a completely different set of responses to protect the vulnerable and to preserve what is of greatest value. There needs to be consequences for behaviors that harm others. It is not good for abusers to abuse; whatever we do to limit abusive behavior of any kind is good for the abuser *and* the abused. Abusers too need to be on a transformational journey and our willingness to confront their behavior benefits the abused, while potentially setting the abuser on the path to transformation. Forbearance does not condone victimization, but it does require a tremendous sense of being grounded in God and having a clear sense of what is ours to do. Being grounded in God means we are free enough from self-referenced concern that we can respond as God leads.

## WE CAN TALK ABOUT HARD THINGS

James 1:19 offers us a very practical description of what forbearance looks like: "Let everyone be quick to listen, slow to speak, slow to anger [or frustration or impatience]." This is presence, plain and simple. But where do we see this taking place anymore? Who is modeling this for us in a culture where the loudest voices are often the most destructive and the wisest voices are either not speaking or getting drowned out? Learning how to talk and listen to one another may be one of the most crucial skills related to forbearance that we can cultivate at this time, and it is a hallmark of transforming community. Where else are people going to learn this stuff if not with us?

We simply cannot take it for granted that people know even the basics of listening these days. But the good news is that listening is a skill that can be taught and modeled so that speaking and listening to one another in this way become the cultural norm in your setting. This will begin to create a feeling of safety in your community, so people grow in their willingness to bring more of themselves to the table. The following are some basics you as a leader can teach and model in all your interactions, both public and private, and then your small groups can become a place where people practice.

- Approach difficult conversations with a posture of mutual influence and shared learning. This requires humility, not just as a perfunctory statement but as a real inner posture.
- Affirm that when we are having a conversation about challenging and controversial topics Jesus is with us as the transforming presence among us. When Jesus says, "Where two or three are gathered in my name, I am in the midst of them," he is referring to situations where there is conflict, and it is there that he promises to be with us in a special way.
- Calm yourself by taking a moment in silence, attending to your breathing, praying, or in some other way getting in touch with your own center.
- Go slow. Make sure there is plenty of time to talk and listen slowly; when the conversation gets going too fast, things can get heated and great damage can be done.
- Lean in and listen with your whole self—heart, soul, mind, senses, feelings, intuitions, imagination.
- Do not interrupt; pause to take in what the other person is really saying before responding.
- Ask clarifying questions. Don't assume you know what the person means or how they are using words.
- Do not formulate your response while the other person is speaking. Ask for space before responding if you need it.
- Do not challenge what others say; rather, ask good questions so you can wonder about things together.
- Use your voice by speaking for yourself, expressing your own thoughts, feelings, and experiences. Stay true to yourself by calmly making "I" statements.

- Express interest and curiosity about the other person and what has shaped their views. Say, "Tell me more about . . ."
- Hold your thoughts, opinions, and even your convictions lightly out of a desire and willingness to be influenced by others.
- Express love and care for the other person. As you stay centered in God, remind yourself that that person's journey is in God's hands and is not yours to control.
- Keep breathing.
- Try to conclude by saying something good. Ashlee Eiland writes, "Good words have power. Good words carry with them the potential to keep meaningful relationships from devolving into distance and dysfunction. They have the capacity to build up confidence and tear down division; to create community in the crevices of vulnerability; to shape safe havens where people are no longer anonymous social media bots to be battled but exquisite image-bearers to be seen, loved and known."[1] It could be as simple as "Thanks so much for sharing with me what you've been thinking about." Or "I am really grateful for this conversation; it has left me with a lot to ponder."

This is what forbearance looks like in practice, and with practice (using a structure like what is provided in *Life Together in Christ*) we can all get better at it!

## FORGIVENESS—WHAT IT IS AND WHAT IT'S NOT

Forgiveness is one of the most difficult and challenging of all the spiritual disciplines. As C. S. Lewis once said, "Everyone thinks forgiveness is a lovely idea until he has something to forgive," and yet, there is no escaping its significance. Jesus taught about it, he included it in the Lord's Prayer ("forgive us our sins as we forgive those who sin against us"), and he actively engaged in forgiveness while hanging on the cross—when it would certainly have been justifiable not to do so! Forgiveness is a nonnegotiable spiritual practice found at the heart of every major religion, and with good reason. As Archbishop Desmond Tutu, chair of South Africa's Truth and Reconciliation Commission, writes, "Forgiveness is nothing less than the way we heal the world. We heal the world by healing each and every one of our hearts. The process is simple, but it is not easy."[2]

Since forgiveness is such a necessary and challenging practice for our transformation, it must be actively and proactively taught, guided, and supported in transforming communities with as much careful nuance as you can bring to it. Because the mere idea of forgiveness can be a little threatening, we will begin by clarifying what forgiveness is *not*.

- Forgiveness is *not* acceptance or approval of what's been done to you. If whatever was done to you was acceptable or worthy of approval, forgiveness would not be needed.
- Forgiveness is *not* a means to bring about reconciliation. It may or may not lead to reconciliation, but forgiveness is its own thing, quite apart from what might take place after that. (More on that later.)
- Forgiveness is not something we do for the person who wronged us. It is something we do for ourselves to free ourselves and others from destructive spiritual bondage.
- Forgiveness is not an avoidance of justice—it creates space for justice to be enacted with purity of purpose that does not include revenge.[3]

Forgiveness is hard because it is a frontal assault on the false self—that part of us that would rather nurse the hurt and the pain, cling to the right to defend oneself, give in to the desire to hit back, get even, withhold, or take revenge. Forgiveness is hard because it takes these normal human responses off the table, and we are left with the humbling awareness that what most needs to be done in our lives, only God can do. To need something so desperately but not be able to accomplish it for ourselves leaves us in the vulnerable position of needing to cast ourselves upon God's mercy.

But forgiveness is also good because, as much as it might seem like it lets the person who has wronged us off the hook, it is really for our own health and wholeness. When we hold someone who has hurt us in unforgiveness, we are in bondage because there is an energetic tie that binds us to them. As Archbishop Desmond Tutu goes on to say,

> Without forgiveness, we remain tethered to the person who harmed us. We are bound with chains of bitterness, tied together, trapped. Until we forgive the person who harmed us, that person will hold the keys to our happiness; that person will be our jailor. When we forgive, we take back control of our own fate and our feelings. We become our own liberators. We don't forgive to help the other person. We don't forgive for others. We forgive for ourselves. . . . [It] is the best form of self-interest. This is true both spiritually and scientifically.[4]

Most of us have probably experienced this; when we refuse to do the work of forgiveness we still think about that person, go over what they did to us, recite things we wish we could say to them, and continue to feel a full range of emotions that are yet unhealed. The grace of forgiveness releases the other person, at least from our side, yes, but it also releases *us* from being bound to them in ways that are destructive to our own psyches. Furthermore, a lack of forgiveness can poison all our relationships because it causes us to put walls around our hearts, at least a little, and to become defensive and shut down.

## FOLLOWING JESUS ON THE PATH TO FORGIVENESS

I suspect many of us avoid forgiveness because we think that if we forgive, that means we have to be in relationship again with the person who hurt us. This could feel especially perilous if that person did something that was cruel, abusive, or untrustworthy and demonstrates no understanding of the damage they've done and/or has no intention of refraining from such behaviors in the future. The good news is that our practice of forgiveness is not contingent on anything anyone else says or does. We can follow Jesus in forgiving those who have harmed us and experience release from this destructive bondage even if the other person (and we ourselves!) are not ready for reconciliation. Forgiveness prepares us to enter a reconciliation process if the opportunity presents itself and is appropriate (who knows what might happen then?), but it does not *require* us to reconcile with that person or allow them back into our lives unless God leads us there.

Finally, in transforming community we *must* emphasize and do our best to help people understand that forgiveness is a process, not something that happens instantaneously. If we imply anything less and fail to give guidance for what the process is, people may be paralyzed by a sense of shame and impossibility, burdened by a heavy sense of failure that they can't do this thing Jesus says we have to do. Forgiveness begins with prayer, and even if we can't bring ourselves to pray for the other person, we can pray for ourselves. We can cry out, "God help me!" "Lord, have mercy on me!" "I don't want to, but I'm willing to be made willing." These requests for help from God along with seeking support from a spiritual director or a therapist can be means of grace for opening ourselves to God.

## FORGIVENESS AS A PROCESS

Archbishop Desmond Tutu's and his daughter Mpho Tutu's *The Book of Forgiving: The Fourfold Path for Healing Ourselves and Our World* is very helpful in describing the deep work of forgiveness. Speaking from firsthand experience with profound discrimination and also the cold-blooded murder of someone very close to them, they describe the first move as *telling the story*—that is, getting in touch with the reality of what happened to us. William Meninger describes forgiveness as a form of realism, allowing us perhaps for the first time to see our life, ourselves, others, and the events of our lives as they really are. This prevents us from pretending it didn't happen, and it's how we begin to take back what was taken from us. When we tell the truth in all its pain and rawness, we lessen the power it has over us.

Telling our story and getting to the bottom of what it means to us and how it has impacted us is not a one-time thing; it is an unfolding that takes place as we gain understanding, make meaning, and accept that this is what happened to us. Then we can *name the hurt and the different ways it has affected us*, hopefully with someone who can be a witness to our pain. This moves us *out of denial and isolation into the grieving process*, which is a very significant place on the journey. Eventually and by God's grace we can *grant forgiveness*, which allows us to *open our hearts again and fully heal.* Then we have a choice as to whether the relationship can be renewed or needs to be released so we can embrace a future that is unfettered by the past.

This is a rigorous approach to forgiveness that does not give oppressors and bad actors a pass, nor should it. This process by its very nature demands accountability for it to even work. It is not good for oppressors to oppress. It is not good for abusers to go on abusing. It is not good for sad, mean people to keep treating others terribly. It is not good for those who benefit from inequality to keep profiting at others' expense. There is no transformation of the human community as long as we allow these dynamics to exist unchallenged. Part of the power of the Truth and Reconciliation Commission's process is that it did not conflate forgiveness and reconciliation. Rather it modeled the significance of creating safe space for the truth to be told so that perpetrators could own what they had done as a first step toward repentance and reconciliation if those involved chose it.

I have described these movements in the briefest possible way to demonstrate what a process-oriented approach to forgiveness really looks like and in hopes that transforming communities will seek out the transformation Archbishop Tutu describes and supports with practices and prayers. There are other models to consider, but one reason Tutu's carries so much heft and weight is because he had so much to forgive and somehow found a way to do it. His wisdom is hard won, coming as it does from one who pioneered a way for whole countries to move forward after experiencing civil conflict, genocide, and oppression.[5]

These movements are not meant to be formulaic; they are ways to continue offering ourselves to God for the work that only God can do. When we are doing what we can do, we can leave the rest up to God.

# 13

# JUSTICE

## *Learning to Love What God Loves*

*The theme of liberation is the largest frame in which to understand spirituality. . . . Liberation is at the heart of both the Jewish and Christian traditions from the very beginning.*

RICHARD ROHR

---

IT PAINS ME to say that my journey toward grasping the significance of justice in the journey of transformation didn't begin in earnest until I was in seminary in the late nineties. There, as part of a more diverse community than the churches and academic institutions that had shaped me, I experienced the privilege of engaging in coursework that highlighted a variety of justice issues including gender, race, socio-economic status, and sexual identity. I was already highly attuned to injustices affecting women, but through these seminary courses my understanding of justice was expanded as I was introduced to liberation theology through authors like James Cone, Delores Williams, Howard Thurman, Gustavo Gutiérrez, and others.

Alongside a diverse mix of teachers and fellow classmates, I was exposed to theological perspectives that emerged from an entirely different set of human experiences than my own, along with rich theological reflections on those experiences. I was forced (in the best way possible) to consider that not everyone experienced life or interpreted Christianity as comfortably as I did. In particular, I was stirred by

James Cone's reflections on Black liberation theology, grounded in the context of his experience of growing up in Arkansas, a lynching state where white supremacy ruled supreme, White people could do anything they wanted to Black people with impunity, and the burning crosses and ghostly figures of the Ku Klux Klan were a familiar reality. Somehow, I had missed learning much about this part of American history and was unfamiliar with the terror that was part and parcel of the Black experience in the United States. I had no idea that such trauma lives on in the collective consciousness of those who have been on the receiving end of such profound violence and injustice.

### THE CROSS, THE LYNCHING TREE, THE CHOKEHOLD

In reading Cone I was humbled and *instructed* by his struggle as a Black theologian to face "the central question of his own existence: how to reconcile the gospel message of liberation with the reality of black oppression? I was black before I was a Christian. My initial challenge was to develop a liberation theology that could be both black and Christian—at the same time and in one voice."[1] When his landmark work *The Cross and the Lynching Tree* was published in 2011, Cone admitted that he had avoided dealing directly with the lynching of Black people in America because it meant "facing the most painful experience I have had as a theologian."[2] But finally, in that work, he did.

I was greatly impacted by his unflinching assessment of the bankruptcy of any theology that does not engage the religious meaning of the African American struggle for justice, which has shaped my own convictions.

> What I studied in graduate school ignored white supremacy and black resistance against it, as if they had nothing to do with the Christian gospel and the discipline of theology. Silence on both white supremacy and the black struggle against racial segregation made me angry with a fiery rage that had to find

> expression. How could any theologian explain the meaning of Christian identity in America and fail to engage white supremacy, its primary negation?[3]

Never again would I be so certain that the way my tradition interprets Scripture carries more weight than the interpretations of those whose life experiences are so different from my own. Never again could I participate in gospel initiatives that failed to give justice for all a central place in their message. Never again would I be able to accept presentations about "the good news of the gospel" without asking, "Good news for whom?" Never again would I accept the discipleship models of White churches that fail to grapple seriously with issues of justice as part of what it means to be a Christian.

James Cone's influence reaches into the perilous days we are living in right now. In Sojourners' listing of the best faith and justice books of the century, Josiah Daniels writes,

> It's hard to over-exaggerate the influence of *The Cross and the Lynching Tree,* as it provides an explicit connection between America's racist past and present that resonates with both religious and secular audiences. At a Black Lives Matter protest for Eric Garner, who was killed after being put in an illegal chokehold by a Staten Island police officer in 2014, someone had written on a sidewalk in chalk: The cross, the lynching tree, the chokehold.[4]

## JUSTICE IS LOVE

My siblings in Christ who have experienced racial injustice are quick to point out that only in the White church would it be possible to avoid issues of justice; in Black, Brown, and Asian churches, issues related to justice are talked about regularly because it is so basic to their need. Because White people assume we will be treated justly, we simply haven't needed to see it, haven't wanted to see it, and have quite effortlessly read right past it. Thank God for theologians like James

Cone, who point out that God has been caring about justice all along and that "love in society is called justice."[5] Thank God for the deep spirituality that grounded Dr. Martin Luther King Jr.'s fight for racial justice as a minister of the gospel who used the power of his pulpit for good. Thank God for contemporary justice fighters who help us understand that "love is the motive but justice is the instrument."[6]

I realize it is a privilege to have gone to seminary and been granted the space and guidance to read and interact with the seminal theological works that inform and undergird my convictions. As new and needed expressions of the fight for justice emerge, it is part of my own ongoing process of spiritual transformation to be present and align myself with these efforts standing on the strong biblical and theological foundations that were formed in the early years of my preparation for ministry. One aspect of the vision for transforming community is that every Christian would have the opportunity and the encouragement to prioritize reading and praying with these great ones of our faith as the foundation for interacting with more contemporary perspectives. I have a dream that it would be a part of every Christian's basic spiritual formation to read King's sermons in *Strength to Love*, Howard Thurman's *Jesus and the Disinherited*, James Cone's *The Cross and the Lynching Tree*, Delores Williams's *Sisters in the Wilderness*, and Walter Brueggemann's *The Prophetic Imagination* and *then* talk about justice in all its needed iterations. If we did, I don't think justice would be the controversial and threatening topic that it is. Justice issues would be part and parcel of what it means to be a Christian, and people wouldn't have to go to seminary to get it.

Pastors and leaders of Christian ministries have a special responsibility to ask, How am I using the power of my platform for the good of all—especially as it relates to issues of justice and equality? What is the example we are setting for our people? How are we inviting them to participate in God's heart for justice?

Recently, David Black, pastor of First Presbyterian Church in Chicago, answered this question for himself when he decided to use the power of his clergy status to bring God's message of love and justice to a particular moment in a particular location—an ICE detention center in Broadview, Illinois. He says,

> I first showed up at Broadview in late August, at the invitation of friends and neighbors who were putting on a small protest and asked me if I would help keep them safe from police and do it as a member of the clergy. I showed up not to protest, necessarily, but to be a pastor in that setting at the invitation of people who are not Christians but recognized what it could it mean to be a clergy in a setting where people's lives are at risk.
>
> People were arrested for exercising their First Amendment rights, and I felt moved to pray. I knelt down in prayer, and the cops declined to arrest me, even though ICE officers were trying very hard to get them to arrest me. Then [ICE officers] moved in and dragged me across the concrete while I was praying for ICE officers who were driving a van and the detainees who were inside the van. The next week when we returned, it was with 50 clergy and 100 other protesters. There was sort of a spark in that moment where I think the clergy of Chicago recognized that there is incredible spiritual power that we wield.
>
> I returned on Sept. 19 with a clergy colleague to support those who were outside the Broadview facility. That morning, [ICE officers] had been shooting pepper balls at protesters and [tear] gassing people.
>
> I was never the smartest seminarian in the systematic theology classes, but I read my Bible every day, and I feel very deeply rooted in the Scriptures and very formed by what I see Jesus teaching us and how he's calling us to imitate him. I was moved in that moment to pray in the verbatim words of Jesus, to warn the ICE officers who were standing on the roof about the spiritual consequences of their actions, in language that was an echo of scriptural prophetic language talking about how generations after them would view their actions, and calling them to repent.

> I quoted Jesus. I said, "Repent and believe the good news, the kingdom of God is at hand." I invited them to an altar call. As I was speaking the words of Jesus that come to us through scripture, they opened fire on me and they shot me [with pepper balls] at least seven times, twice on the head, also on my torso, my arms, my legs, and very rapid fire.
>
> Immediately there were other people nearby who were strangers to me, who rushed in to shield my body with their bodies. When I was shot on my head, the first time I was kind of stunned; the second time, I collapsed.
>
> I'm the center of the spectacle right now, but this story is not about me. If they are doing this to pastors who are praying and protesters who are singing songs and holding hands and chanting and peacefully showing up to voice their conscience—journalists, teachers, mothers, elders—then it makes me shudder to imagine what they might be doing to our neighbors behind closed doors and in these outsourced internment camps, in [places like] El Salvador.
>
> To me, stepping into that moment was the purest expression I could find in my faith, to pray for those that I felt were my enemies, to seek their blessing and conversion.[7]

Black did not expect his presence on a sidewalk in Broadview that day to become a viral moment. I'm sure that when he left home that morning, he did not expect to be attacked for being where he was called to be as a clergy person. But from inside his own relationship with God, he knew where he needed to be, and God used that to draw further attention to one aspect of injustice in our world that needed to be confronted. One of the most important things we can do in transforming community is use the power of whatever platform we have to draw people into a transformational journey that includes grappling with the question of how we can participate in God's love by working for justice in any area where we might have influence or some ability to make a difference.

## GRAPPLING WITH THE SIN OF INJUSTICE

Gary Haugen, founder of International Justice Mission, offers this helpful definition of injustice. "The sin of injustice is defined in the Bible as the abuse of power—abusing power by taking from others the good things God intended for them, namely, their life, liberty, dignity, or the fruits of their love or their labor. . . . When a stronger person abuses power by taking from a weaker person what God alone has given that person—God judges this as sin."[8] Of course this definition applies to people groups that dominate, exploit, or enslave others based on race and ethnicity, "explorers" who have "discovered" new lands and then expelled the Indigenous people who were already there, countries that invade other countries to take by force what doesn't belong to them, human traffickers that kidnap or manipulate women and children for their own financial gain, racial profiling whereby masked ICE agents can abduct people off the streets and transfer them around the country without due process, or the inhumane treatment of immigrants who are seeking a better life. The list goes on.

Naming injustice as the sin that it is means we cannot just pretend it doesn't matter or that it is some sort of side issue for us as Christians. As Rich Villodas, pastor of New Life Church in New York, writes,

> The starting point for any Christian conversation on race must be the purpose of the gospel. The gospel we proclaim must be big enough to engage the realities of racial fragmentation. However, it's often not seen this way. Sadly, there is often a hyperspiritual perspective held by many Christians, who see racial justice and reconciliation as optional or ancillary to the gospel.[9]

Discrimination, inequality, and inequity of any kind "steal" from others the inherent dignity, freedom, and opportunity to flourish that God intends for them. Diminishment of other humans in these ways is, by its very nature, deforming to the human person. You can't invite people into a transformation journey while at the same time treating them unjustly and expect it to *work*. That would be the mother of all mixed messages!

To participate in the divine nature is to love justice as God does and to partner with God in *the work* of ensuring justice for all. This is one of the major outcomes of the transformational journey as Quaker Thomas Kelly describes it: "He plucks the world out of our hearts, loosening the chains of attachment. And he hurls the world into our hearts, where we and He together carry it in infinitely tender love."[10] That God-induced tender love produces a passion for justice that is no less than love in action.

Can you imagine a parent who would want a different set of benefits for one of his or her children than another? When we grasp justice as an outworking of love, we don't need any more reason than that to make it a priority in transforming community. This work belongs to all of us who call ourselves Christians.

> God is calling his people to a pathway out of fear and triviality *through the struggle for justice* in his world, . . . and it is a call to all his people. It's not a call to the handful of social justice zealots or slightly odd issue advocates in our faith community. Many churches miss out on God's transforming call by putting the handful of justice agitators in their congregation on some ministry subcommittee where they can do "their thing" without, hopefully, doing any harm. This effectively inoculates the rest of the congregation and directs everyone else right back into their Christian cul-de-sac, where round and round they go.
>
> Spiritually healthy and dynamic churches, on the other hand, have learned to equip the whole community of faith to do the things that matter to God.[11]

## RACIAL HEALING AS SPIRITUAL FORMATION

The Transforming Center is a majority White space; we know that. *And*, by God's grace, we are a much more diverse community now than when we began. With gratitude for the gracious presence of those among us who bring diversity (all kinds) and for the gifts they bring, I am aware of God's steady guidance in clarifying for us that the journey toward justice is inextricably interwoven with our journey of transformation. We have been impacted at every turn by people whose life experiences are different from our own and have discovered that the diversity journey and the justice journey are really one and the same. The fact that we regularly create space in our communities for sharing about differing experiences in our bodies means that inevitably experiences of discrimination, oppression, lack of equity, abuse, and injustice are shared. Often with trembling and tears.

The way we hold these conversations and why we hold them lead us beyond debating, finger pointing, defensiveness, and trying to prove our points to *being impacted* by others' experiences of injustice, discrimination, and being treated as "less than." In this space the openness and receptivity to one another is palpable as we lean forward to hear others share about their most vulnerable life experiences and receive experiences that, in many instances, are so different from our own. This sharing becomes part of our collective experience at every level of our community's life as we learn how to hold these experiences and each other with great love and respect, care, and concern. And then we are challenged with how to respond. Such moments take us deeper into community and to the edge of our own knowing about what to do with what we're hearing.

It can be uncomfortable and painful to sit in that space of hearing about injustice in our world, how we have hurt and been hurt. These things are hard to share and to receive. And yet, it also brings about healing that is strangely and deeply unifying. As one of our community members, Afrika Afeni Mills, writes, "The work of racial healing is not optional for followers of the Way of Jesus. It is a way of being—a deeply raw, courageous, and redemptive process—that is essential to formation into the likeness of Christ."[12] Lament is one of the ways we sit with it together and open ourselves to God's healing work.

**THE POWER OF LAMENT**

Lament is the Christian practice that gives us something to do when we don't know what to do.[13] It is that unsettling biblical tradition of prayer that includes expressions of complaint, anger, grief, despair, and protest to God.[14] Our Christian faith offers up the prayer of lament as a way of being with God, ourselves, and each other in times of incomprehensible loss, violence, and inhumanity. There are more than fifty psalms of lament in our Scriptures (more than any other genre of psalms) plus an entire book of our Bible called Lamentations. When we practice lament, we shout or cry or whisper our most pointed interrogations to the God we know loves us but whose ways we don't always understand.[15]

Lament is powerful because it invites us to get in touch with our hardest emotions and then to *address God directly* with our grief, confusion, and questions about how God might redeem all that is wrong. Rather than merely talking among ourselves or brainstorming solutions before we fully understand the problem, we are talking to God amid our distress as the psalmist does in Psalm 44:23-24—"Why do you sleep, O Lord? . . . Why do you hide your face?" We are getting very specific about what is disturbing us, along with prayers asking in no uncertain terms for what we desire to see happen. Praying from the middle of our disillusionment and desire requires a particular kind of courage because it takes us right out to the edge of our faith. What if God doesn't do anything? What if God does something different from what I expect? How do I even know if God is hearing me? Oftentimes we don't ask for things to be different because we're really not sure anything can change or get better. So instead, we go numb and refuse to even talk to God about it.

Lament is a step of faith toward a God we believe exists, who loves us, and whom we cannot fully comprehend and control. When the horror we are experiencing leaves us with the deepest kinds of questions, we approach God anyway, saying with the first disciples, "To whom can we go? You have the words of eternal life" (John 6:68).

Lament, practiced rightly, *creates space for the voices of those who have suffered to speak and be heard.* When injustice, sin, and wrong-headedness can no longer be ignored, oftentimes the leader-types in the non-oppressed group want to appropriate (or, more accurately, misappropriate) the moment by offering up their own take on the situation, using it as a time to pontificate, appear insightful, or position themselves as saviors. Without even realizing it, we may use it as an opportunity to be seen as successful and on top of things. No doubt there are good intentions fueling such activity, but when we grab the leadership in these moments, we inflict another kind of hurt; now we rob others of the sense of agency and personhood that comes through having a voice.

In his detailed study of the book of Lamentations, Soong-Chan Rah points out that in our efforts to right wrongs,

> we often believe our task is to speak for the voiceless. But maybe we need to follow the book of Lamentations and move the ones who suffer to front and center. The prophet-narrator (the writer of the book of Lamentations) has much to say, but the real movement and progress is that we hear the voice of those who suffer, . . . empowering those who suffer to find their voice. The movement from an advocate speaking on behalf of others to the sufferers speaking up for themselves offers hope to all who suffer.[16]

## A WORD ABOUT SILENCE

"Silence is violence" has emerged as a significant message in current protests, and it is true. For instance, when a dominant group (like White people) refuses to speak up and stand up for the rights of their Black brothers and sisters when they have endured the knee of the White community on their necks, keeping them down and bringing about slow death, it *is* a form of violence. It signifies a lack of solidarity, an unwillingness to get involved, the turning of a blind eye toward injustice. This silence is a form of collusion; when we do not speak up about sin and evil within the systems we are a part of, we are supporting those systems through our presence and participation.

But silence can have other meanings as well. Sometimes silence is an expression of humility, as in the humble posture of someone who doesn't know very much about a topic listening to someone who does. Sometimes silence means it is someone else's turn to talk, and if you don't stop the flow of your own words, they will never get to. And sometimes silence is the deepest kind of reverence for that which is too deep for words, realizing that to rush in with trite phrases and easy answers would violate the moment.

Sometimes silence has to do with being quick to listen and slow to speak. This tension between "silence as violence" (complicity) and silence as humility and reverence is a dynamic we can navigate together if we are to be in real relationships with one another. Those who have suffered do not want the oppressing group to speak for them about their experiences. They want to bring out the truth of their own existence *in their own words.* These are moments when those who have been hurt, oppressed, and violated need to speak and lead while those who have been part of the dominant group need to be humble, step aside, and give control to others. That in itself will make it a healing moment.

## LET US EXAMINE OUR WAYS

Lament, rightly practiced, leads to confession. In Lamentations 3:40, for instance, those who are grieving terrible loss and violence make a powerful turn toward corporate confession: "Let us test and examine our ways and return to the Lord." "Spiritual renewal emerges as God's people engage in corporate confession of sin, and sincere repentance moves the community toward a changed and renewed life. . . . Confession acknowledges our need for God and opens the door for God's intervention. Confession in lament relies on God's work for redemption."[17] Here we take responsibility for confessing personal sins and omissions but also the corporate sins of our unjust systems. "If individuals have contributed to a system of injustice, confession of a sinful social system must be offered to address sin in its proper context."[18]

If lament is to be true, it must lead to self-awareness and confession as we reflect on questions like, How did we get here? What was my part in it? What can we do to make it right?

One of the most important components of this self-awareness is awareness of our history as Christians and how an American version of Christianity has been complicit with racism from our earliest days. Jemar Tisby writes,

> European colonists brought with them ideas of white superiority and paternalism toward darker-skinned people. . . . They erected a society and a version of religion that could only survive through the subjugation of people of color. By surveying the church's racist past, American Christians may feel the weight of their collective failure to consistently confront racism in the church. This should lead to immediate, fierce action to confess this truth and work for justice.[19]

### LAMENT THAT LEADS TO ACTION

No matter how jaded and cynical we've become, as Christians we believe in a God who is in the business of transforming people and relationships, communities, and cultures. This means that such honest confessions can and should be accompanied by expressions of faith and confidence in God's power and intention to reconcile and redeem, to disrupt and eventually heal. This means that when we join with God, this is the redemptive work we are joining.

Psalm 44 concludes with this faith-filled request to God: "Rise up, come to our help. Redeem us for the sake of your steadfast love" (v. 26). Such a faith-filled prayer comes from recalling past experiences of God's love, faithfulness, and redemptive work even in the midst of all that seems unfixable. We turn our hearts toward hope in God rather than merely trusting in what we ourselves can come up with. We acknowledge the rich partnership that exists between God and humankind, going all the way back to creation and God's mandate to the first man and the first woman to do good and fruitful things with God's creation.

The practice of lament is prophetic in nature because we are speaking forth the mind of God. We are declaring, "What is happening here is wrong! This is not how God intended it to be!" The prophetic aspect of lament calls us to name sin for what it is, to repent and turn in a new direction. It positions us to participate humbly in the coming of God's kingdom as we pray, "O God, may it be so. May your kingdom come on earth as it is in heaven *and* in this specific aspect of our lives, as it is in heaven. Amen."

Prophetic lament captures the pain of injustice and the reality of suffering and declares a word that points beyond such destructive realities to *right action* that lays down clear tracks toward justice, equality, and flourishing for all of humanity. That word needs to be delivered by the right kind of leader in a way that catalyzes unity and shared momentum toward a common good, rather than inflammatory rhetoric, defensive maneuvers, partisan manipulation, and violence. This is a leader who has undergone the deepest kind of transformation and rises to speak from a spiritual center, an inner authority that transcends partisanship and elevates our discourse above argumentative, competitive, self-serving braying.

Dr. Martin Luther King Jr. is a leader who was able to move people from lament to right action. In 1967 he gave a speech at Stanford titled "The Other America," in which he outlined very specific things that would need to change for justice to prevail. He described two Americas—one that White Americans experience every day in which they have unobstructed opportunities for life, liberty, and the pursuit of happiness in all its dimensions, and another in which Black Americans struggle to experience basic economic support and civil rights, let alone the justice and equality that contribute to human flourishing. George Floyd's life and murder illustrated this troubling reality. At the time of his death, he was experiencing the triple threat experienced by the Black community: economic vulnerability (he was unemployed), systemic health risks and comorbidities disproportionately affecting the Black community (he had tested positive for Covid-19 along with other underlying health issues), and racial profiling and police brutality (the cause of his death). This is "the other America" White people do not know and cannot comprehend.

Toward the end of King's life, he had a growing clarity about the importance of legislative action *plus* enforcement and accountability. This hard-won wisdom was born of his experience and ongoing reflections as a justice leader, and we are seeing the truth of it today. King's life and teachings demonstrated that lament, rightly practiced, leads to necessary action that confronts principalities, powers, and systems, combining personal transformation with institutional and legislative change. Knowing what is required for justice to rain down, we need Christians who will accept the calling to engage in government, politics, the legal system, and law enforcement so they can work at this level.[20] This, too, is being in God for the world.

For some reason that's hard to fathom, God chooses to partner with—and even at times be limited by—us, his human creation. We all have choices to make about whether we will participate in the Holy Spirit's work of moving us beyond the chaos we are in now to the beloved community for which we were created.[21] Our participation in these efforts is central to cultivating transforming communities. This means that part of lament is asking, What is mine to do in the field God has given me to work and to cultivate? Soong-Chan Rah rightly challenges us, "Lament will not allow us to revert to easy answers. There is no triumphalist and exceptionalist narrative of the American church that can cover up injustice. There are no easy answers to unabated suffering. Lament continues."[22]

## WALK THE LINE

It has been a daunting task to write about a topic on which mountains of inspiring words have been written and spoken by great thinkers and leaders more qualified than I am to address such weighty matters. At the same time, realizing how important justice is to the journey of transformation has compelled me to try and say something. What I know now is that whenever and wherever people are truly opening to God's transforming work, a passion for justice will bubble up because God cares about it so much.

We have experienced a straight line between "welcoming the one who is strange to you" and cultivating a passion for justice. Welcoming those with different life experiences than we have and engaging those differences fully and honestly makes the need to grapple with justice issues inevitable. But you can count on the God of justice to meet you there and show you what is yours to do. We will need to get beyond our grandiosity so we don't become paralyzed by all that needs to be made right in our world *and* so we don't take on too much. We will need to accept that no one person, community, or organization can do everything that needs to be done in our world. It is only as we know ourselves to be one small part of the body of Christ that we can do what is ours to do and trust the body of Christ as a whole to accomplish what's needed.

Sometimes people who journey with us are surprised that we hit justice issues so hard in our Transforming Community experience, even suggesting that we "need to stay in our lane." Clearly, they have a different idea of what spiritual transformation is all about than we do! But we keep asking the questions anyway. How have we loved God and led whole communities of Christ-followers for so long and failed to attune our hearts and our priorities to God's heart on these matters? Have we really loved God with all our hearts when we have not loved God's children and treated them with the dignity, respect, and equality they deserve as much as we do? What part of Micah 6:8 have we not understood and failed to prioritize in our life together? And if what the Lord requires of us is "to do justice and to love kindness and to walk humbly with your God," what does that look like on any given day?

## WHEN GOD BLESSES US WITH DISCOMFORT

As I ponder that last question, I can't help but think of two brave women who illustrate that even the smallest step in the right direction can make a difference. The first is Rosa Parks, an active member of the civil rights movement whose life illustrates how one relatively simple decision made by an ordinary person can make a huge impact on the movement as a whole. The way she tells the story, it was her body that led the way. One day she was riding home from work on a bus as she always did, and she was, quite simply, tired. On this day, she also had a solid sense of her own worth and that her tiredness mattered as much as anyone else's, so when a White person boarded the bus that was now full, she refused to give up her seat as societal norms dictated. Her body knew what it knew, and she obeyed it.

Discernment of this kind often begins with something our body knows, and when Rosa Parks coupled what she knew in her body with the courage to do something different, it became a major spark in the civil rights movement. There were many other days when Rosa Parks had given up her seat on the bus just as societal expectations dictated—until one day she didn't.

Who knew that such a simple, honest action could accomplish so much? On some days, maybe the work of justice is as simple as that.

I also think of Bishop Mariann Budde and how she used a fifteen-minute homily to speak truth to power. In the worship service at the National Cathedral on Inauguration Sunday in 2025, she spoke directly to President Trump, who was seated in the front row alongside Vice President Vance. From her position of spiritual authority as the Episcopal bishop of Washington, she addressed him directly, firmly, and with respect.

> "Let me make one final plea, Mr. President," Budde said in her sermon. . . .
>
> "Millions have put their trust in you. And as you told the nation yesterday, you have felt the providential hand of a loving

> God. In the name of our God, I ask you to have mercy upon the people in our country who are scared now," Budde said.[23]

Trump and his allies quickly criticized the bishop's remarks, with one Republican congressman saying that the American-born Budde should be "added to the deportation list." Despite the backlash, Budde told National Public Radio (NPR) that her remarks were sincere, and she did not have any regrets in bringing them to the president's attention.

> "I don't hate the president, and I pray for him," Budde said. "I don't feel there's a need to apologize for a request for mercy. I regret that it was something that has caused the kind of response that it has, in the sense that it actually confirmed the very thing that I was speaking of earlier, which is our tendency to jump to outrage and not speak to one another with respect," she continued. "But no, I won't, I won't apologize for what I said."[24]

Nor should she. Leave her alone, she has done what she could.

# 14

# PUTTING IT ALL TOGETHER

## *Discerning a Way of Life in Community*

*The spiritual radiation of a community depends on the commitment of its members to the transformational journey and to each other. To offer one another space in which to grow is an integral part of this commitment.*

Fr. Thomas Keating

---

As we come to the conclusion of this book, I want to offer some questions to ponder about what you are aiming for in your community: Is spiritual transformation an elective, or is it essential? Is it a program or a priority? A department or a value that permeates the whole community? What follows is the story of how First Church approached these questions.

First Church was a large mainline church in the heart of a major southern town; its historic steeple had been a beloved part of the cityscape for decades. Many of its members were from second- and third-generation families who had been born into the church and had held positions of influence and power through the years. If one were to visit on a Sunday, it would be hard to miss the affluence and generational wealth of significant members of the congregation, along with tributes to several well-known politicians who had grown up there. All of this contributed to a deep sense of pride about the church's history and influence within the community.

The senior pastor, Rick, was somewhat traditional in his approach to leadership—adhering to the long-held traditions of the church and denomination while at the same time trying to introduce ideas that would facilitate church growth. Every so often he would attend a church growth conference and return with lots of energy to implement new strategies. The congregation had gotten used to weathering these periodic bursts of enthusiasm; they, too, wanted their church to grow as long as it didn't mess with their sacred cows—Sunday school classes that had been together for thirty to thirty-five years, traditional worship services with vestments and a robed choir, high-profile guest preachers and musicians, potlucks and social events that kept everyone feeling connected.

By attending the latest church growth conferences and reading voraciously, Rick was able to stay on top of church trends, especially as it had to do with finding ways to be more relevant. He implemented the addition of a contemporary worship service on Saturday nights, featuring guitars, drums, an electric piano, new song choices, and leaders dressed casually in jeans and T-shirts. Establishing this new service didn't happen without some controversy, but Rick had gotten it done and felt pretty good about it.

## A NEW TREND OR SOMETHING MORE?

Somewhere along the way Rick started noticing that discussions about "spiritual formation" were cropping up in different places; even though it sounded somewhat mysterious at first, he eventually decided this was simply another way to talk about discipleship. As it turns out, one of his younger associates (let's call her Tricia) had a great deal of interest in and passion for "spiritual formation" and had included an emphasis on this in her seminary training. When Tricia asked for more freedom to champion this value in their congregations and make it more of a priority, it seemed like a fine thing to do.

The problem came when Tricia began to press for clarity about the importance of spiritual formation in the congregation's life and priorities. Rick had assumed that spiritual formation would be one department among many with folks choosing to participate as they wished, but his young associate kept insisting that spiritual formation should not be *elective* but essential to what their church was about. She clarified that, technically speaking, spiritual formation was happening all the time; the only question was whether it was *trans*formation or *de*formation, and she wanted to be clear about which side of that equation their church was on.

Rick's young colleague seemed to think that people would jump on board based on her enthusiasm and conviction alone—but this simply did not happen. Members of the congregation struggled to grasp what spiritual formation really was from a biblical, theological, and practical point of view. For his part, Rick tried very hard to understand his young colleague's vision and to satisfy her intense desire to see spiritual transformation positioned appropriately in the church's spiritual and organizational priorities, but they never could quite come to an agreement on what that would look like. Because spiritual formation was not Rick's "thing" and he had delegated it to his younger colleague, he failed to grasp it for himself or to communicate well about it from his position as the senior pastor. At one point, in a moment of poignant realism, he admitted with a sigh, "I'm just a church growth guy," by which he meant numerical growth, not necessarily spiritual growth.

Soon other staff members observed the tension around this subject; some agreed with the senior pastor that spiritual formation should be a set of elective classes and retreats people could choose from. Others resonated with the associate who felt it should be an organizing principle across all ministries and functions of the church. Eventually the younger associate got tired of fighting and left the church to pursue her passion in other ways. Bits and pieces of what this young leader had tried to implement are still in evidence in the church's life with varying degrees of buy-in, but to this day there is still uneasiness about what really happened around all this. Even now they are not clear on where spiritual formation fits in their life together.

**ELECTIVE OR ESSENTIAL?**

The story of First Church is a cautionary tale about the confusion that ensues when leaders fail to grapple with the role of spiritual formation in a community's life. This confusion can play out in several ways. One is that spiritual formation can be reduced to a "menu" of options people are invited to choose from—or not—based on preference, personality, the seriousness with which they are taking their spiritual journey, and so on. Often when I am invited to visit with churches and denominations, they are excited to show me what they are doing in the area of spiritual formation. Most often "what they are doing" is providing a list of elective classes, retreats, and experiences that primarily have to do with the quieter and more personal spiritual disciplines, and sometimes the list is quite impressive!

The problem, though, is that this approach is far too narrow in terms of how spiritual formation gets defined and positioned within the community's priorities. It can get relegated to the status of being something of an add-on rather than central to the life of the community. It can also get reduced to a personality type (introverts) rather than being seen as an all-encompassing value. Dallas Willard contradicts this tendency in his writing. While acknowledging that the church's track record for solving social and individual ills may not appear historically outstanding, he affirms his belief that our transformation into the image of Christ holds the only answer for society—still. But then he asks this penetrating question, one we as leaders must continue to grapple with: "What then is keeping Christianity from being that guide to life which it alone can be?" He answers his own question:

> Christianity can only succeed as a guide for current humanity if it does two things. First, it must take the need for human transformation as seriously as do all modern revolutionary movements.

> The modern negative critique of Christianity arose in the first place because the church was not faithful to its own message—it failed to take human transformation seriously as a real, practical issue to be dealt with in realistic terms. Second, it needs to clarify and exemplify realistic methods of human transformation.[1]

A transforming community understands its *primary reason for existence* as no less than being part of a revolutionary movement that is a guide for humanity in discovering realistic methods of human transformation. When we make spiritual formation a separate department or reduce it to a program or an elective, it sends a subtle message that spiritual transformation is happening here and not there. It begs the question: If this is the spiritual formation department, then what is everybody else doing? However, if we can find agreement that spiritual transformation is central to the message of the gospel and therefore central to the mission of the church, spiritual transformation becomes a value to be lived throughout all aspects of the community's life—a priority that permeates everything. This means that wherever you poke or engage it, the community bleeds spiritual transformation through its shared language, shared commitments, and shared embrace of practices that open us to God together.

So the first element of a strategic approach is asking and answering the question about whether spiritual transformation is elective or essential. Do not skip getting to the bottom of this question. The answer will be a guiding light for your community over time, especially when the going gets tough or when you have important directional matters to discern.

## WE ARE THE CHAMPIONS

The second strategic consideration that needs to be clarified is whether the vision for spiritual transformation in community will be intelligently and enthusiastically championed by the senior pastor/leader along with other key leaders and influencers. It will take consistent leadership and buy-in across the board, but the senior leader bears a special responsibility to be the champion for it, even if she or he is working with and through other empowered staff. We have already addressed this in concept, but here, as you think about strategy or intentional approaches, this needs to actually be discussed and decided. Anything less risks communicating that spiritual transformation is a passion project rather than being central to the community's purpose and mission. Not only are leaders experiencing spiritual transformation for themselves and leading from experience, they are also willing to take responsibility for keeping this priority in front of the community.

International Justice Mission (IJM) is a good example of this. A global organization that protects people in poverty from violence, IJM also identifies itself as a community of Christian spiritual formation, and their founder and CEO, Gary Haugen, is clearly the one who champions it. He realized early on that in an organization with such an intense mission focus "the problem of prayerless striving" loomed large on the horizon. That awareness initiated the beginning of 11:00 prayer, during which the whole organization stopped what they were doing and gathered to bring the cares and concerns of the ministry before the Lord. Several years after that, Gary had a sense that God had more of his presence and power to pour out on IJM but that they weren't ready to receive it, so they introduced what came to be known as "8:30 stillness." This means that half an hour before work starts people are in their offices, but instead of working, they use this time to prepare themselves to receive the power and presence God has for them. Eventually they also added quarterly days of prayer to receive deeper empowerment from the Holy Spirit.

I have been with IJM in several different capacities over the years and have observed that, while Gary has good people around him who help carry out this priority, he is is clearly the impetus for the consistent and deepening focus on transformation in Christ's presence. I could feel Gary's conviction in these words from a conversation we had recently:

> For the work that IJM is doing, we need people who are more spiritually transformed than our churches are producing. We need the fruit of the Spirit to be more manifest. We need

> supernatural passion for justice, supernatural hope that justice is possible, supernatural courage to face the cost of it, supernatural perseverance, because this is going to take a long time. We're going to need supernatural love because people are going to get messy in the middle of all this. And we're going to need supernatural wisdom, because it's going to get complicated. That's another way of saying that we need to be much more like Christ for this incredibly demanding mission that we're doing, because it is scary and hard. We need to provide supplemental spiritual formation.[2]

Spiritual transformation is an organic process that goes far beyond mere behavioral tweaks. In this process the Spirit of God works deep and fundamental changes at the core of our being, moving us from behaviors motivated by fear and self-protection to trust and abandonment to God. From selfishness and self-absorption to freely offering the gifts of the authentic self. From the ego's desperate attempts to control the outcomes of our lives to the ability to do God's will even when it is foolishness to the world around us. Our churches and Christian ministries need this kind of reality lived and modeled by leaders at every level. This alone will change what our communities become. Truly the best thing we bring to transforming community is our own transforming selves and the inner authority that comes from the witness in our own lives. We must always be speaking of what we know and testifying to what we have seen and experienced. Any additional strategy will come quite naturally after that.

## SPIRITUAL TRANSFORMATION: HOW IT HAPPENS IN THE LIFE OF A PERSON

Once we have settled the all-important question—Is spiritual transformation elective or essential?—and clarified that the senior leader(s) will be the champions for it, our next strategic effort will have to do with establishing shared understanding of how spiritual transformation happens in the life of a person, so that everyone involved is clear about what kind of process they are prioritizing and facilitating.

As we talked about early in this book, *it all begins with desire*—that is, helping people get in touch with their spiritual longings, the desires of the heart that God longs to meet (Psalm 37:4). Teaching, preaching, and small group discussions on the role of desire in the spiritual life are essential. It is important that leaders model what it is like to work with desire as a spiritual dynamic, as they will not be able to foster effective conversations about desire within their church community if they are not comfortable with it personally. Start by *teaching and discussing this at the leadership level,* achieving comfort there first. Give ample time for pastors and leaders to share their desire for themselves and for the community. *Do not rush this step.* Make sure you give people enough time, space, and spiritual guidance to claim their own desire rather than just falling into line.[3]

Then, speak into that desire by *casting vision for what is possible,* using every means available—preaching, teaching, conversations and guided experiences in small groups, Christian education settings, retreats, etc. *Allow desire to deepen into intent* by encouraging people to stay with their desire long enough to consider what it might be like to arrange their lives for what they say they really want. *Give time and space for intent to deepen into decision-making* by introducing the Christian practice of establishing a personal rule of life. Offer guided experiences with the practices, relationships, and attitudes that open us to spiritual transformation and then provide real guidance for putting together a personal rule of life.[4] The goal in a transforming community would be that someone could walk up to any person in the community and say, "Tell me about your rule of life," and they would be able to do so.

As part of your teaching on the Christian tradition of crafting a rule of life, *encourage discernment about how our spiritual transformation is for the sake of others in the body of Christ and in the world God loves.* This is a major outcome of spiritual transformation, and there should be some evidence of this in our rule of life. This might include simply noting how one is serving or intends to serve within the body of Christ with one's spiritual gifts and how one is engaging with the needs of the world in any number of different ways.

One's rule of life can and should be reviewed annually (at least) or when major changes take place in one's life. Creating space for this could be introduced as part of the community's rhythm—maybe at the beginning of the school year, at the New Year, or at the beginning of Advent as the start of a new church year.

Finally, be sure to *structure a system of support for developing a rule of life based on being in touch with desire and then living it out over time*. This could include one-to-one spiritual direction, group spiritual direction, or groups convened for the express purpose of being spiritual companions for one another. Be careful here not to assume that your typical Bible study groups will provide this. They probably won't unless given specific guidance for how this kind of companioning is different from what they've been doing.[5] Recommended and assigned readings could be a part of this structural support, and I would suggest using spiritual formation resources strategically. Recommend or assign them as part of a larger strategy so everyone can see where these resources fit into the community's priorities, see how they support their shared commitment to spiritual transformation, and have a strong sense of togetherness in the journey toward becoming a transforming community. An effective flow could be to work through *Sacred Rhythms* first so people are learning and gaining experience with basic spiritual practices (nine chapters, nine months, take the summer off) and then move to *Life Together in Christ* in the fall to begin implementing a structured approach to longer-term spiritual companioning for this journey.

Figure 14.1 is a graphic representation of the process of spiritual transformation in the life of an individual.

*People change incrementally . . .*
*over time . . .*
*with others*
*in the context of spiritual disciplines*
*that open us to God.*

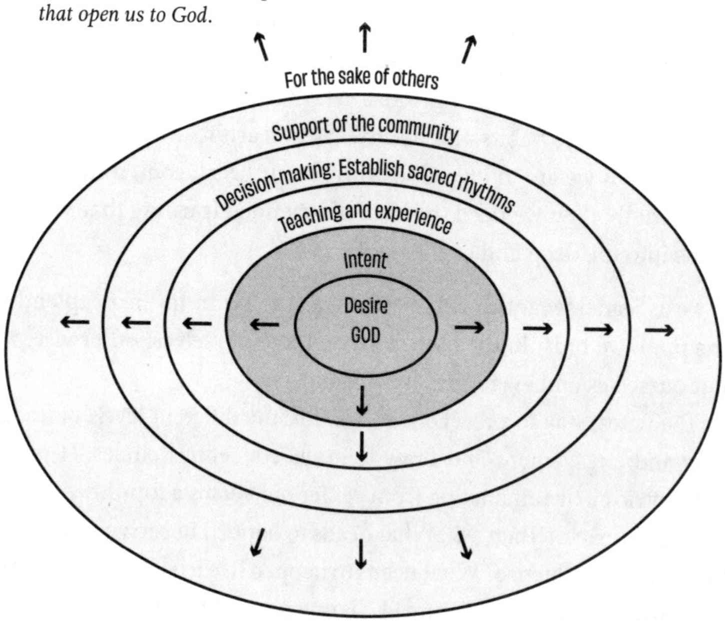


**Figure 14.1.** How spiritual transformation happens in the life of a person

## SPIRITUAL TRANSFORMATION: HOW IT HAPPENS IN THE LIFE OF A COMMUNITY

So, how does a whole community get organized for all this? My best idea is to *work from the center out.*

Spiritual transformation in your community doesn't begin with the hiring of a new spiritual formation pastor. It doesn't begin with the appointment of a committee to "look into these things." It doesn't even begin when we start offering a few spiritual formation electives or retreats. It begins when the core leaders in a church or organization take a step back and give serious attention to their own process of spiritual transformation (or the lack thereof) and commit themselves to a more intentional process of spiritual transformation, determined to lead from that place.

Anglican theologian W. H. Vanstone once observed that

> the church is like a swimming pool in which all the noise comes from the shallow end. But most of the wisdom is to be found in the deep end, among those who have taken the time and cultivated the habits and disciplines to learn to swim in deeper waters. If we are to love God with all our heart, soul, mind and strength, then we need the kind of sustained learning that leads us into the deep end of the pool.[6]

If we as leaders want to help others learn to swim in the deep end of the pool, we must know how to swim there ourselves; otherwise, we put ourselves and everyone else in danger!

The wisest way to proceed is to identify the different levels of leadership and engagement and draw them as concentric circles. (I prefer concentric circles emanating from center out versus a top-down/hierarchical approach.) Then ask, What needs to happen in each circle of relationship and influence? What needs to happen in each leader so they are prepared to lead others? Figure 14.2 is one illustration of what this might look like in a church. This diagram can be adapted for other types of organizations using whatever designations fit the organizational structure.

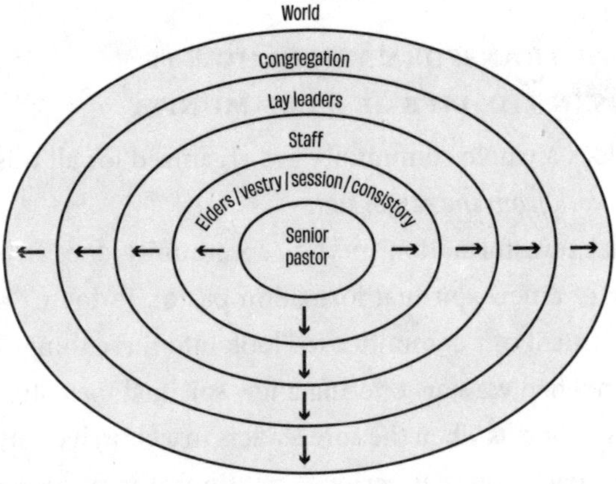


**Figure 14.2.** The progress of spiritual transformation within a church or organization

## USE EVERY MEANS AVAILABLE

After achieving some sense of unity at the leadership level, you can begin unfolding an intentional process of engaging your community around spiritual formation themes and practices.

Work wisely within your community's structure and polity to:

- Cast vision. At least in the beginning, this should probably come from the senior leader or an outside presenter who is highly respected by the community.
- Teach. Really flesh out the vision in age and developmentally appropriate ways.
- Provide training and guided experiences in how to practice the spiritual disciplines and how to put together a rule of life and then provide support for living it out.
- Establish small groups for spiritual companioning and give clear guidance.
- Articulate and model commitment to spiritual transformation at all levels of leadership.
- Implement a process of aligning all aspects of the community's life with the values and practices of transforming community, working closely with board and staff.
- Utilize new-member gatherings and congregational meetings to keep articulating, clarifying, and seeking alignment around the priority of spiritual transformation in your community and how that will be lived out.
- Practice periodic noticing. Establish a regular rhythm of providing further transforming resources and opportunities and to check in about whether the culture and practices of your community continue to be transforming or deforming. One aspect of our periodic noticing in the Transforming Center is that we incorporate into our annual reviews a check-in with our staff about our spiritual practices and rules of life. We are very careful to frame this as a

way we care about each other's spiritual health and well-being and not a "performance" thing that could affect employment.

- Humbly receive feedback from all levels of the community's life rather than trusting only what we are aware of from the ivory tower of senior-level leadership.

## A COMMUNITY THAT PRACTICES

In the end, a transforming community is simply a community that practices. In the Wesleyan tradition, spiritual practices are understood as "means of grace"—ways of opening to God's grace, which is always there for us and is able to accomplish more than we could ever ask or think. For Wesleyans, grace is not just one of God's attributes; it is a dynamic energy, a force in which God does something *in* me and *through* me (with my consent, of course) that I cannot do for myself. It is pure gift, which means we cannot earn it, but we *can* find ways to open to it.

Engaging spiritual practices as means of grace is a way of creating channels for opening to God's work of transformation in our lives. It's like we are digging a deeper well to tap into a water source flowing underground or carving out a new trench to direct the flow of water where we want it to go. Similarly, the spiritual practices, postures, and experiences around which we orient our lives can become conduits that open us to the flow of God's grace. And it's not just individuals who can choose to order their lives this way; whole communities can order their life *together* around the habits and practices that open us to the grace of God's transforming work.

In Christian tradition, crafting a rule of life was not so much for individuals as it was a way to help whole communities order their lives together around practices they believed would be fruitful for opening to God's transforming grace at work among them. But developing a rhythm of such spiritual practices takes time and intentionality. It takes time and wise guidance to learn about and explore a variety of spiritual disciplines and experience the dynamics of each one. Then, it takes more time to experiment with arranging the disciplines in a way that fits one's life with beauty and flow—like a dance, a beautifully arranged symphony, or the ebb and flow of the tide. It's best if people can be given a chance to try each discipline one at a time so they can work with it for a while, rather than trying to change too much too fast. Once people have experienced some of the basic disciplines they can be encouraged to incorporate the practices in a way that is realistic and personal based on stage of life and other factors, balanced, and flexible. In Christian tradition, we call this arrangement a rule of life, or sacred rhythms.

As we teach and encourage people to incorporate spiritual disciplines into their lives, remember how important it is that they do so based on their spiritual desires. The spiritual life is not about "oughts" and "shoulds" imposed from the outside; it emerges from desires that God has placed deep within us. Our job as spiritual leaders is to keep helping people stay in touch with their spiritual desire and then to present spiritual practices that correspond to those desires. For instance, solitude, silence, and prayer correspond with the desire for intimacy with God. *Lectio divina* corresponds to the desire to hear a word from the Lord. Self-examination corresponds to the desire for deeper levels of transformation. Sabbath-keeping corresponds to the desire for rest and a way of life that works, and so on. As much as possible, do not let your teachings about spiritual disciplines get decoupled from spiritual desire. Otherwise, you will only be substituting one set of legalistic practices for another. This is nuanced business, and this is our job as leaders of transforming communities.

## DISCOVERING HOLY VALUES AND SACRED RHYTHMS IN COMMUNITY

Transforming community does not happen by accident, nor is it maintained and cultivated in a haphazard way. It is led by leaders who are clear that spiritual community is what they are called to, who embrace the values that undergird it, and who are brave enough to commit to practices that help us live out our values in concrete ways.

Every community will have some values that are already in place. Step one is to to look at those again, name how they contribute to spiritual transformation, and make sure they still hold. Step two is to add a few more that are more specifically related to your commitment to becoming a transforming community. Some of your values will be very general, appropriate for any Christian community or ministry organization, while others will be more specific to your unique calling as a community. Take all the time you need with this; it may take a few meetings to really land on what is most important to all of you.[7]

If articulating values in this way is new for your community, it might be good to introduce a few first and begin living with them before by making claims you're not sure you can live up to. Gordon Cosby, founding pastor of Church of the Savior in Washington, DC, offers this piece of advice from fifty years of leading the same community: "Our written commitment has grown out of our life together. The life occurred first and then it was put down in a written commitment. To make a formal commitment without having drunk deeply of the life of the group is simply to take a husk that can mock us. Only in commitment can there be real belonging."[8]

Step three is to make sure you have a practice or practices to go with each value. A value is just a nice-sounding idea unless you have concrete activities and behaviors that make it real. For instance, the first value we committed ourselves to in the Transforming Center is "spiritual transformation in community." The practices we are committed to that are associated with this value are fixed-hour prayer in community and each of us having a personal rule of life, as well as a communal rule of life, that we check in regularly about with each other. (If you're interested, see the appendix for an example of the guiding values and practices that have shaped the life of the Transforming Center over the years.)

After you have done your work articulating values and the practices that will help you live them out, you may want to consider making a covenant around them or taking time for prayers of commitment. This is another way of making it real. Whatever you do, making sure that these values and commitment are in writing for everyone to have, pray through, and come back to as needed is essential.

## FROM BUSYNESS AND BURNOUT TO INCARNATIONAL LIVING

Some members of your community may not be ready for the rigors of a truly transformational journey, but I wouldn't be too concerned about that. You can kindly let them go. In the short term, you may experience a decrease in numbers while doing the work of becoming a transforming community, and it may require a multiyear process. But the good news is that those who are ready to engage the process with intention will become increasingly grounded in God, more committed to the community they are a part of, and clearer on what their unique mission in the world really is. Because they are living in good-for-the-soul rhythms of transformation, discernment, and mission, they will be sustained for the long haul of ministry and engagement with the needs of the world, rather than burning out prematurely. They will be getting better and better at discerning exactly what part of God's kingdom work they are being called to participate in. And they will be constantly renewed through the sacred rhythms they have in place as individuals and as a group. Simply put, they will be on an intentional journey of spiritual transformation so they are discerning and doing the will of God together.

When Christians gather on the basis of their desire for transformation in Christ's presence and are willing to bring intentionality to it, people change—whole communities change!—in deep and fundamental ways. And their existence within their larger, geographical community becomes a transforming element in the world around them. Evangelism, then, is understood as an invitation to spiritual transformation in the here and now, not just the promise of something better in the afterlife. The power of their witness is the transformation taking place within individuals, the quality of the community's life together, and the heart of Christ they are incarnating in the world around them. Christ's kingdom is *always* best validated by the transformation taking place in the lives of his followers.

A transforming community is radically incarnational in that its members believe it is possible to *be Christ* in the world. Rather than merely seeking to become "like" Christ, they embrace the fact that we can become "participants of the divine nature" (2 Peter 1:4) and then incarnate that nature with others. They know there are concrete ways they can open to the transforming presence of Christ so that increasingly it is Christ who is living uniquely through them. Members of transforming communities know it is not what they *do* that will change their world fundamentally as much as who they *are*. As they embody their transforming, Christ-in-you selves, their very lives demonstrate the power of the gospel. Through them the spirit of Christ lives and works through his body here on the earth now. Through their life together they are sustained in the mystery of faith so they can be in God for the world.

In such a community, it is understood that every Christian is a minister: that is, in God for the world in a way no one else can be. "Your pastor is not the minister. According to Ephesians 4:12, your pastor's job is to equip *you* for the work of ministry, and to use your gifts to build up the body of Christ in love. You are the ones living in your world with your circle of relationships—circles your pastor can never touch. You are the one to be God's presence in the world."[9]

## TRANSFORMING COMMUNITIES TRANSFORMING THEIR WORLD

I close with an example of what it can look like when transforming communities are in God for the world. The story is told by Reverend Otis Moss III, senior pastor of Trinity United Church in Chicago, writing about the day his church received an unwelcome visit from another congregation on a Sunday morning after he took a stand on *Roe v. Wade*. Rev. Moss knew that Christians have differing views on this topic, but he felt that this particular group was using the rhetoric of hate. Catching both the leaders and members of his congregation by surprise, the protesters held signs with what Moss describes as "outrageous claims about abortion and our church" and others "shouted racist epithets through megaphones." Church members had to wade through this crowd to get to church.

> I was furious, and I knew I wouldn't be the only one. On the South Side of Chicago, some citizens have not yet been won over to the nonviolent methods of Dr. King. I knew some of our "cousins" from the community, if provoked, would use more aggressive styles of conflict resolution. No matter that the [protesters] had attacked us, that we had justice on our side, or that I longed to put those so-called "Christians" in their place—they would be able to portray us to the media as violent, accessing racial stereotypes to undermine our community. That could stir up even more anger and draw great scrutiny and harassment.
>
> I ran back into the church and found the members of the choir who were still in the atrium, preparing for their customary procession into the sanctuary. I gathered them together and gazed on the group, the seriousness of the situation surely etched over my face. I leaned forward and began talking: *This is what I need for you to do. Muster up the kind of faith our ancestors had. We are going to march outside and surround the protesters, but we are not going to touch them. We're going to sing to the glory of the God so loudly that our voices, the voices of love, are going to drown out the shouts of hate.*
>
> The choir loved it. They could confront the frightening forces of bigotry and intolerance with song. They went out there, a hundred strong, and got right in the faces of the [protesters] singing "This Little Light of Mine." Try to imagine a sixty-eight-year-old grandmother, all of five foot four, getting in the face of a menacing, rather stout six-three gentleman, clapping and singing with all her power as the protester tries to gather his composure. That man was almost pushed into the street because the power of the song made him lose his balance.

> Four elderly women surrounded the "megaphone man." He couldn't get a word out. They just kept singing and clapping. . . . We created a wall of sound so strong that the congregants could file into the sanctuary without hearing the horrific chanting. In my sanctified imagination, I saw the loving sound waves of gospel music wrestling the sound waves of hate. Somewhere between the lawn and the sidewalk, the words of hate decided to change course and join a new choir. The words of hate were not destroyed by the sound of joy; they were transformed in midair.
>
> I instructed the deacons to ask the protesters to join us in prayer—a simple request, one group of believers to another. As I expected, the church group rejected the chance to join us in lifting up the name of Jesus. But that didn't stop of us from praying for them. They had offered us hate, but we offered them grace. The deacons joined hands and began to surround the protesters with Pentecostal prayers—that is, prayer deep from one's soul, designed by the spirit to place even a nonbeliever in a space of reflection. The atmosphere changed. The protesters were overwhelmed by something they were not used to: the spirit of God's love. Looking half drunk, they climbed clumsily into their vans and drove away.[10]

And there you have it—transforming leaders of transforming communities who are transforming their corner of the world. That, friends, is the whole point of toiling and struggling to become a transforming community.

*Epilogue*

# THE QUESTIONS WE'RE WILLING TO ASK OURSELVES

*In the spiritual life, the questions we are willing to ask ourselves are more important than the answers we think we know.*

Ruth Haley Barton

---

One final question we as leaders in the body of Christ need to sit with has to do with distinguishing between the church as an institution and the church as the living, growing, breathing body of Jesus. We need to ask, *Can the institutionalized church and institutions of any kind be transforming communities, given their propensity toward self-preservation, the drive to preserve the image of success at all costs, and the need to manipulate and control outcomes, which develop over time?*

This may be a startling question to end with, and I want to assure you that I have written this book because I believe the answer to this question is yes. But I also think we need to do the work of thinking about the process by which something becomes an institution and what happens when it does. We need to bravely ask questions such as, Can institutions be structurally closed to being grasped by God, just as individuals can be? Can something that has become an institution be committed to the Tradition of following the God who is always doing something new? Can we hold our current expression of church lightly enough to let us recognize and receive the new thing God is doing, even if it messes with the institutional aspects of what we're doing? These questions, if we are willing to ask them may just open a door or a window so a fresh wind of the Spirit can blow through. We all need to ask ourselves: Can institutions such as churches and ministry organizations become transforming communities, or is there something in the very nature, the DNA, of an institution that works against it over time? And are we able to distinguish between the institution the church has become and the actual body of Christ on the earth now?

These questions have been running in the background of my mind throughout the writing of this book, and I think it *is* possible for any church, ministry, family, or small group to become a transforming community, but it will come at great cost and require extreme vigilance. In leadership circles we like to talk about mission drift, but I would also like to introduce the idea of "essence" or "identity" drift, which is, in the end, much more serious. While these questions might sound discouraging, I think our doubts about whether this is possible can actually be profitable. They can keep us honest, humble, and vigilant in asking the right questions, even when such questions are deeply uncomfortable, and even when we have our doubts.

## IS OUR FAITH BIG ENOUGH TO INCLUDE DOUBT?

In the movie *Conclave*, Cardinal Lawrence, dean of the cardinals, offers this powerful word to his fellow cardinals as they enter into the process of electing a new pope:

> To grow together we must be tolerant. God's gift to the Church is its variety, its diversity. One sin which I've come to fear above all others: certainty. Certainty is the great enemy of unity. Certainty is the deadly enemy of tolerance. Even Christ was not certain at the end. . . . Our faith is a living thing precisely because it walks hand in hand with doubt. If there were only certainty and no

doubt, there would be no mystery and therefore no need for faith. Let us pray that God will grant us a pope who doubts and let us ask for a pope who sins and asks forgiveness and carries on.

If you've seen the movie, you know his conviction on this point was severely tested by the time the conclave was over; no doubt his own words came back to haunt him when faced with greater complexity than he could have imagined. But fortunately, his convictions held up under extreme duress and carried him through. May we also be leaders who can tolerate doubt, who ask forgiveness when needed, and who then carry on. May our doubts *and* our convictions carry us through. The adventure continues.

**I Hold My Life Up to You Now**
*Oh God of wonder*
*of mystery*
*of adventurous journeys*
*Help me not to let my life slip away from me*
*without doing that thing I am meant to do*
*without taking the journey that is mine to take*
*without risking everything to gain everything.*
*O God of possibility,*
*I hold my life up to You now*
*as much as I can*
*as high as I can*
*in this mysterious reach called prayer.*
*Come close,*
*lest I wobble,*
*fall short,*
*hold back.*
*It is not days or years I seek from You,*
*not infinity or enormity,*
*but small things and simple awareness,*
*that You are in what I am*

*and in what I seek.*
*It is not new time that I seek from You,*
*but new eyes and a new heart,*
*fresh courage and clearer intent,*
*and You,*
*always You.*
*O God who continually makes all things new,*
*make something new* of me *and of our community*
*for Your glory*
*for the sake of others*
*and for the abundance*
*of this life*
*we all share.*

—Ruth Haley Barton
January 2025

# GRATITUDE

**This book has been a hard one**—for all sorts of reasons—but mostly because it is almost *impossible* to capture in words over twenty-five years of guiding transforming communities with real people in real time as they open to the work of the Spirit together. I have led twenty (count them!) twenty-seven-month transforming community experiences over the last twenty-five years, and every one of them has been different because the people who come together are different and because the work of the Spirit is unique every single time. In the end, the only way I could finish this manuscript was to accept the limits of time, space, words, and the process of book writing itself, trusting that it will be enough of an offering to at least get people started and moving in the same direction together.

My deepest gratitude this time around goes to my long-suffering editor, Cindy Bunch. She literally pulled me and this book across the finish line. Her patience with all my missed deadlines, her partnership in restructuring the book during the editing process, and her fearless leadership in rallying the InterVarsity Press team working within constricted deadlines and truncated processes are the only reasons this book is here now. Thanks to her and to the whole IVP team for working with me to write, publish, and sell my books. I am honored by your hard work.

To each and every person who has taken the brave journey of transforming community with me. Everything I have written in this book I have learned and confirmed with you. What a privilege it's been to journey with you!

To the staff and board of the Transforming Center, whose schedules have been ordered, reordered, and at times upended because of what it has required to write this book. Your grace has been God's grace to me. There are not enough words to describe how I feel about your love and support.

To Bob Mulholland, to whom this work is dedicated, and to all my teachers, many of whom are referenced in this book. Throughout my life, when *this* student has been ready, the teacher has appeared. I thank God for each of you. My life has been so profoundly enriched by your faithfulness to the craft of teaching and writing—for the sake of others.

To my friends, who have stood by patiently praying, supporting, and waiting until I could be the kind of friend I want to be again.

And to my family. You are those who have been through the great ordeal, and you have endured. I can't wait to be a normal person again—living my normal, chaotic, achingly beautiful, full-of-love life with all of you.

*Appendix*

# TRANSFORMING CENTER GUIDING VALUES AND PRACTICES

*These guiding values and principles are the product of many years of the Transforming Center board and staff working together to articulate them and live them out. We started out with the first five, adding to them and reshaping them over time. This is intended to be a living document, not a static statement, so we revisit our values and related practices every year to notice how we are doing at living them out and making any needed edits and adjustments. This annual practice is crucial for making sure these are not just words on a page, but principles to be lived.*

---

***Spiritual transformation in community.*** We are a community of men and women gathered around the presence of Christ for the purpose of transformation so we can discern and do the will of God. *What we do* flows out of *who we are* in Christ. Learning to come together and stay together in unity is our first and most enduring task as we pattern our relationships after Christ's relationships with his disciples. "He loved his own until the end" (see John 13:1; 15; 17). Through our commitment to community we incarnate the body of Christ on the earth now; to compromise community would be to compromise our very essence and then we would not have much that is of value to offer to others. Practices: fixed-hour prayer and a shared rule of life.

***The best thing we bring to leadership is our own transforming self.*** The ability to *be* a community and grow in unity is a direct result of a continuing process of spiritual transformation. Thus, each individual in the community is committed to their own personal spiritual disciplines (solitude, silence, prayer, reflection on Scripture, self-examination, confession, personal discernment, caring for the body, etc.) and also to corporate spiritual disciplines that support and catalyze our spiritual transformation in community. Our corporate disciplines include engaging in one or more Transforming Community experiences, fixed-hour prayer, shared silence, reading and reflecting on Scripture, retreat, sabbath, self-examination and confession, communal discernment, and celebration. While we know that none of us will achieve perfection this side of heaven, our commitment to these practices assures that we are bringing a transforming self (not a deforming self) to our life together in leadership community.

Practice: We routinely check in with each other about our rule of life/spiritual rhythms both in private conversations, group interactions, and supervisory relationships.

***Sane rhythms of work and rest.*** This commitment is anchored in our practice of keeping the Sabbath for the purposes of rest, worship, and delight. In addition to being one of the Ten Commandments (which many Christians violate routinely!) we experience sabbath as a precious gift from God. It is a means of grace that helps us to live within our limits, to find rest and replenishment, and to delight in God's good gifts. Sabbath-keeping fosters within us a sense of trust in God—trust that if we live our lives on God's terms for us by working six days and ceasing on the seventh, God will make the work we have done "enough" and provide what is needed.

Our commitment to sane rhythms of work and rest is part of what ensures that we bring rested, alert selves to the tasks and responsibilities associated with leadership and discernment. As part of our practice, it is routine for us to talk about our pace of life and whether it is enabling us to remain healthy or whether we are approaching dangerous levels of exhaustion. We seek to make scheduling decisions based on this kind of awareness and discussion.

***Unity within our diversity.*** One of the delights of the kingdom of God is all the different ways God created God's children in God's image (Genesis 1:26-28). Further, in Christ, "there is no longer Jew or Greek; there is no longer slave or free; there is no longer male and female, for all of you are one in Christ" (Galatians 3:28). We strive to live out this reality in our retreats, resources, and relationships by intentionally seeking out the richness of diversity that includes (but is not limited to) gender, race, age, sexual orientation, education level, ability, veteran status, immigration status, national origin, political affiliation, leadership position, ministry context, personality type, denomination, marital status, parental status, theological understanding and viewpoints, geographic location, socio economic status, and spiritual gifting.

We are convinced that one of the most spiritually profitable things we can be and do is provide a safe space that holds and honors the rich diversity that exists within the body of Christ—particularly as that has to do with topics on which Christians disagree. In fact, to engage in Transforming Community is to *expect* that we will be walking together in mutually influencing relationships with those who are different than we are, and those who are the same, knowing this to be a vital spiritual practice. To that end, we invite different thoughts, perspectives, and life experiences into our communities, believing that holding this space with love and respect, while modeling this for others, is the most edifying thing we can do for the body of Christ and its leaders at this time (John 17:20-26). We do not have to think alike in order to experience transformation in community; thus, we expect every member of the Transforming Center and its communities to be loving and respectful to all in the body of Christ.

***Discerning God's will together.*** Discernment is an increasing capacity to recognize and respond to the presence and the activity of God, both in the ordinary moments of our lives and in the larger decisions of our lives. Discernment takes place in and through the Holy Spirit, the third person of the Trinity, who has been given to us to mediate the real Presence of the living Christ, who desires to lead his Church. One of the main functions of the Holy Spirit is to expand Jesus' teachings from the moment in which they were given to the moments in which we find ourselves right now. As the Spirit helps us discern the demands of love in our current context, the will of God continues to be revealed among us in fresh ways. Thus, we are committed to the *habit* of discernment—seeking to be attentive and alert to God's activity among us day by day—and naming that together so we can seek to respond faithfully. We are also committed to the *practice* of discernment in community—proactively seeking God's guidance together when we need specific direction for decision-making.

Because discernment takes more time and a different kind of attention than mere decision-making, living out this value requires commitment to a clear process for leadership discernment and the discipline to carry it out. (See *Pursuing God's Will Together: A Discernment Practice for Leadership Groups* for a full description of the practice of leadership discernment to which we are committed.) We recognize that not all decisions need a formal discernment process, so we work to identify what needs a structured process versus traditional decision-making.

***Listening to fear and resistance.*** An important aspect of discerning God's will together is our commitment to listening to inner dynamics such as consolation and desolation, fear, and resistance. We all experience fear, particularly as we enter more deeply into community and calling. Fear causes people to behave strangely or even badly (to give in to "fight, flight, or freeze" reactions, self-protection, manipulation, etc.). When not acknowledged, fear causes us to shrink back when perhaps God is calling us forward; however, it can also alert us to situations that are truly dangerous. Becoming a leadership community in which it is safe to express fear enables us to (1) exercise wisdom and ask, *Are the consequences of the decision or action detrimental to anyone or the organization?* (2) hear God's challenge for us to be courageous, or (3) pay attention to areas where our trust in God or each other is weak and needs to be strengthened. When we experience fear in our work setting, we are encouraged to share it openly with the staff team or supervisor so it can be processed together.

***Lived experience.*** We will not teach theories or things we merely wish were true; we will teach only that which we are experiencing ourselves *to some degree.* "We speak of what we know and testify to what we have seen" (John 3:11). Sometimes this means we choose not to teach on certain topics—even if it would be a great topic!—because we know we are not yet living them effectively.

***Self-knowledge, repentance, confession.*** Closely related to our commitment to spiritual transformation and discernment in community is our commitment to increasing levels of self-knowledge, a willingness to take responsibility for becoming aware of negative patterns that affect interactions in community, and dealing with our own inner dynamics appropriately as we become aware of them. Since spiritual transformation takes place primarily in those places where we are not like Christ and in transforming community, others become agents of God's troubling grace, giving us many opportunities to see ourselves more clearly, to repent, and to confess our sins one to another so that we might receive grace and healing. Thus, we seek to acknowledge and respect the profound role that brokenness plays in the unfolding of the spiritual life and in the formation of true spiritual community. We believe that coming face-to-face with our weakness and sharing it together prayerfully opens us to the gift of community and releases God's power among us, within us, beyond us (2 Corinthians 12:7-10). This fosters humility among us as we learn and serve together.

Without a shared willingness to name sin, to cultivate self-awareness relative to what caused our negative behavior, and to confess our sins one to another as needed, communities are prone to splinter and fall apart under pressure—an inevitability that undermines Jesus' deepest desire for us—that we would be one and that as Christians we would be known by our love (John 17).

***Truth-telling and truth-hearing.*** God desires truth in the inward being because truth leads to freedom, spiritual transformation, and deeper levels of discernment. All truth, no matter how delicate or painful or seemingly inconsequential, can contribute to the process of transformation and to the ability to discern faithfully. Since the Holy Spirit has been given to us to guide us into truth, we seek to offer the truth to one another in love, directness, and gentleness rather than hiding truth or "spinning" the truth; anything less than this kind of honesty places the community in great peril (see the story of Ananias and Sapphira in Acts 5). Because truth-telling is such a deeply held value and practice, it guides us and gives us courage to go ahead and say the hard thing with grace and love and to support each other in doing so.

***Conflict transformation.*** One of the most important aspects of long-term community is very concrete commitments regarding what we will do when we experience significant disagreement. What is our commitment relative to discerning together even through conflict or differing perspectives on what God is doing in us and among us? How do we move through conflict and disagreement in ways that help us (1) open to the presence of Christ among us ("where two or three are gathered [to deal with conflict], I am there among them" [Matthew 18:20]), (2) honor God and the community, and (3) pursue deeper levels of transformation rather than capitulating to what is worst within us? What is the role of the group in calling individuals and the group back to these commitments during difficult times and what is a biblical and spiritual process that we agree to adhere to?

Commitment to engaging conflict in a way that changes us *for the better* and deepens our unity in Christ is a more challenging commitment than "conflict management" or conflict avoidance; *agreeing to this principle in theory* is very different from *living it out* with real people in the midst of a real conflict. It requires a certain level of spiritual maturity and commitment to community to move beyond human tendencies to avoid conflict, to blame others, and to leave when the going gets tough. We recognize it is only by God's grace that we are able to seek unity and deeper levels of transformation in the midst of conflict and disappointment, and we choose to rely on that grace.

***Kindness.*** The commitment to truth-telling must also be balanced with love and kindness. Kindness is a basic characteristic of mature spirituality but often the Christian community is unkind. Choosing to enter into a spiritual community requires a certain tenderness and gentleness with each other. Many people, particularly pastors, have been treated badly in churches and Christian organizations. Wouldn't it be something if we could at the very least be a place where people (including ourselves) encountered true kindness and gentleness over the long haul? Even if that's all we accomplished, it would be very significant!

***Celebration.*** Celebration is the spiritual discipline associated with gratitude. Thus, we look for every opportunity to celebrate God's presence with us and God's activity among us. In our life together and in our retreat ministry, we always set aside one evening that is specifically designed for celebrating our life together in community and God's transforming work among us. Celebration fosters joy—which is a fruit of the Spirit we all need more of!

***Community covenant.*** To the best of our ability, we covenant to uphold and live out these values together, taking time every year to reaffirm them. This fosters a sense of being mutually responsible for holding the group accountable to what we have agreed on and for calling the group back to the covenant when any aspect of our adherence slips. Because community at the leadership level is so challenging, the process of articulating covenant commitments and embracing them together in God's presence is of utmost importance. Although we continue to add and fine-tune our guiding values and principles, it is essential that we covenant together around those values that are clear to us and that we *can* agree on. We enter into this covenant for the sake of our community that is one expression of the body of Christ here on the earth, for the integrity of the mission God has entrusted to us, and for the sake of others. *Thy kingdom come . . . on earth and in our community as it is in heaven.*

# NOTES

### 1. LONGING FOR MORE IN COMMUNITY

[1] Clarence Heller, *A Piece of Goodness,* email message to author, July 11, 2024. Used with permission.

[2] Arbor Research Group and ChurchSalary, *The Impact of COVID-19 on the American Church,* https://pages.churchsalary.com/covid-study-download. Cited in Jeff Brumley, "New Study Details Church Divisions Created by COVID Pandemic," *The Christian Century,* May 2024, 14.

[3] Brumley, "New Study Details," 15.

[4] Brian McClaren, "A Responsibility for Our Tradition," *Daily Meditations,* Center for Action and Contemplation, October 24, 2025, https://cac.org/daily-meditations/a-responsibility-for-our-tradition/.

[5] By missional, I am not referring to misguided attempts to wipe out others' cultural and religious traditions or the colonizing of Indigenous people groups; I simply mean to become witnesses of what we have experienced with Jesus (as in Luke 24:48) and to do the good works for which were created, which God prepared beforehand to be our way of life (Ephesians 2:10).

### 2. ARRANGING OUR LIVES TOGETHER FOR SPIRITUAL TRANSFORMATION

[1] Brian C. Taylor, *Spirituality for Everyday Living: An Adaptation of the Rule of St. Benedict* (Liturgical Press, 1989), 17.

[2] Taylor, *Spirituality for Everyday Living,* 17.

[3] M. Robert Mulholland Jr., *Invitation to a Journey: A Road Map for Spiritual Formation,* rev. ed. (InterVarsity Press, 2016), 166.

[4] Elaine Heath, *God Unbound: Wisdom from Galatians for the Anxious Church* (Upper Room Books, 2016), 11, 60.

[5] Adam Russell Taylor, "It's Time to Rethink American Churches," *Sojourners,* April 8, 2021, sojo.net/articles/it-s-time-rethink-american-churches.

[6] Alan Jamieson, *A Churchless Faith: Faith Journeys Beyond the Churches* (Society for Promoting Christian Knowledge, 2002), 28.

[7] Dietrich Bonhoeffer, *Life Together* in Dietrich Bonhoeffer Works—Reader's Edition, vol. 5 (Fortress Press, 2015), 13.

[8] Rose Mary Dougherty, SSND, *Group Spiritual Direction: Community for Discernment* (Paulist Press, 1995), 7.

[9] This section and the first paragraph of the following one rely on my article "On the Road to Becoming a Transforming Church," *Beyond Words* (blog), n.d., https://transformingcenter.org/2017/07/road-becoming-transforming-church. The article draws from the story of Oak Hills Church as told by Kent Carlson and Mike Lueken in their book *Renovation of the Church* (InterVarsity Press, 2011).

[10] Barton, "Becoming a Transforming Church."

[11] Barton, "Becoming a Transforming Church."

[12] Barton, "Becoming a Transforming Church."

[13] Barton, "Becoming a Transforming Church."

[14] See chapter one of my book *Sacred Rhythms* (InterVarsity Press, 2006) for a more complete treatment of this subject and these Scriptures.

[15] Henri J. M. Nouwen, *The Way of the Heart: Desert Spirituality and Contemporary Ministry* (HarperSanFrancisco, 1981), 35.

## 3. BELIEFS THAT SHAPE THE SOUL

[1] Kent Carlson and Mike Lueken, *Renovation of the Church* (InterVarsity Press, 2011), 39.

[2] This is an expanded version of Robert Mulholland's definition in *Invitation to a Journey,* rev. ed. (InterVarsity Press, 2016), 31. See also Galatians 4:19; Romans 8:29; 12:1-2; 2 Corinthians 3:18.

[3] Mulholland, *Invitation to a Journey,* 28.

[4] Steve L. Porter, "Sanctification in a New Key: Relieving Evangelical Anxiety Over Spiritual Formation," *Journal of Spiritual Formation and Soul Care* 1, no. 2 (2008): 129.

[5] Dallas Willard in a personal communication with the author, November 2005.

[6] Parts of this section and the next rely on appendix two, "A Biblical Perspective on Spiritual Transformation," from my book *Pursuing God's Will Together* (InterVarsity Press, 2012), 240-45.

[7] Cindy Lee, *Unforming: De-Westernizing Spiritual Formation* (Fortress Press, 2022), 12.

[8] Kent Carlson, "Précis," *Journal of Spiritual Formation and Soul Care* 4, no. 2 (2011): 205.

[9] Mulholland, *Invitation to a Journey*, 32.

[10] Richard Foster, *Renovaré Perspectives*, April 1999.

[11] Mulholland, *Invitation to a Journey*, 187.

## 4. CHRIST FORMED IN US

[1] Parts of this section rely on my article "Martin Luther King Jr.'s Strength of Soul," *Beyond Words* (blog), n.d., https://transformingcenter.org/2011/01/martin-luther-king-jr-'s-strength-of-soul.

[2] Richard Rohr, *A Lever and a Place to Stand* (Paulist Press, 2011), 15-16.

[3] Martin Luther King Jr., *Strength to Love* (Fortress, 1963), 56.

[4] King, *Strength to Love*, 150-51.

[5] Henri J. M. Nouwen, *Spiritual Formation: Following the Movements of the Spirit* (HarperCollins, 2010), 124.

[6] Kelly Brown Douglas, "What Does It Mean to Be a Christian in These Times?" *Christian Century*, February 2025, 29.

[7] As quoted in Ron Rolheiser, "The Gospel Unfolding in History," ronrolheiser.com, August 24, 2008, https://ronrolheiser.com/the-gospel-unfolding-in-history.

[8] Richard Rohr writes about at-one-ment in many of his works including Richard Rohr, *The Divine Dance* (SPCK, 2016), 131-40.

[9] Ronald Rolheiser, "The Cross as Revealing the Non-Violence of Christ," ronrolheiser.com, February 10, 2002, https://ronrolheiser.com/the-cross-as-revealing-the-non-violence-of-christ.

[10] Rolheiser, "The Cross as Revealing."

[11] Ronald Rolheiser, *Sacred Fire: A Vision for a Deeper Human and Christian Maturity* (Image, 2014), 15.

[12] Ronald Rolheiser, "The Passion of Jesus," March 30, 2015, https://ronrolheiser.com/the-passion-of-jesus.

[13] Robert Mulholland, *Invitation to a Journey: A Road Map for Spiritual Formation*, rev. ed. (InterVarsity Press, 2016), 170, 172.

## 5. LIVING FROM THE CENTER OUT

[1] Dietrich Bonhoeffer, *Life Together* in Dietrich Bonhoeffer Works—Reader's Edition, vol. 5 (Fortress Press, 2015), 55.

[2] Ruth Haley Barton, *Invitation to Solitude and Silence: Experiencing God's Transforming Presence* (InterVarsity Press, 2004); *Sacred Rhythms: Arranging Our Lives for Spiritual Transformation* (InterVarsity Press, 2006).

[3] Gunilla Norris, *Sharing Silence: Meditation Practice and Mindful Living* (Bell Tower, 1992), 19.

[4] Henri Nouwen, *Bread for the Journey: A Daybook of Wisdom and Faith* (HarperOne: 1997), entry for January 22.

[5] Fr. Thomas Keating, *Intimacy with God: An Introduction to Centering Prayer* (Crossroad, 1994), 155.

[6] Thomas Kelly, *A Testament of Devotion* (HarperSanFrancisco, 1941), 100.

[7] Two of my favorite books on fasting are Lynne M. Baab, *Fasting: Spiritual Freedom Beyond Our Appetites* (InterVarsity Press, 2006) and Scot McKnight, *Fasting*, Ancient Practices Series (Thomas Nelson, 2009).

[8] Chapter six of *Sacred Rhythms* goes into much more detail about how to practice self-examination and how it culminates in celebration of the goodness of the created self *and* confession of all that is not like Christ.

[9] Bonhoeffer, *Life Together*, 89.

[10] For more on communal leadership discernment, see Ruth Haley Barton, *Pursuing God's Will Together: A Discernment Practice for Leadership Groups* (InterVarsity Press, 2012).

## 6. WITH GOD IN OUR BODIES

[1] Stephanie Paulsell, "Honoring the Body," in *Practicing Our Faith: A Way of Life for Searching People*, Dorothy Bass, ed. (Jossey-Bass, 1997), 16.

[2] Paulsell, "Honoring the Body," 14-15.

[3] The rest of this chapter is an adaptation of my work in "Flesh and Blood Spirituality: Honoring the Body as Spiritual Practice," *Covenant Quarterly* (August/November 2018): 29-39.

[4] Paulsell, "Honoring the Body," 5.

[5] Saint Irenaeus, *Against Heresies* 4.20.7.

[6] M. Robert Mulholland Jr., *Invitation to a Journey*, rev. ed. (InterVarsity Press, 2016), 56.

[7] David Benner, *Soulful Spirituality: Becoming Deeply Alive and Fully Human* (Brazos Press, 2011), 79.

[8] Benner, *Soulful Spirituality*, 9-10.

[9] See Ruth Haley Barton, *Embracing Rhythms of Work and Rest: From Sabbath to Sabbatical and Back Again* (InterVarsity Press, 2022).

[10] Elouise Renich Fraser, *Confessions of a Beginning Theologian* (InterVarsity Press, 1998), 31.

[11] Benner, *Soulful Spirituality*, 9-10.

[12] I distinguish dealing with issues of race, class, gender, and sexuality only on special occasions (like national holidays or in response to a current tragedy or court case) from grappling with these challenging in-the-body experiences regularly and routinely as part of our life together in transforming community.

[13] Barbara Brown Taylor, "Our Bodies, Our Faith: Practicing Incarnation" *The Christian Century*, January 27, 2009, 24, www.christiancentury.org /our-bodies-our-faith-practicing-incarnation.

[14] For further reading on this topic, I strongly recommend Atul Gawande, *Being Mortal: Medicine and What Matters in the End* (Metropolitan Books, 2014).

[15] Benner, *Soulful Spirituality*, 12.

## 7. CHOOSING TO WALK TOGETHER

[1] This section is adapted from my work *Life Together in Christ: Experiencing Transformation in Community* (InterVarsity Press, 2014).

[2] Rose Mary Dougherty, SSND, *Group Spiritual Direction* (Paulist Press, 1995), 14.

[3] M. Robert Mulholland, *Shaped by the Word: The Power of Scripture in Spiritual Formation* (Upper Room Books, 2001).

[4] Barton, *Life Together in Christ.*

## 8. TRANSFORMING WORSHIP

[1] Manuel Luz, *Honest Worship: From False Self to True Praise* (InterVarsity Press, 2018), 7-8.

[2] "A Liturgy for Evening Prayer," in *The Upper Room Worshipbook: Music and Liturgies for Spiritual Formation,* comp. and ed. by Elise S. Elsinger (Upper Room Books, 1985), 114.

[3] Rory Noland, *Transforming Worship: Planning and Leading Sunday Services as If Spiritual Formation Mattered* (InterVarsity Press, 2021), 11.

[4] Noland, *Transforming Worship*, 23.

[5] These characteristics and questions are adapted and expanded from my forward to Rory Noland's book *Transforming Worship,* 4-6.

[6] Michael Potemra, "A Remarkable Liturgical Synthesis," *The Corner*, National Review Online, April 3, 2011.

[7] Marilyn McEntyre, *Midwinter Light: Meditations for the Long Season* (Broadleaf Books, 2024), 156.

[8] Barbara A. Holmes, *Joy Unspeakable: Contemplative Practices in the Black Church* (Fortress, 2017), xx.

[9] Ronald Rolheiser, *Our One Great Act of Fidelity: Waiting for Christ in the Eucharist* (Doubleday, 2011), 27.

[10] Rolheiser, *Our One Great Act,* 27-28, emphasis added.

[11] Rolheiser, *Our One Great Act,* 19-20. Although these are my words, they are heavily reliant on Rolheiser's insights.

## 9. OUR LIFE TOGETHER UNDER THE WORD

[1]Dietrich Bonhoeffer, *Life Together* in Dietrich Bonhoeffer Works—Reader's Edition, vol. 5 (Fortress, 2015), 25.

[2]Justo L. Gonzalez, *Santa Biblia: The Bible Through Hispanic Eyes* (Abingdon, 1996), 13-15.

[3]M. Robert Mulholland Jr., *Shaped by the Word: The Power of Scripture in Spiritual Formation* (Upper Room Books, 1985), 29.

[4]Bonhoeffer, *Life Together*, 34.

[5]I am deeply indebted to Scot McKnight's *The Blue Parakeet: Rethinking How You Read the Bible*, second ed. (Zondervan, 2018) for many of the ideas in this paragraph.

[6]Henri Nouwen, *The Way of the Heart* (HarperCollins, 1981), 52, 55.

[7]Frank A. Thomas, *They Like to Never Quit Praisin' God: The Role of Celebration in Preaching* (The Pilgrim Press, 1997), 3.

[8]Thomas, *They Like to Never*, 31.

[9]Barbara Brown Taylor, "Featured Author of the Month," Nashville, TN: Cokesbury, February 2009.

[10]Rory Noland, *Transforming Worship: Planning and Leading Sunday Services as If Spiritual Formation Mattered* (InterVarsity Press, 2021).

## 10. WORKING WITH STAGES OF FAITH IN THE FAMILY OF GOD

[1]These are Fr. Thomas Keating's categories as found in *The Human Condition: Contemplation and Transformation* (Paulist Press, 1999), 13.

[2]Richard Rohr, "Surrender," *Richard's Daily Meditations*, November 4, 2009.

[3]M. Robert Mulholland Jr., *Invitation to a Journey: A Road Map for Spiritual Formation*, rev. ed. (InterVarsity Press, 2016), 94.

[4]This section is adapted from my book *Sacred Rhythms: Arranging Our Lives for Spiritual Transformation* (InterVarsity Press, 2016).

[5]Mulholland, *Invitation to a Journey*, 111.

[6]Mulholland, *Invitation to a Journey*, 115.

[7]Sue Monk Kidd, *When the Heart Waits: Spiritual Direction for Life's Sacred Questions* (HarperOne, 2006), 102-3; Daniel Day Williams, *The Spirit and the Forms of Love* (Harper & Row, 1968), 206.

[8]Janet O. Hagberg and Robert Guelich, *The Critical Journey: Stages in the Life of Faith* (Sheffield, 1989), 12.

[9]Pierre Teilhard de Chardin, *Hearts on Fire: Praying with Jesuits*, Michael Harter, ed. (Loyola Press, 1993, 2004), 102-3. Used with permission.

## 11. PARTAKERS OF THE DIVINE NATURE

[1] M. Robert Mulholland, "For the Sake of Others" (teaching and handout), Transforming Center, May 2011.

[2] Thomas Merton, *New Seeds of Contemplation* (New Directions, 1972), 114.

[3] Anthony Bouchard, "Here's What Happens Inside a Caterpillar's Chrysalis," *Labroots*, September 22, 2019.

[4] The Greek word translated "knowledge" here is *epignōsis,* which signifies a deeper, more complete, or full knowledge, often implying experiential understanding rather than just factual knowledge. The Greek word *doxa,* translated "glory," refers to the radiance of God's character, the essence of a person, who someone is at the center of their being, their nature.

[5] Michael J. Gorman, *Inhabiting the Cruciform God: Kenosis, Justification, and Theosis in Paul's Narrative Soteriology* (Eerdmans, 2009); as quoted by Robert Mulholland, "For the Sake of Others" (teaching and handout), Transforming Center, May 2011.

[6] Thomas Merton, *New Seeds of Contemplation* (New Directions Books, 2007), 279.

[7] Jonathan Wilson-Hartgrove, "God Doesn't Love Your 401(k) and Other Hard Truths: Economics for Disciples," *Christian Century,* September 8, 2009, 22.

[8] Scot McKnight, *The Blue Parakeet: Rethinking How You Read the Bible*, second ed. (Zondervan, 2018), 14.

## 12. PRACTICING FORBEARANCE AND FORGIVENESS

[1] Ashlee Eiland, *Say Good: Speaking Across Hot Topics, Complex Relationships, and Tense Situations* (NavPress, 2024), 5.

[2] Desmond Tutu and Mpho Tutu, *The Book of Forgiving: The Fourfold Path for Healing Ourselves and our World* (HarperCollins, 2014), 5.

[3] Tutu and Tutu, *Book of Forgiving,* 40.

[4] Tutu and Tutu, *Book of Forgiving,* 16.

[5] Anti-apartheid activist and Nobel laureate Archbishop Tutu was chair of South Africa's Truth and Reconciliation Commission from 1995 to 1998, where he pioneered a new way for countries to move forward after experiencing civil conflict and oppression.

## 13. JUSTICE

[1] James Cone, *The Cross and the Lynching Tree* (Orbis Books, 2011), xv, xvi.

[2] Cone, *Cross and the Lynching Tree,* xviii.

[3] Cone, *Cross and the Lynching Tree,* xvi, xvii.

[4] Josiah R. Daniels, "The Best Faith and Justice Books of the Century (So Far)," *Sojourners,* December 2025.

[5] Cone, *Cross and the Lynching Tree,* 71.

[6] This quote has variously been attributed to Reinhold Niebuhr, Martin Luther King Jr., and Bryan Stevenson.

[7] David Black, as quoted in an interview with Josina Guess, "The Chicago Pastor Who Confronted ICE in a Viral Video," *Sojourners,* October 23, 2025.

[8] Gary Haugen, *Just Courage: God's Great Expedition for the Restless Christian* (InterVarsity Press, 2008), 46.

[9] Rich Villodas, *The Deeply Formed Life: Five Transformative Values to Root Us in the Way of Jesus* (Waterbrook, 2020), 49.

[10] Thomas R. Kelly, *A Testament of Devotion* (HarperCollins, 1941), 19-20.

[11] Haugen, *Just Courage,* 38-39.

[12] Afrika Afeni Mills, "An Invitation to Racial Healing as Spiritual Formation," Missio Alliance, August 15, 2025, https://missioalliance.org/an-invitation-to-racial-healing-as-spiritual-formation/.

[13] This and the next few sessions draw from my work in the following posts: "Part 1: Lament That Leads to Partnership in God's Transforming Work," *Beyond Words* (blog), n.d., https://transformingcenter.org/2020/09/a-spirituality-of-racial-justice-and-healing-part-1-from-passive-lament-to-prophetic-lament; and "Part 2: Lament That Leads to Justice: Celebrating Martin Luther King Jr.'s Transforming Leadership," *Beyond Words* (blog), n.d., https://transformingcenter.org/2023/01/part-2-beyond-lament-in-celebration-of-transforming-leadership.

[14] Kathleen D. Billman and Daniel L. Migliore, *Rachel's Cry: Prayer and Lament and Rebirth of Hope* (United Church Press, 1999), 6.

[15] What follows is highly reliant—with gratitude—on Soong-Chan Rah's masterful work *Prophetic Lament: A Call for Justice in Troubling Times* (InterVarsity Press, 2015).

[16] Rah, *Prophetic Lament,* 179.

[17] Rah, *Prophetic Lament,* 130-31.

[18] Rah, *Prophetic Lament,* 131-32.

[19] Jemar Tisby, *The Color of Compromise* (Zondervan, 2019), 24.

[20] In addition to *Where Do We Go from Here? Chaos or Community* (Beacon Press, 2010), by Dr. Martin Luther King Jr., I also recommend Eugene Cho, *Thou Shall Not Be a Jerk: A Christian's Guide to Engaging Politics* (David C. Cook, 2020), and Michael Wear, *The Spirit of Our Politics: Spiritual Formation and the Reformation of Public Life* (Zondervan, 2023).

[21] This phrase is from the title of Dr. King's final work, *Where Do We God from Here? Chaos or Community.* Dr. Bernice King has identified this as her father's seminal work, the one that should be read if you can only read one.

[22] Rah, *Prophetic Lament*, 210.

[23] Alaina Wise, "Bishop Mariann Budde tells NPR 'I Won't Apologize' for Sermon Addressing Trump," NPR, January 22, 2025, www.npr.org/2025/01/22/nx-s1-5270918/bishop-mariann-edgar-budde-trump-interview.

[24] Wise, "Bishop Mariann Budde."

## 14. PUTTING IT ALL TOGETHER

[1] Dallas Willard, *Spirit of the Disciplines: Understanding How God Changes Lives* (Harper & Row, 1988), ix.

[2] Gary Haugen, conversation with the author, November 3, 2025.

[3] Chapter one of my book *Sacred Rhythms: Arranging our Lives for Spiritual Transformation* (InterVarsity Press, 2006), describes this process in more detail.

[4] *Sacred Rhythms* is designed to provide step-by-step guidance for this—from desire to practices to crafting a rule of life.

[5] Both *Sacred Rhythms* and *Life Together in Christ* offer concrete help with structuring this kind of support.

[6] L. Gregory Jones, "Swimming in the Deep End," *The Christian Century*, July 5, 2000, www.christiancentury.org/article/swimming-deep-end.

[7] For a much more detailed treatment of this process, see part one in Ruth Haley Barton, *Pursuing God's Will Together* (InterVarsity Press, 2012).

[8] Gordon Cosby, *Good Is a Timely Word: From the Preaching of Gordon Cosby* (Moonchpa Publishing, 2001), 108-9.

[9] M. Robert Mulholland, Transforming Center retreat, June 3-5, 2012.

[10] Otis Moss III, *Dancing in the Dark: Spiritual Lessons for Thriving in Turbulent Times* (Simon & Schuster, 2023), 98-101.

TRANSFORMING | Resources®

## *More from Ruth Haley Barton*

***Strengthening the Soul of Your Leadership***

***Pursuing God's Will Together***

***Longing for More***

***Sacred Rhythms***

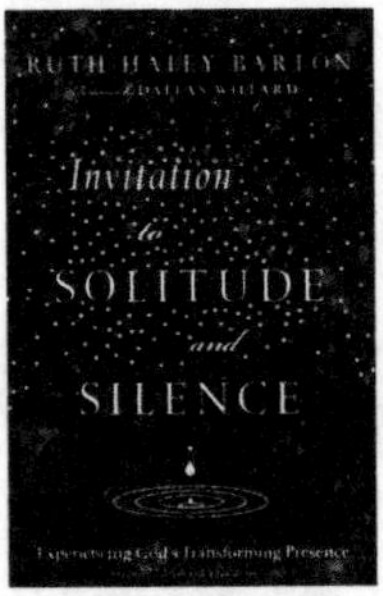


***Invitation to Solitude and Silence***

***Invitation to Retreat***

***Life Together in Christ***

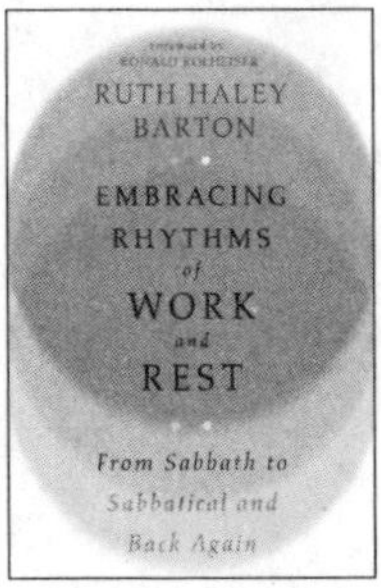


***Embracing Rhythms of Work and Rest***

*To learn more about transforming resources, communities, and events, visit*

***transformingcenter.org***

## TRANSFORMING | Resources®

*Transforming Worship*

*Spiritual Disciplines Handbook*

*Invitations from God*

*The Deeper Journey*

*Invitation to a Journey*

*To learn more about transforming resources, communities, and events, visit*

***transformingcenter.org***

ivp formatio

## BECOMING OUR TRUE SELVES

The nautilus is one of the sea's oldest creatures. Beginning with a tight center, its remarkable growth pattern can be seen in the ever-enlarging chambers that spiral outward. The nautilus in the IVP Formatio logo symbolizes deep inward work of spiritual formation that begins rooted in our souls and then opens to the world as we experience spiritual transformation. The shell takes on a stunning pearlized appearance as it ages and forms in much the same way as the souls of those who devote themselves to spiritual practice. Formatio books draw on the ancient wisdom of the saints and the early church as well as the rich resources of Scripture, applying tradition to the needs of contemporary life and practice.

Within each of us is a longing to be in God's presence. Formatio books call us into our deepest desires and help us to become our true selves in the light of God's grace.